Text Book of Digital Marketing

OrangeBooks Publication

1st Floor, Rajhans Arcade, Mall Road, Kohka, Bhilai, Chhattisgarh 490020

Website:**www.orangebooks.in**

© Copyright, 2024, Author

All rights reserved. No part of this book may be reproduced, stored in a retrieval system, or transmitted, in any form by any means, electronic, mechanical, magnetic, optical, chemical, manual, photocopying, recording or otherwise, without the prior written consent of its writer.

First Edition, 2024

TEXT BOOK OF DIGITAL MARKETING
FUNDAMENTALS

AVIJIT KUMAR ROY | ARITRA KUMAR ROY

OrangeBooks Publication
www.orangebooks.in

Basic Digital Marketing Course

**Avijit Kumar Roy (Process Consultant) |
avijitkumarroy@gmail.com | +91 9836976920**

Learn the basic fundamentals of digital marketing, and help grow your business or career.

About this course

Master the basics of digital marketing. There are 7 Focus areas having 26 modules to explore, packed full of practical exercises and real-world examples to help you turn knowledge into action.

Details of 26 Modules to Be Covered

Focus Area – I: Take a Business Online (4 Modules)

Module – 01: The online opportunity 1
Module – 02: Your first steps in online success 10
Module – 03: Build your web presence 27
Module – 04: Plan your online business strategy 52

Focus Area – II: Make It Easy For People to Find a Business on The Web (5 Modules)

Module – 05: Get started with search 75
Module – 06: Get discovered with search 100
Module – 07: Make search work for you.. 120
Module – 08: Be noticed with search ads 135
Module – 09: Improve your search campaigns 152
Module – 10: Get noticed locally 170

Focus Area – III: Reach More People Locally, on Social Media or on Mobile (7 Modules)

Module – 11: Help people nearby find you online...................... 181
Module – 12: Get noticed with social media 196
Module – 13: Deep dive into social media.. 215
Module – 14: Discover the possibilities of mobile...................... 231
Module – 15: Make mobile work for you... 243
Module – 16: Get started with content marketing....................... 264

Focus Area – IV: Reach More Customers with Advertising (4 Modules)

Module – 17 : Connect through email 291

Module – 18 : Advertise on other websites 314

Module – 19: Deep dive into display advertising 328

Module – 20: Make the most of video 341

Focus Area – V: Track and Measure Web Traffic (3 Modules)

Module – 21: Get started with analytics 363

Module – 22: Find success with analytics 378

Module – 23: Turn Data Into Insights 392

Focus Area – VI: Sell Products or Services Online (2 Modules)

Module – 24: Build your online shop 413

Module – 25: Sell more online 422

Focus Area – VII: Take a Business Global (1 Module)

Module – 26: Expand internationally 436

Module – 01: The Online Opportunity

Today's world is a digital one, with nearly half of the global population online. With so many people using the internet, it makes sense for a business to tap into digital. Find out what opportunities exist and how a website, videos or social media could help you reach your goals.

Lesson 1.1

Introduction

Key learning

Dive and explore how you can make the most of online opportunities. This introductory video will give you a brief overview of what you can learn throughout the course and highlight some of the benefits of building or polishing your digital skills.

Knowledge:

Today, our online experience is so much more than just checking emails. From talking to friends and family to doing the weekly food shop, discovering new holiday destinations and researching things to do locally, the online world is very much a part of our daily lives.

As the time we spend online increases, so do the digital opportunities available. The online experience is constantly evolving thanks to content creators, businesses and app developers who are able to find new and innovative ways to help us shop, learn, and connect. So, whether you own a business yourself or would like to work for one, now is a great time to jump in and see how you can get involved in the digital world.

But where do you start?

This Course provides you with a simple way to navigate digital marketing concepts and gain the knowledge you need to feel confident. Whether it's content marketing, online advertising, mobile marketing or selling products online, The Course is organised into bite-sized Knowledge Capsule and Self-Assessment Question and Answer Sessions, and Self Engagement Projects related to the existing modules of the course, so that it's easy for you to either pick up new skills or brush up on your existing knowledge.

Learn how to build an online business strategy, improve how a website ranks on search engines, and use analytics tools to understand online performance. Whatever your interest, there's a topic here to help you meet your online goals.

The digital marketing topics have been created to allow you to learn at your own pace. Take the lessons in chunks or complete multiple topics at once – whenever and wherever you want.

No matter what your skill level is or what you'd like to achieve, this Course will help you build your digital marketing skills. Improve how your business performs online, boost your CV, or just jump in to learn something new.

Check your knowledge 1.1

Doing business online offers all of these great benefits (apart from saving money on your heating bills – hey, it can't do everything). Being online lets you reach out to new customers and build better relationships with customers you already have. You can sell locally or globally (or both), and use state-of-the-art analytics to find out what your customers really want and need. Sounds good, right?

Question 1 of 1

Doing business online brings lots of fantastic opportunities – it can really help your company in new and exciting ways.

Once your business is online, what opportunities can you take advantage of?

1. Finding lots of new customers – everyone's online these days
2. Selling your products or services straight from your website or app
3. Delivering targeted advertising to customers
4. Saving money on your heating bills
5. Learning more about what your customers love
6. Using analytics to power your online sales

(Answer: 1,2,3,5,6)

Activity 1.1

Find out more! Visit the International Telecommunication Union (ITU) website to look at some of the statistics about the digital shift. Then, visit the "Think with Google" website (www.thinkwithgoogle.com) to look at a wealth of data on people's online habits, from browsing to shopping to social media.

Lesson 1.2
Your Digital Opportunity

Key learning

It's never been easier, cheaper or more beneficial for your business to get online. Don't be intimidated by the breadth of opportunities in digital. In this lesson we'll look at:

- the core components of a digital presence
- how they relate to YOUR business
- how to get started.

Knowledge:

So, you've seen how digital has transformed our daily lives, but now, let's get practical. What do the growing number of online opportunities actually look like for you?

In this lesson, we'll discuss the core components of digital, how they relate to YOUR business and how to get started.

Let's say you're a mechanic whose business has grown strictly through referrals and word of mouth. So far, you've not had any digital presence, but now you want to take your business to the next level. How will being online help your business succeed?

One of the biggest advantages to being online is reaping the benefits of search. Having a digital presence means you'll be visible when people go online and search for a business like yours.

So, let's assume someone searches for "mechanic Swansea" and your shop appears in the results. How can this benefit your business?

Well, the possibilities are virtually endless. When a customer clicks a link to your website there's so much, they can learn about you.

They might watch a video you posted about car maintenance that demonstrates your knowledge.

They could read testimonials from happy customers.

They might look through your pricing guide, find your shop on a map or find out you offer free towing within a 40-mile radius.

Maybe they'll fill out a form to ask a question or request a quote.

They might even click over to your social media sites where they'll find even more tips, photos and videos.

You might not start by having all these features on your website, but these examples should give you a sense of the many ways you can benefit from being online. And guess what? There's more!

Your online presence can also give you valuable insight into prospective customers: what they want, and how to give it to them. How? Well, digital allows you to show targeted advertising to people right when they're looking for what you offer.

For example, using search advertising, you can show ads to potential customers. Such as people searching for "auto repair Swansea." You can also restrict the ads to show within a certain geographic radius of your shop. You can learn to use analytics tools to find out if people clicked on your ad, visited your site, and took certain actions. Like filling out a form or watching a video.

Exciting, right? But how do you get started? Well, first, don't be intimidated: the tools and technology available today are easy to learn, easy to use and easy to acquire. Many are even free. In fact, for many businesses, the biggest challenge to being online isn't getting used to the tools, but putting together a plan. We've got lots of videos that are going to help you do just that, but let's run down a quick list of the major things you want to consider.

The first is scope. Web, mobile, social... there are so many options. Where do you want to start, and where do you want to go?

Next is Technology and Content: Decide if you'll handle the technical and creative aspects of the site yourself-which may take more time-or get help, which may take more money.

Finally, you'll want to consider Cost and Time: Set a realistic budget and an achievable schedule with clear milestones-and commit fully to both.

Every day, thousands of small business owners are making the web work for them. The opportunity to reach customers from around the corner and around the globe is too big to ignore.

It's time to take the plunge and go digital!

Check your knowledge 1.2

By going online, Karl can make his business more visible, and use targeted ads to specifically advertise to local people within a certain distance of his garage. He can have conversations with potential customers and get insights into their behaviour. Being online wouldn't necessarily reduce the need for customer conversations as Karl's business involves a lot of face-to-face communication. But it will help people looking for mechanics to find him in the first place. He can modernise his company logo any time – it's not specifically related to being online.

Question 1 of 1

Karl, a 50-year-old mechanic, runs the local garage in a small town and is considering taking his business online.

1. How could going digital benefit his business?
2. He'd be more visible to customers
3. He can target ads at local customers
4. It's easier to communicate with customers
5. Less need for customer conversations

More insights into customers' online behaviour

He can modernise his company logo

(Answer: 1,2,3,5)

Activity 1.2

Create a wish list of your digital presence:

What components are you already using?

What would you like to add? Start writing down your ideas, and take the first step towards developing a digital plan.

Check your knowledge 1.A

Question 1 of 4

The increased use of the Internet presents a lot of potential for which types of businesses?

1. All businesses
2. Small business owners
3. International businesses
4. Local businesses

Question 2 of 4

Taking a business online can involve many different steps. When starting out, which activity could be a part of this process?

1. Sending flyers with your web address to customers
2. Creating a business listing in online local directories
3. Increasing print and billboard advertising
4. Building a team of digital advertising experts

Question 3 of 4

Which of the following is the easiest way for visitors to learn about a business while visiting a website?

1. Getting a free 'taster' of one of your products when they sign up to receive emails
2. Listening to an audio file that auto plays whenever someone visits your site
3. Browsing your product pages and reviewing the Frequently Asked Questions page
4. Reading the terms and conditions for your products on your site

Question 4 of 4

What is a key benefit of having an online presence for a business?

1. The ability to sell products directly to customers through social media
2. Being visible when people search for a business like yours
3. Sending users emails to update them on new products
4. Being able to offer new customers promotional discounts

(answer: 1 – 1, 2 – 2, 3 – 3, 4 – 2)

Module – 02: Your First Steps in Online Success

There are many ways to promote a business online. But before you can get started, you should familiarise yourself with how these digital channels work, which options are best suited to you, and how to set up a clear plan or strategy that will help you achieve your goals and assess your results.

Lesson 2.1
Your Online Goals

Key learning

Taking your business online offers a lot of opportunities, but with so many options, it's easy to spin your wheels and lose focus. Setting specific goals can help as you begin to navigate the digital world.

Knowledge:

Every business has different objectives. It's good to know exactly what you want to achieve online, as it can help you set the right priorities and put your plan into place. Because you don't want to feel too overwhelmed.

There are lots of clear ways digital can help your business. Such as, building relationships on social networks, selling online, finding new customers. Or even keeping existing ones. It's good to start by asking yourself a simple question: why, exactly, do I want to be online? Imagine you own a hair salon. Your ultimate goals could be: to cut more people's hair, sell more premium services than the standard haircut and sell more of the products you offer. But before anyone can walk through your door, they have to know you exist. This is a great goal that digital can help with. So, let's start with that one: getting the word out in the digital world. One easy win is listing your business in local online directories. So, when people look for hairdressers on search engines or online maps, your business will show up. Then you might decide to build a website to share information about your business. This could be things like your opening hours, your location, your prices and the services you offer. Maybe even photos and videos that could entice new customers to walk through your door. You could set up a social media page on Facebook or Twitter where you could post photos of your creations, offer special deals and really connect with your customers.

As you start achieving these goals, and more people become aware of you. Your goals may naturally evolve and you might want to shift your focus toward turning visitors into paying customers.

You could add new features to your site. Things like online appointment scheduling, a "reviews" section where people can say nice things about you, or even an ecommerce store to sell your hair and beauty products online.

Now that you're using digital to attract visitors, and turn them into customers, you could start expanding your business by investing in online advertising.

Whatever your ultimate digital goals are, or where you currently stand, your priorities will naturally change and grow with your business.

Now to make sure you're meeting your objectives, it's really important to measure your progress along the way.

This is called "analytics". Analytics lets you know what's working well, and what could be tweaked.

We'll dive into this more later, but with digital you've got lots of options for measuring your success.

So, let's recap. Before you dive into the digital world, think about exactly what you'd like to achieve. Then, prioritise different online opportunities to help you accomplish your goals.

In the next few videos, we'll help you plan. First, by looking at different ways you can establish a digital presence.

Next, the different ways to market yourself online.

And lastly, how you can measure and improve your digital endeavours.

Check your knowledge 2.1

Being online could help Hamish attract customers to his new salon, gather customer feedback and let everyone know about his extended opening hours. Having an online presence wouldn't necessarily help with buying a new range of products.

Question 1 of 1

Hamish is a successful hairdresser. He's decided to grow his business by opening another salon.

Hamish doesn't have an online presence yet, but thinks this might help.

Which of his business goals could being online help him achieve?

1. Attract new customers
2. Gather customer feedback
3. Source new hair colouring products
4. Advertise extended opening hours

(answer: 1, 2, 4)

Activity 2.1

Whether you've got an online presence already or not, do some thinking and write down the three biggest goals you want to achieve by getting more involved in digital.

Lesson 2.2
Building Your Online Presence

Key learning

Let's take a look at all the options for launching your business online, step by step. We'll cover:

- local listings
- social media and video
- websites and mobile apps.

Knowledge:

We're going to look at the first step to going digital: staking your claim online.

You've got lots of options for building a digital presence, including things like local listings, websites, mobile apps and social media. If you get these basics right, it could make a world of difference. These days, it's easy for anyone to make a home online. But while a website might be the first thing that comes to mind, you don't necessarily need to start there. Let's say you're a hairdresser, for example. Your first step to finding customers online, and being found online, might be to list your shop in local online directories like Google My Business. Then, when someone searches Google for hairdressers in your area, you'll appear in the results - no website required! You could also start a Facebook page to give potential customers a glimpse into your business and what you can do, like photos or videos of some happy customers with great hairstyles that you've created. If this is all a bit much, don't worry. We've got loads of videos here to help you explore social media in more detail.

There's a lot you can do without a website, but at some point, you might want to build a home of your own on the web, a one-stop-shop where your customers can find everything, they need to know about you online. Great, let's get going! The most important thing to think about as you start to plan your site is what you want people to do there. For example, do you want them to ring you? If so, include your phone number prominently on every page. Perhaps you want them to find your physical shop? Well, include a map and driving directions. Maybe you want them to make appointments online? That's a feature you can build in. Or, lastly, you might want them to actually buy products from you online, by placing an order or submitting a payment. That's called e-commerce, and there are a range of options - from simple to more complex - that we'll discuss in more detail in other videos.

Websites aren't the only online homes anymore. These days many businesses create mobile apps for customers which they can keep on their smartphones or tablets.

Apps open up all kinds of digital doors - for example, you can create loyalty programmes or automatically send reminders about upcoming appointments.

Right, to be clear: If you want people to find you on the web, you need to stake your claim online.

That can be a listing in a local business directory, a presence on social media sites, a simple website or one with e-commerce, a mobile app - or all of the above.

Whatever you choose, this is the place where people find you, get to know you, and hopefully become your customers.

Check your knowledge 2.2

There are many options when it comes to using digital tools, and technology is always changing. Websites and social media can be used to reach existing and potential customers. You can use these channels to get your messages to as many people as possible. Using emails and apps, you can choose who gets which message and when. So, when Hamish wants to reward regular customers or gather feedback, an app or an email will do the job. A map could help new customers find the salon.

Question 1 of 4

Gather customer feedback

1. An online gallery
2. Email survey
3. A map
4. Social media page

Question 2 of 4

Tell customers about the extended opening hours

1. An online gallery
2. Email survey
3. A map
4. Social media page

Question 3 of 4

Show customers Hamish's latest hair looks

1. An online gallery
2. Email survey
3. A map
4. Social media page

Question 4 of 4

Help local customers find the new salon

1. An online gallery
2. Email survey
3. A map
4. Social media page

(Answer: 1 – 2, 2 – 4, 3 – 1, 4 – 3)

Activity 2.2

Create an inventory, or a wish list – for your digital presence.

What items are you already using?

What would you like to add?

Jotting down your ideas is the first step towards developing a digital plan.

Lesson 2.3
Marketing Your Online Presence

Key learning

You're online, so now it's time to bring in the customers you want. We'll review how to best help them find you, using some tried--and--tested online marketing avenues:

- search engines
- other websites
- social media
- email.

Knowledge:

OK, so you've established your online home, and now you're looking for ways to bring more customers to your virtual front door.

Let's discuss some great strategies to do just that using search engines, other websites, social media and email.

So, let's talk about you, how are you going to get customers to find you online?

There are a few ways to do it using digital.

Let's start with search engines. When people type something in a search engine, they're letting it know exactly what they are looking for.

If you offer relevant services and products, search engines will show your business in the search results.

Now, there are two main ways you can use search engines, and we've got lots of info to share on both.

The first is search engine optimisation, or SEO, which helps you promote your business in the unpaid search results.

The second is search engine marketing, or SEM, which lets you buy ad space in the search results.

SEO is all about getting your site in front of the right people who are searching for your products and services.

Now, there are lots of ways to do this, we'll explain them in detail later on, but the key is knowing what words people actually type in - the keywords. They are the most relevant words to your business.

Understanding these will help you improve how you show up when these words are searched.

SEM, on the other hand, is when businesses pay to advertise to people searching for specific keywords online.

Most major search engines use an auction system, where lots of different businesses compete to show their ads by bidding on the keywords they'd like to target.

Search is a great way to reach people, but we do lots more on the Internet. We read news, check sports scores, browse recipes, watch videos and generally browse lots and lots of interesting content across the web.

Alongside all of this content you might see ads. This is called display advertising.

Display ads appear everywhere online, and come in many formats like text, images, video, and ads you can click on and interact with.

They can be a great way to get your message out there and you're able to choose the people you want to see your ads, and the websites and pages you'd like them to appear on.

Social media sites like Facebook or Twitter are another option for boosting awareness of your business, and they're especially useful for building relationships with customers.

On most networks you'll create pages or profiles for your business. You can then connect with lots of people by starting meaningful conversations and sharing content you've created whilst growing your business' online social life.

Before we wrap this up, let's not forget one more pretty important way businesses can use digital: email marketing.

We're not talking about junk email, or "spam" that clutters up your inbox, but sending relevant information and offers to people who have already said they'd like to hear from you.

You can get people to sign up, or "opt in" to receive emails from you. Then the rest is up to you. You can send coupons to people who have made an appointment on your site, advertise special events, or promote sale items.

Knowing all the ways you can find people online - and knowing how they can find you - can help launch your business big-time.

The more types of digital marketing you try, the more opportunities you'll have to reach your most valuable customers, wherever they happen to be in the digital world.

Check your knowledge 2.3

Search engine marketing (SEM) is different to search engine optimisation (SEO). In SEM, the business pays to enter an auction. They then bid for advertising space on a website, and whoever wins gets to show their search ad. Tagging keywords within your content could increase the chance of your website appearing higher up in search engine rankings. This is called search engine optimisation (SEO) and is a free way for Hamish to reach more potential customers. However, neither provide free marketing space or optimised website design.

Question 1 of 4

Buy ad space on a search results page

True / False

Question 2 of 4

Bid for keywords to display your content in search engines

True / False

Question 3 of 4

Tag keywords within your website content

True / False

Question 4 of 4

Optimise your website's design

True / False

(answer: T, T, F, F)

Activity 2.3

Write down the ways you attract visitors now, and how you'd like to find them in the future.

Then for each, list the types of customer you want to target, and ideas for the advertising messages you'd like to show.

Lesson 2.4
Analyse and Adapt

Key learning

To go digital and do it the right way, you need a well-thought--out and flexible plan. In this lesson we'll talk through:

- setting realistic expectations
- tracking and measuring how you're doing
- adapting to changes in technology and your industry.

Knowledge:

By now, you know how important it is to figure out what you want to get out of digital, how to establish your online presence, and start using digital marketing to drive people to your digital home.

But it's also important to make sure that your digital plan is geared toward the long haul. Let's go over a few ways to do that: setting realistic expectations, tracking your results and adapting to changes in technology and your industry.

The first thing to remember: don't expect too much too soon. It can take a bit of time to set up your digital presence and get noticed online.

So, if you're a hairdresser launching your very first website, your online shampoo sales probably aren't going to go through the roof straight away.

It takes time for search engines to find you, and for you to implement and improve your digital marketing plan. So, try not to set unrealistic goals you're unlikely to meet.

A crucial part of any online plan is to measure what you're doing and make sure it's working. This is called 'analytics,' and it can show you how people are finding your website and what they do when they get there.

We've got lots of videos that dive into the details of analytics, but generally, knowing where your online visitors come from can help you figure out which of your marketing campaigns are working and which ones aren't.

If you know what people do once, they're on your website, it can help you figure out if your investment in digital is working.

For example, in your hair salon, you don't just want people to find your homepage, you might want them to do lots of things like: watch your clever how-to videos, make appointments, get driving directions to your shop, or actually buy something. Tracking what people do on your site can help you to understand what's working and what's not, so you can make changes and continually improve what you're doing. A final point to mention: it's important to remember that the online world is constantly changing. New tools, technologies and tactics pop up pretty much daily. So, a good plan combines the basic concepts that don't change that often, with forward-thinking to keep up with the latest and greatest.

Similarly, when things change in your industry, make sure your online world is kept up to date.

Are you offering the latest hot trends in hairstyling? If hair dyes become the next big thing, you can quickly update your adverts to show customers what you can do.

To set yourself up for success online, you need to look before you leap. And don't stop looking! A good plan will consider three things: first, know your online goals, and set yourself realistic expectations. Next, use analytics to track and measure what you're doing and how it's working. And last, always keep up-to-date and adapt to changes in technology and the industry you work in. If your plan tackles all these things and you stay flexible, you'll be well on your way.

Check your knowledge 2.4

Analytics can tell Hamish a lot of things about how people interact with his website, like which parts are popular and where the user is coming from. But without asking the user, analytics can't find out if there is anything specific, they don't like. Using this data, Hamish can draw conclusions and then adapt his approach. For example, if lots of people access his site from a mobile device, he could make sure his website is responsive, or launch mobile-friendly display ads.

Question 1 of 4

Show which pages of a website are most popular.

True / False

Question 2 of 4

Log which items of the website are clicked on.

True / False

Question 3 of 4

List which parts of the website a user doesn't like.

True / False

Question 4 of 4

Identify where in the world visitors are logging on from.

True / False

(answer: T, T, F, T)

Activity 2.4

Write down the digital goals you believe you can accomplish within six months.

Next to each goal, estimate the costs, time and resources you'll need to achieve them.

Then, ask yourself:

are you dependent on any one technology?

That could be a sign that you could be more flexible.

Check your knowledge 2.A

Question 1 of 4

Which tool helps you measure the success of your website?

1. Keyword Planner
2. Ad Gallery
3. Ad Preview Tool
4. That's right! Analytics can help a business improve its online activities. By tracking what people do on your site, you can start to understand what's working and what's not.

Question 2 of 4

Which of the following statements is true when it comes to taking a business online?

1. Stick to what you are doing and don't make changes
2. The same content works across online and offline platforms
3. Use analytics to make informed decisions
4. Use analytics to track your customers across the Internet

Question 3 of 4

Which term best describes the business activity that occurs when website visitors buy products or services from you online?

1. E-commerce
2. Display advertising
3. Search engine marketing
4. Pay per click

Question 4 of 4

Which of the following statements is true when marketing your business online?

1. You need a website to show up in search results
2. You'll reach a similar client base to the one you have in the real world
3. You'll be seen by the same volume of customers whether you use search advertising or not
4. Social media is a great way to engage your audience

(answer: 4,3,1,4)

Module – 03: Build Your Web Presence

From websites to local listings, mobile apps to social media, there are lots of ways to be found online. If a website is the best fit for your goals, you'll need to have a basic grasp of how they work. Even more importantly, having design and usability best practices under your belt will help you build a website that tells your story well, and allow your customers to find what they need.

Lesson 3.1
Choosing Your Online Presence

Key learning

There's more than one place for people to find you online. In this lesson we'll explore just how important being online is these days, as well as some common ways to do it, including:

- websites
- local business listings and review sites
- social media
- mobile apps.

Knowledge:

In this lesson, we'll introduce you to all the ways you can create an online presence-from websites and social media to local business listings and review sites.

You can see just how important it is these days to be online, so let's get going. The most obvious way to "go digital" is with a website. Early websites weren't much more than online brochures that described the who, what and where.

Today's websites can do much more. Your site can help people do research, chat with experts, read customer reviews, watch videos, buy things, track orders – and much, much more. If you decide that a website makes sense for you, the key is to think about what your site actually needs to do in order to support your business goals. We've got a whole lesson coming up where we'll talk about that in detail, but for now, don't worry about whatever today's shiny new technology is if it's not going to directly contribute to your goals.

Of course, it's also possible to do business online without a website. If you own a bakery, for example, you want customers to be able to find you, website or not.

Think about the last time you had a craving for a carrot cake. You probably searched for something like 'bakery near me' and reviewed your options.

You might see a website for a local bakery... or you might discover a good option in local listings.

Some businesses use local listings to create a digital presence, using products like Google My Business and Bing Places for Business. These types of directories let businesses publish details like descriptions, reviews, maps and images.

These listings are usually free, and are a good way to help your business appear on results pages when people search.

Beyond local listings, there may be review sites for your specific type of business where people can leave feedback - and you can respond. Rave reviews will give you the edge over the competition.

You can also use social media as your digital presence. People all over the world use Facebook and Twitter pages to complement - or in some cases replace - a website.

Another way you can reach customers online is through their mobile. You've probably downloaded apps or games on your mobile phone. You can create and offer these apps to customers yourself.

Apps can take advantage of a mobile device's unique capabilities, like GPS, mapping and phone, to connect with customers.

If a customer installs your app on her mobile, the next time she's near your shop, the app might send her a special offer, thanks to GPS.

Apps could even let her place an order right then, so when she comes in she can skip the queue, pick up her order and pay by tapping her mobile against the till. Mobile apps are often used as loyalty tools, to encourage existing, frequent customers to come back... and maybe get a free coffee with that carrot cake.

So, to recap: whether you use a website, local business listings, social media, mobile apps, or all of the above, the trick is to decide what you want customers to do, then create a home that accomplishes those goals. Together, these things work as your digital storefront: your space to interact with customers online.

We've got lessons covering all of these areas, but for the next little while we'll be focusing on websites: you'll learn the basics like how websites work, how to pick and register a proper domain name, and how to make whatever you decide to do online as friendly as possible to your digital visitors AND support the goals of your business. And if you keep watching, we'll cover all of this and more.

Check your knowledge 3.1

A social media profile is a quick, simple and cheap way for Addie to establish an online presence. This should be the first step she takes to help customers engage with her and her business. After Addie has established her social media profile, she can then look at longer-term investments such as building a mobile app, which could help customers find out more information and place orders.

Question 1 of 1

Addie runs a local bakery. After getting the business up and running over the last six months, she's now ready to create a digital presence.

1. What do you think Addie should set up first: a social media profile or a mobile app?
2. Social media profile.
3. Mobile app.

(answer: 1)

Activity 3.1

Write down all the places your business currently "lives" online, from listings, to social media sites, to your own website, if you have one.

Now, write a wish list of options you'd like to include in the future.

Next to each, jot down ideas about what you might include there, like content and functionality.

How can you encourage customers to interact with you online?

Lesson 3.2
How Websites Work

Key learning

If your business needs a website, the first step is to understand the basics. Here's a quick summary of what you'll need to know:

- what web servers do
- how domain names work
- how your website uses these.

Knowledge:

Welcome to our lesson on how websites work. We'll run down the basics- without getting too technical, promise! - on web servers and domain names, what they do for you and how to find what you need to get started. A website is your business's home on the Internet. It's where potential customers can come and learn about your business and what it has to offer them. Let's say you decide to open a bakery in the real world. First you'd have to rent a space to house it, right? A website is no different. Only you're not renting space on a high street, you're renting space on a server.

There are loads of services out there that take care of this automatically... but here's a quick overview so that you have an idea about what's happening behind the scenes. OK, hang with us, here comes a bit of technical information.

A server is a computer connected to the Internet, with software that allows it to store or 'host' the pieces of your website: the code, the images, the video clips and anything else that makes up your site.

It's called a server because it 'serves' up the right content when requested - that is, when someone wants to view a page on your website.

There are many companies and services that will rent you space on a server and host your website. Just like a brick-and-mortar shop, you pay an ongoing hosting fee, which is a bit like paying rent, leaving them to take care the technical aspects of running a server so you don't have to.

Every single server in the world has its own address. This is called an IP address, which is short for internet protocol. All you need to know is, it's a long string of numbers that means any device connected to the internet can talk to the server and find it. Luckily, you don't need to understand what they're saying to each other; all you need to do is choose a nicer name to reference that numeric IP address. Which brings us nicely to the second part of this session: the web address, or 'domain name.' Your domain name is how potential customers will find you, the same way people would find our real-world bakery: by the sign above its door. It's the thing you type into the browser window to get to any website. Like www.google.co.uk or www.yourbusinessnamegoeshere.com. Let's take a minute to break it down. Everything after the 'WWW dot' is actually what's known as the domain name. It's the part that lets people find your website, so it's pretty important. Any device that searches for this address- a tablet, a smartphone, a laptop - is communicating with the server. The server then sends that device all the correct pieces it needs to display the website - things like images and code - so that whoever is on the other end of the device can view your pages. When someone types your web address into their browser, here's what basically happens. First, their browser figures out which server holds the content, and heads over to that server. The browser then says, "Hey, would you mind giving me all the elements I need to show a person this web page?" The Server replies, "Sure, I'm sending along 5 images, 2 scripts, and a few additional files." The browser puts all the pieces together, and the person sees your nicely formatted web page. And that's pretty much it, except they'd actually be talking in really confusing bits and bytes, not English. But that wouldn't make any sense to us, so...

To sum up: Deciding to build a website for your business starts with understanding how it all works together: a server 'hosts' your site, and a domain name helps people find it.

Check your knowledge 3.2

To launch a website, you need to get what's called hosting space. Think of it like a plot of land for a house. Sometimes you have to pay a fee. In some cases, it's free. So do shop around before making your choice. This 'plot of land' is one of many within a server. Think of a server as a street where many companies rent out space for websites. A bit like sharing the same postcode. Each server has what's called an IP, or internet protocol, address. This is made up of a string of numbers that can be located by any device that has internet access. Every website has a domain name. This is everything after the www. or World Wide Web part. You can think of this as the physical address of your house. But what if someone wants to find you, or in this case your website? They'd use a browser like Google Chrome. This locates and retrieves the website information, and then displays it. How long a website takes to load depends on things such as the amount and type of information, and internet speeds.

Question 1 of 4

An IP address is made up of a string of numbers that can be located by any device connected to the internet.

True / False

Question 2 of 4

A browser figures out where online content is hosted and displays it to the user.

True / False

Question 3 of 4

Every website is hosted on a server.

True / False

Question 4 of 4

When users navigate to a website it is known as 'hosting'.

True / False

(answer: T, T, T, F)

Activity 3.2

Every website with a domain name has a corresponding numerical identifier called an IP address.

Want to see it in action?

Open a web browser (Preferably other than Chrome) and enter this string of numbers in the address bar: 172.217.16.195

What do you see?

(Full IP address details for 172.217.16.195 (AS15169 Google LLC) including geolocation and map, hostname, and API details.)

Lesson 3.3
Key Website Ingredients

Key learning

A website consists of many parts. Build and blend them right, and you're sure to succeed. In this lesson, we'll cover:

- your name
- the website's organisation
- text, photos and other interactive elements.

Knowledge:

In this lesson we'll talk you through some crucial early decisions you'll make about your website: choosing a website name and planning how your site is structured. The goal is making it easy for customers to find their way around and get what they want. Because a happy customer equals a more successful business, right?

Ready to go?

First up, your domain name. That's what people will type into a web browser to find you.

When choosing a domain name, you first need to check if the one you want is available. There can only be one TastyBakery.com on the web, for example, and if someone has already claimed it, you won't be able to use it.

So, how do you know if the name you want is taken? Just do a search for 'domain registrar' and click on one of the results. There should be a tool on the site that lets you see if someone is already using the name you want. And, if they are, it may suggest another similar name that's available for you to use.

A good domain name is one that people can easily remember. Keep it as short, relevant and as to-the-point as possible.

You may be able to get a variation of the name you want by choosing a different extension, which is the fancy name for the bit at the end. You're probably familiar with the '.com' or '. co.uk' extensions, but you might find others that are available or a better fit. For example, non-profit organizations often use '.org.' What this also means is that although 'TastyBakery.com' may be taken, 'TastyBakery.net' may still be available. OK, that's the name sorted. Let's have a look at some other common parts of a website, like the home page. This is the first page people see after they type in your domain name and get to your website. The home page is your shop window, where you invite people in and explain what you're all about. A home page also directs visitors to other pages of your website through what we call 'navigation'. Your navigation headings may run across the top of a page or down the side. Either way, it's a menu that lets people travel from one part of the site to another.

How you organise the site is very important. Start by thinking about the websites you visit regularly. How are they organised?

Now, decide what kind of content you want to offer, and then group it together in ways that make sense. Incidentally, many website-building tools offer business website templates that can help you get started.

One easy place to start? The pages and sections you see on most websites: things like 'About' and 'Contact' pages. Your website's Contact page might include your address, phone number, email and a map with directions.

The About page might tell the story of your business and include photos of some of your best work. There's no right or wrong way to organise a site, but you'll always want to put yourself in your visitor's shoes. What's he or she looking for? What are they trying to accomplish on the website?

Now, you want to set things up so it's super-easy for visitors to find the information they need, like the bakery's working hours, or complete important goals, like submitting an online order.

Let's check out what you'll see on the pages themselves.

First, you'll notice those navigation signposts, like the About and Contact headings. They should appear on every page of your site so that people can always get to where they want to go, or back to where they've been.

Of course, there will also be words, or text: headlines, paragraphs, bulleted lists. And you might also have things like images and video.

Text and images can also be set up to link to other pages on the Internet when they're clicked. These are known as 'hyperlinks', or shortcuts to other pages either on your site or elsewhere on the web. Many websites also invite customers to interact, with features like forms to submit questions, maps with turn-by-turn directions to your store or shopping baskets to buy products directly. Your website - your digital storefront - is a great opportunity to connect with customers. Choosing the right domain name, organising the site logically and including nifty features can help your visitors find exactly what they're looking for.

Check your knowledge 3.3

Question 1 of 1

What are "hyperlinks"

Text and Objects chances when clicked

Link set up to text and images on to other pages on the Internet when they're clicked. Text and images provide detailed information when clicked.

(answer: 2)

Activity 3.3

Visit the websites you look at regularly and create a list of things you'd like to include on your own site.

Pay close attention to how the information is organised on these sites, and where the information appears on the web pages.

Lesson 3.4
Websites And Your Business Goals

Key learning

When creating your website, consider how to combine your business goals with what your visitors want. In this lesson, we'll talk about:

- using your site to further your business goals
- thinking like a customer
- telling your story online.

Knowledge:

It's time to take a look at meeting your customers in the middle-that is, how your website can unite your visitors' wants with your business needs. We'll walk through how to think like a customer and design your website accordingly, all without losing sight of your own goals.

So, you're starting to design your site. As you do this, keep your goals in mind, but also consider what your visitors are looking for. Marrying what you want people to do on your site and what they want to do is the secret to success.

Here's an example. Think of the last time you went to a website looking for a phone number. Maybe you wanted to ring a shop to ask a question or get directions. Was the number easy to find?

If you're a business, be sure to put your phone number in a very visible location-maybe even highlight it-on every page of your site. You might even consider adding some text encouraging visitors to "call now." And make your Contact page easy to find, in case that's their first stop.

Also, it's a good idea to allow mobile users viewing your site to call you with just one click.

So, back to our local bakery. Let's say you want more locals to visit the shop. Meanwhile, your customers want to know how to find you when they're craving some fresh baguettes. Including maps on your website along with specific directions can make you both happy.

So, what other things visitors might be looking for on your website? Prices? Special offers? Certifications to show you're qualified to provide a service?

By making sure all of these things are easily available, you match your business goals with your visitors' needs.

And if you're interested in learning how to measure what your visitors are doing on your website with analytics, check out our lessons on that topic, too.

Now let's talk about content, or the actual words on your pages.

The words you use should be so much more than just a sales pitch. In most cases you want to avoid technical jargon and chest-beating about how great you are.

Instead, explain how you can meet the needs of your customer or solve a problem they have. By framing it in terms of what you can do to help visitors, your content will be much more engaging, not to mention more helpful.

To achieve this, write in a tone that's confident, but not intimidating. Unless your audience is made up of astrophysicists, explain concepts in everyday language.

Tell a story to help connect with your visitors. Things like testimonials or videos starring satisfied customers whose problem you solved, or letting people write reviews about your products and services directly on your site can really help.

Remember, every second counts. People won't be on your website for long, and they may scan words quickly or not at all. But images, headlines and clear navigation can help them find exactly what they're looking for before they move on.

Design and build your website with your business goals and your visitors' desires in mind, and it will have a much better chance of success.

Check your knowledge 3.4

Addie needs to write in a tone that's confident, but not intimidating. For her business, everyday language would be suitable, but it may not be appropriate for businesses such as law firms. The tone Addie uses should tell the story of the business and what it offers. The second option uses far too much business jargon. A vision statement might work for a tech startup, but for a bakery it's too confusing. In this description, there is no mention of the fact that the business is a bakery. Option three comes across as arrogant and over-confident. It's trying to provide a sales pitch, rather than explaining how the business could meet the customer's need.

Question 1 of 1

Addie is drafting a description for the About Us page of her bakery website.

Which do you think works best?

1. Love cake? So do we. Here at Knead to Know Bakery we have a passion and reputation for creating the most delicious cookies, cakes and bread.
2. Our business is driven by our vision and objective - to commit to sustainable, local produce that engages with and builds community spirit.
3. We are the best bakers in town. Just like that!

(Answer: 1)

Activity 3.4

Make a list of some of your best customers whom you might be able to call on to share a testimonial or a story about how you've helped them.

Perhaps you can add a reviews or testimonials section to your website!

Lesson 3.5
Make Your Website Easy to Use

Key learning

Visitors to your website should be able to navigate and interact with your site easily – that's called usability. Bring them back again and again by:

- providing simple and clear navigation
- creating a consistent layout
- writing relevant and effective content.

Knowledge:

Welcome to our lesson on website usability. That's digital speak for making it easy for visitors to find what they're looking for and accomplish what they want. We'll go over the best ways to improve usability, from how to provide simple and clear navigation to the importance of a consistent layout. We'll also explain how your writing can make your site more effective.

Sound good?

First, let's look at navigation: the stuff that guides visitors around your site.

Good navigation means arranging your site in a way that makes sense for your visitors.

If you have a physical shop, like a bakery, think of how your goods are grouped there. Big items like cakes and pies might be in one area, while individual treats like croissants and cupcakes are in another.

On your site, you can organize things the same way, and have the main menu navigation tell visitors what they'll find in each section, like signs in your shop.

In spite of all of this, your site may not make perfect sense to everyone. That's why including a search box might be a good idea, especially if your site has lots of pages or products. Put the search box in the same place on every page of your site, so it's easy to find, and visitors who are in a rush will always be able to find it, and whatever they're looking for.

One last thing to consider about navigation: When people visit any site on the web, they expect things to work a certain way.

Say you're browsing a site and you want to get back to the home page- what do you do? Click on the logo.

This is something visitors will expect, and it's common to nearly every website, so be sure your logo is clearly displayed on every page, and that a click on it takes them "home."

That's navigation navigated. Now let's talk about style and the way your site looks and feels. Everyone has their own tastes, but there are some general guidelines to follow.

First, consider your page layout. It should be consistent across your site, with similar fonts, images and other design elements.

When it comes to color, you may be inclined to go bold to grab attention. But online, most people are used to reading dark text on a light background. You've worked hard to create your content-make sure your visitors' eyes don't cross when they try to read it.

You also need to be conscious of where on the page your content ends up. Don't make people scroll down too far to see the important stuff. Use headers and bulleted lists to help them quickly scan your pages and decide if it's worth their time to stay.

Write for your audience. Are they a highly technical bunch? Then jargon is A-OK. Otherwise, write for the everyman.

Another tip? Encourage visitors to take an action while visiting your site. This is called - can you guess it? - a "call to action," and it can help them understand what to do next.

Want them to pick up the telephone? Tell them to "Call now." Hoping they'll pay you a visit? Point them to "Get directions to our store." Or nudge them to make a purchase with a "Buy now!"

So, let's review. When you're creating a website, try your best to make it easy to use. Give visitors a clear roadmap to your site's pages, keep design consistent throughout, write content that speaks their language, and give them the experience they're looking for.

Check your knowledge 3.5

Visitors to Addie's website should be able to quickly find what they need. Addie can do this by using a side menu and a search bar. For best practice, these should stay in the same place on every page of the website. Visitors should also be able to get back to the homepage quickly. For a lot of websites this is done by selecting the logo. About Us information is useful for drawing people in but isn't needed for every page.

Question 1 of 1

Addie wants to make her website easy to navigate.

Which of the following features should Addie include on every page of her website?

1. Side menu
2. About Us information
3. Bakery logo leading to homepage
4. Search field

(answer: 1,3,4)

Activity 3.5

Make a list of things you'd like people to do on your website, like find your phone number, fill out a contact form or watch a video.

Then, ask a friend or relative (who hasn't seen your website) to try to accomplish those tasks.

If possible, watch them as they navigate your site.

Can they, do it?

Are some areas of the site difficult to navigate?

Can you find any places that might be improved?

Lesson 3.6
Website design do's and don'ts

Key learning

When designing your website, watch out for mistakes that often chase customers away. In this lesson, we'll outline some ways to avoid frustration, such as:

- quick-loading pages
- mobile-friendliness
- general accessibility.

Knowledge:

You've heard the expression "you only get one chance to make a first impression," right?

Well, it holds true online, too.

This lesson can help you avoid common mistakes in your website design that can drive visitors away.

We'll cover how to make sure your pages load fast, making your site mobile friendly, general accessibility and the quality of your content.

First, you need speed. Internet users aren't famous for patience, and if your pages take too long to load, they'll leave.

There are lots of technical things that you, or whoever builds your website, can do to speed things up, like choosing the right technologies and hosting solutions.

But there are also some simple fixes.

If you have images on your pages, use the smallest ones you need. Ditch large, high-resolution files if they're only going to appear as thumbnails.

Plenty of software programs can resize or compress images to make them smaller, and this translates to faster loading times.

Simplify your design. Generally, the more you limit what your visitors' browsers have to download and re-use, the faster pages will load.

Use the same background image across many pages, and ask whoever is building your website to be efficient with code and scripts.

If you want to test how you're doing, try opening the site on your mobile- using a data connection, not WiFi - and see how quickly it loads.

Next, make sure your website is easy to use on a mobile. More and more people are using their smartphones as their primary device for browsing the web, and if your site is difficult to use on these devices, you'll potentially lose customers.

The easiest way to have a mobile-friendly website is to build it that way from the start, using an approach like "responsive design," which automatically detects the type of screen being used and displays the site accordingly-doing things like stacking text and photos vertically on a smartphone being held upright.

If you want to get a sense for whether your site is mobile-friendly, try Google's Mobile-Friendly Test tool.

Keep in mind things like swiping or tapping, which are unique to touchscreens. Be sure the components of your website respond properly to these kinds of "inputs."

Using widely recognised icons and making content clear and well organised will help visitors using smaller screens to find what they need.

Next, make it easy to find your address and phone number. Many devices are equipped with GPS and mapping features, which can help visitors on-the-go. And of course, when accessing your website from a mobile, it should be easy for visitors to give you a ring.

You'll also want to remember that people will be viewing your site on different browsers-like Chrome or Firefox-and different platforms, like Windows or Mac.

Do a test run from as many computers, devices and browsers as you can. Does your site look right in every case? Are you prompted to download plug-ins? That's an extra step that may send visitors away.

Last, remember that your website is not just for selling-it's for solving.

Imagine you're a visitor. Ask yourself, why am I here? What am I trying to do? What problem am I trying to solve?

For example, if you own a bakery that makes custom cakes, someone is probably visiting your site because they need one.

You could write pages about your decorating style and inspirations. But a testimonial and photos from a real-life customer might be a better bet.

So those are some common mistakes that trip up many websites. To avoid them, make sure your pages load quickly, and look and behave properly, no matter what device and browser a visitor uses.

And think of your customers when you create content. Answer their needs, and you have the best chance of bringing them in.

Check your knowledge 3.6

Here's the right order: - 2-minute HD advertising video for the bakery - Large high-res, full-screen background image - 20-second explainer animation - Low-res compessed thumbnail image - Twitter button that links to Twitter page - Text descriptions People expect websites to load quickly and might leave if they take too long, so you want to make pages load fast while keeping the overall design you want. Choosing the right media mix and hosting solution can help with this. You should design your web pages efficiently using compressed images and not too many large files such as videos. It's good to test how long it takes for a business website to load on different devices and connections before it goes live.

Question 1 of 1

To make the homepage of her local bakery website interesting, Addie wants to add some media elements to it.

Different elements will cause the page to take longer to load, so she needs to get the right mix for the site.

Can you put the following elements in order from the ones with the longest load time to the shortest?

1. Click and hold to drag the items into the right order, then select Submit.
2. Text descriptions
3. 2-minute HD advertising video for the bakery
4. Large high res, full screen background image
5. 20 second explainer animation
6. Low res compressed thumbnail image
7. Twitter button that links out to twitter page

(answer: 2,3,4,5,6,1)

Activity 3.6

Pick a few of your favourite websites and load them on different devices and browsers.

How do they look?

Do they take a long time to load or require additional software?

Do their designs make it easy to find information?

Check your knowledge 3.A

Question 1 of 6

Which of the following statements is true when it comes to developing a web presence for a business?

1. Customers can learn about a business by downloading a mobile app, but they can't place an order using an app
2. Building a new website requires a large budget
3. Mobile apps enable your customers to purchase your products without being on your website
4. All businesses must have a website to sell products

Question 2 of 6

What is a web server?

1. The customer service representative you can call when you have questions about your website
2. The answer you get when you search a term on the web
3. A computer connected to the Internet with software that allows it to host all the components of your website
4. The device that determines the speed of your mobile connection

Question 3 of 6

Fill in the blank: A _____ is a shortcut to other pages on your site or elsewhere on the web.

1. Hyperlink
2. Return link
3. Menu bar
4. Breadcrumb

Question 4 of 6

Which of the following is something you'll probably want to exclude from your website?

1. Prices
2. A lot of deep scientific information and detailed statistics

3. Special offers
4. Certifications to show you're qualified to provide a service

Question 5 of 6

Which of the following is an example of a 'call to action' on a website?

1. A list of phone numbers customers can use to get in contact with you
2. A 'Get directions to our store' button which when clicked, redirects to a map displaying directions to the store based on the customer's current address
3. An icon button that takes the customer to your social media accounts
4. A hotline phone number that helps users complete their purchases

Question 6 of 6

What should you consider when developing your website content?

1. What your customers are looking for
2. Your latest promotions and discounts
3. Your brand values
4. Whether the content will go viral or not

(answer: 3, 3, 1, 2, 2, 1)

Module – 04: Plan Your Online Business Strategy

From identifying your goals to knowing how to track your progress, this topic will show you how to put your best foot forward when creating a digital business strategy. Learn how to stand apart from the competition and how to impress customers at every point of their experience.

Lesson 4.1
The Benefits of an Online Strategy

Key learning

An online business strategy can boost your chances of digital success, helping you to define clear goals and focus your online activity. In this lesson, we'll explore:

- how an online business can benefit from a business strategy
- best practices when creating a business strategy
- examples of common goals and popular strategies to achieve them.

Knowledge:

So, you want to know more about online business strategy, or perhaps improve your current strategy?

In this lesson, we'll explore how creating an online business strategy can have a positive impact, what a good strategy looks like, and common things you can implement to achieve your business goals.

An online business strategy helps get all the ideas out of your head and into a usable format. This can help define objectives to work towards, and increase your clarity and focus.

Imagine you've set a new fitness goal to become more flexible. Now, going for a 10-mile run may be great for your cardio, but it won't help you achieve that bendy yoga position you've got your eye on.

In order to do that, you'll base your workout around key areas that will help you achieve your goal, in this case becoming more flexible. Running may be a part of it, but stretching is more likely to help you succeed. Likewise, identifying actions tailored to your goals will provide you with a better understanding of how to meet your business needs.

So where do you start?

The first step is to clearly define your goals. Perhaps you'd like to increase sales by 20%, or identify 100 potential customers? Setting goals will provide you with direction and a clear path to follow.

Next up is articulating what your business stands for. This can be represented by a simple sentence, generally referred to as a mission statement. For example, this might be "to inspire healthier communities" or "to provide fun spaces for everyday fitness".

You also need to identify your Unique Selling Point (or USP) - this is what makes you stand out from your competition online. Find out what makes you different by looking at businesses doing similar things, and work out what sets you apart. For example, if customer service is what sets you apart from your competition, this is your Unique Selling Point.

Understanding what you want to achieve can help you make the right decisions at the right time. Here are some typical goals and the strategies that can be used to address them:

Increase sales: If your goal is to improve online sales, driving more traffic to your website can help.

There are many many ways to achieve this, from paid advertising to content marketing.

Next up: Increase awareness of the business or brand

Social media is a popular way to increase brand awareness to both new and existing customers. It provides a platform to express your values, personality, and engage with your audience.

Finally: Grow your email marketing list

To encourage customers to sign up to email marketing, try clearly communicating what your audience can expect to receive, whether it's exclusive content or member-only updates.

So how do these benefits stack up in real life? Let's take a look at Rachel's Kitchen, who used a strategy to maximise their impact online.

If this lesson has got you thinking about your own online business strategy, be sure to explore the additional resources at the end of this topic to learn more.

Check your knowledge 4.1

You're right! Well, done. Sam will find it easier to put together his online strategy once he's figured out the company's goals, written a mission statement and identified the company's USP. Once his strategy is in place, he can launch his website, develop a targeted digital marketing campaign, and establish a client base.

Question 1 of 3

What should his first step be?

1. Define business goals
2. Create an email template
3. Find an investor
4. Ask the bank for advice

Question 2 of 3

What should his second step be?

1. Launch a blog
2. Hire an assistant
3. Design a logo
4. Write a mission statement

Question 3 of 3

What should his third step be?

1. Launch an advertising campaign
2. Identify his USP
3. Launch a newsletter

4. Hire an accountant

(answer: 1 – 1, 2 – 4, 3 – 2)

Activity 4.1

Now that you understand why developing a business strategy is important, have a think about your online presence and what it is you want to accomplish.

Answer the following questions to help identify your goals, mission statement and USP.

1. Goals - What do you want to achieve by being online? (i.e., more sales or greater brand recognition)

2. Mission Statement - Which values are important to the business? (i.e., fair trade or protecting the environment)

3. USP - What makes you stand out against your competitors? (i.e., customer service, price point or quality)

Next time you're surfing the web or social media, take a look at other businesses and note what makes them stand out.

Try listing brands that resonate with you and see what you can learn from them.

Lesson 4.2
Taking A Business Online

Key learning

When taking a business online, understanding how customers browse on the web is an important factor in ensuring your online efforts are rewarded. In this lesson, we will explore:

customer behaviours online, and how these overlap with offline behaviours the "See, Think, Do, Care" framework, and how to use this to help understand the online customer journey how to group your audiences using audience segmentation.

Knowledge:

In this lesson we will look at the differences between online and offline customer behaviours. We'll also cover how audience segmentation can help you choose where to focus your digital efforts when moving online.

So, what are the key differences between a customer in a physical shop and a customer online?

Imagine you just set a personal goal to improve your fitness, and now need new running shoes. In the offline world your journey might go a bit like this:

You visit the local shopping centre, going from shop to shop. Ultimately, you make a decision based on price, quality, returns policy, friendliness of staff, and stock availability. You process all that information, head back to the store with the shoes you liked best, and make the purchase.

When it comes to online purchasing, you're likely to engage in four distinct stages throughout your online shopping journey. These principles are described in the "See, Think, Do, Care" framework, and offer a useful way to identify where a business should invest effort in connecting with customers. Let's take a look at our shoe shopping example, while highlighting these four stages:

In the SEE stage, you notice that some of your friends have taken up running, and are posting maps of their favourite routes on their social media accounts. This inspires you to start running yourself. In the THINK stage, you get your phone and type 'what are the best running shoes for beginners?'. This introduces you to a whole lot of online content, from blog articles to targeted ads, giving you more factors to base your decision on. Eventually, you make your purchase, which makes up the DO stage, and perhaps post a photo on social media. This last step of sharing your purchase is part of the CARE stage.

Keep in mind that customers don't necessarily experience all four stages every time - your individual journey might begin at the THINK stage, or end at the DO stage.

Now let's combine offline and online activities together. Imagine you are in the sport shop having just tried on the new running shoes. You get out your phone and search for them online - perhaps checking if they are cheaper elsewhere. The chances are you might buy online after visiting a physical store- an approach called 'showrooming'.

Understanding the differences and similarities between online and offline shopping can help you create a more balanced online customer experience.

So how can you identify where to focus your efforts online? To choose the right channels, find out who you're talking to, when you should talk to them, and what you should talk about. This is called audience segmentation.

You can segment customers in many ways, from basic demographics like age and gender, to specific interests. For example, segmenting customers by location may benefit an e-commerce store if certain products are only available to ship to specific areas. Segmentation can also help with your online advertising; as most channels allow you to target paid advertising to specific audiences, based on information like what an audience likes or dislikes. You can also make your ads appear only to people within a certain radius of your shop or business, which can be handy when offering promotions to local shoppers.

To wrap up, when it comes to taking a business online, think about the customers and put yourself in their shoes: which channels do they use most? How do you engage differently with them online and offline?

Check your knowledge 4.2

That's right, great work! Although Omar has a successful market stall, his goal is to develop his online business- so focusing only on his offline marketing skills wouldn't help. Selling at a cheaper price on the website could be a risky decision so early on. While some retailers do engage in this practice, others price match. Given that e-commerce is new to Omar, it would be less risky to keep the online and offline pricing the same to start. Identifying all audiences will allow him to decide when he should engage with them, and what he should talk about - helping to increase his chance of success online. Lastly, while paid online advertising might be an effective channel, Omar should consider all possible options and see which fits his business needs best.

Question 1 of 4

He should focus on duplicating his successful offline marketing efforts to an online audience

True / False

Question 2 of 4

He should sell at a cheaper price on the website to attract more customers

True / False

Question 3 of 4

He should identify his various online and offline audiences, and how best to engage them

True / False

Question 4 of 4

He should consider paid online advertising as the sole means of promoting his business online

True / False

(answer: F, F, T, F)

Activity 4.2

Think about the last product that you bought online and then look back at the See, Think, Do, Care framework explored in this lesson.

Map your journey through the touchpoints you encountered before making your purchase. Think about:

1. What initiated your interest in the product? (See)
2. How did you go about doing your research? (Think)
3. What finally made you hit that 'Buy Now' button? (Do)
4. Did you leave a review or post an image of your purchase online (Care)

Now think back to your business scenario: what types of content could you use at each stage of the customer journey to encourage people to make a purchase?

Lesson 4.3
Understanding Customer Behaviour

Key learning

Create the best possible online experience for customers by understanding how to make the most of the moments when they interact with a brand. In this lesson, we'll explore:

- what customer touchpoints are
- how to map common online customer journeys
- how to identify customer touchpoints that generate business goals.

Knowledge:

Customers are the key to success, which is why understanding and nurturing them is so important. In this lesson we'll look at the importance of customer touchpoints, how to use them to map the journey customers take online, as well as how improving the customer experience can help you achieve your goals.

So how can you make a customer's experience better? Let's start by explaining customer touchpoints and why they're important. A touchpoint is any stage when a customer, or potential customer, comes into contact with a business.

Touchpoints are used a lot in offline business, particularly in retail. They can be receipts, bags, signage, customer service counters, and many other points along the way. Online, they can be a valuable way for businesses to build brand loyalty and trust. When a customer encounters a touchpoint multiple times, such as online ads, this provides consistent value and creates ongoing positive associations with a brand.

While people don't all look and think the same, the way they buy things, and the touchpoints they interact with, have many similarities. To understand online user behaviour, you need to establish what those touchpoints are and where they take place.

To identify them, try mapping the journey a customer takes. Once you know the steps they take to get to you, you can plan how to impress them at every stage. Imagine a marathon - once you know the route, you can plan in strategic points to rest, drink, or top up your energy levels. The purchase journey is the same - knowing the route gives you an understanding of exactly how you need to strategise your online approach.

Because there are so many potential interaction points, figuring out the journey may seem overwhelming at first. To make it easier, try putting yourself in the customer's shoes.

Ask yourself:

- where do I go when I need answers?
- where do I normally spot new brands or businesses?
- what helps me make a purchase decision? and
- do I see a brand again after I've made the purchase?

Another option is to ask customers directly about the route they took to find you. A simple face-to-face or online survey can break this journey down step-by-step, making it clearer and easier to visualise.

Once you understand the route a customer takes, it's all about making sure the relevant touchpoints chosen are effective in drawing people in. If you have a website, does it tell a potential customer what they want to know whilst keeping existing customers interested? The more value a site has to someone, the more likely it is they will want to return to it.

Social media is another great tool to develop touchpoints and can help give a business character and a personal feel. Remember your customers are real people - so connect with them in a way that's relatable and engaging.

Once your touchpoints are set up, remember to regularly review how they're performing. For example, if your product or service is suddenly becoming popular with a new audience, like teens, you may need to make adjustments to your touchpoints, so that they resonate directly with that age-group.

To wrap up, here are some quick reminders to help you work on your own touchpoints:

- ➢ think about the journey you take as a customer when you buy something, and apply this information to your business scenario
- ➢ if you can, talk to customers to get real-world info on the touchpoints they encounter
- ➢ analyse touchpoint performance and optimise your message if required, so that the customer's needs always come first.

Check your knowledge 4.3

That's right, great work! The customers have been experiencing difficulty in navigating the website, so Holly and her team should look at how they can improve the website's design and page layout. Customers also found contact information difficult to locate. Holly can make this information easier to find by creating a clear 'Contact Us' page, and by including contact details in the footer of every page. She can also include it in her email marketing campaigns, which will allow customers to contact the business without having to visit the website.

Question 1 of 1

Holly owns a dance studio. To improve sales of dance classes, she is reviewing how her marketing team could update the company's online presence.

As part of the rebrand, the team listened to customer feedback and mapped customer journeys. They identified two things online customers generally struggled with: navigating the website and finding the business's contact information.

Which of the brand's touchpoints should Holly modify to help address her customer's feedback?

1. Website layout
2. Instagram account
3. Instructor's Blog
4. Email marketing

(answer: 1,4)

Activity 4.3

Think about the customer journey and how touchpoints affect it.

Taking your business or a business of a well-known brand as an example, put yourself in the customer's shoes and map out the customer journey from start to finish.

At every touchpoint, make sure to answer the following questions:

What value does this touchpoint provide you as a customer?

Does this touchpoint match up to your expectations of the brand?

How could this touchpoint be improved to provide the customers with a better experience?

Lesson 4.4
How To Stand Out from The Competition

Key learning

Understanding the competition is a key component of your online strategy, enabling you to position a business correctly in the marketplace. In this lesson, we'll explore: how to identify what makes a business stand out in a busy marketplace why Unique Selling Points (USPs) are important and how to construct them online tools available to help you research the competition.

Knowledge:

Healthy competition keeps us on our toes and increases our drive for success. In this lesson, we'll explore how to identify what makes a business stand out online, why you should be checking out your competitors, and what tools can help you get ahead of the game.

Let's start with this question: what makes you stand out?

Imagine you own a basketball gear shop. What would make your brand distinct compared to other sports shops selling basketball equipment?

Maybe your shop's exterior is painted in bright red, or you have an eye-catching window display, or perhaps you've even hired someone to shoot some hoops outside to grab people's attention as they walk by.

As a physical store you need to stand out. The same is true in digital. When we identify what makes us different from the competition online, we call that our Unique Selling Point, or USP.

A Unique Selling Point is a clear statement that describes the benefits you offer, how you might solve your customer's needs, and what distinguishes you from the competition.

4 key questions to ask yourself when defining your USP are:

1. who is my target audience?
2. who are my competitors?
3. what problems does my target audience have? and
4. how can I solve them?

Once you ask these questions, you can piece together a concise statement that incorporates the answers. Here are a few pointers to remember.

Speak in a human voice. Be as natural and relatable as you can and remember, you are trying to attract people, not robots.

Shout about it. Your USP should be displayed on your website, social media, and other marketing materials. A good USP won't appeal to everyone, but that's ok. Build a USP that is tailored and speaks directly to your target audience.

Other things to consider while working on your USP are your strengths and weaknesses.

To do this, use a SWOT analysis, which will help ensure business decisions are well informed. SWOT stands for Strengths, Weaknesses, Opportunities and Threats.

Ask yourself:

- what is it we're good at? These are your strengths
- what can we do better? These are your weaknesses
- how can we grow, change and improve? These are your opportunities
- what is happening or could happen, both internally and externally, that might affect us negatively? Those are the threats.

While constructing your USP, it's a good idea to check what the competition is up to. When starting a competitor analysis, make sure to utilise the free tools available online. Start with search engines, which can offer the most immediate answers.

Simply search for your key terms and make note of:

- who appears in the top results on search engines for your product or service
- which keywords appear on their website, that is, what words are they using in the page titles on their website, and
- what messaging they use on their social media.

Another way to stay up to date with what competitors are doing is through signing up to alerts systems. Free tools like Google Alerts show you who is talking about certain topics online, so they help you keep your finger on the pulse. Try setting up alerts for key products or services, as well as your own business and competitor names. You'll then receive notifications when the terms you enter are discussed online, and be able to see how your business or the business you work for compares.

Let's take a look at how these tips can be applied to help you stand out online:

So, what makes you different online? Use the tips from this lesson to find out what your competition is doing, and use a SWOT analysis to identify what makes you stand out.

Check your knowledge 4.4

You're right! Great work. Ensuring Bobbi's company has a strong USP could help it attract new customers online. Being unique is an effective way to stand out in an already crowded marketplace. Bobbi could also look at what her competitors are doing to find out what's working well for them, and what isn't. This would provide her with a broader market view, and would highlight potential opportunities which she could use to formulate a strategy for her own company's growth. By conducting a SWOT analysis, she can identify opportunities that will allow the business to grow - as well as highlight weaknesses she could resolve.

Question 1 of 1

Bobbi owns a protein shake company, which has been trading for 3 years. Her products are stocked in a number of gyms, but the company has not seen much growth in recent months. Bobbi would now like to break into the online market to boost product sales.

Which of the following actions should Bobbi take to identify opportunities for online business growth?

1. Hire a financial planner
2. Identify a USP
3. Ship to new countries
4. Build a SWOT analysis
5. Distribute feedback forms to suppliers
6. Review competitor websites

(answer: 2,4,6)

Activity 4.4

It's time to see what the competition is up to.

Take ten minutes out of your day and use a search engine to research the following terms:

1. A business name - this will show you the competition for keywords and branding.
2. A product or service - this will show you who the competition is for that product or service.
3. Include your location - this highlights competitors who are local to you, that offer the same services.

These searchable terms are 'keywords' that are associated with a brand or product.

These keywords are what people will use to find a business or product online, so it's important to know who or what else appears when customers search the web.

Lesson 4.5
Using Goals to Improve Business Performance

Key learning

When marketing your business online, it's important to use the data and metrics available to evaluate how your online activities are performing. In this lesson, we'll explore:

- why setting goals and KPIs is so important to online businesses
- how to construct a KPI using the SMART framework
- how to analyse data gathered to help improve online marketing efforts.

Knowledge:

In this lesson, we'll cover how setting and tracking specific goals can help you understand and improve business performance. You'll also learn about Key Performance Indicators and how these can be used to evaluate the effectiveness of processes most important to achieving your goals.

Let's dive in: Key Performance Indicators, or KPIs, are quantifiable measurements used to focus attention on the metrics most important to meet business goals. They are also useful in helping a team understand how progress will be tracked and measured.

There are many ways to construct KPIs, but they should all be measurable, practical, achievable, and provide direction. So, what does a KPI look like in the real world?

Meet Ryan. He owns a chain of fitness centres called 'Fit Gym'. He needs to make sure that he has enough customers to keep the business growing. To do this, Ryan wants to sign up at least 50 new members per gym a month. This would be his goal. To help achieve this goal, Ryan now needs to set KPIs that will measure the efforts his staff make towards meeting this target.

Here are the KPIs Ryan has identified for his sales staff, based on actions that can help improve membership sign-up rate.

The sales team should:

- reach out to 20 prospective customers per day
- respond to all online queries on social media and email within 15 minutes of receiving them during working hours; and
- renew or upsell 8 existing gym memberships per month.

Analysing results against these KPIs will accurately assess which employees meet the expected standard, and help identify who needs additional sales training.

When you consider your business or the business you work for, remember that a KPI can be anything that gets you closer to achieving your goal. From sales calls to posts on social media, email list sign-ups to customer satisfaction ratings, make sure you choose the KPI that best fits your needs.

So how do you know what your KPIs should be, and how do you measure them? KPIs should be specific, measurable, attainable, relevant and time-bound. By creating them this way, you can ensure they will be clear and achievable. Try creating your own KPIs and see if you can answer the following:

a) Is this KPI specific enough?
b) Can it be measured?
c) Can employees attain this?
d) How relevant is it to the wider business objective?
e) And lastly, when is it due to be delivered or carried out?

An example KPI could be to increase sales figures by 25% compared to last year. This is both specific and measurable, and reviewing your previous sales figures will allow you to determine whether or not it's attainable. Increasing sales is key for business growth, which would be an overall business objective, and comparing year on year makes it timely.

Remember to evaluate both KPI results and the KPIs themselves on a regular basis, and respond to the data accordingly. For example, if Ryan's sales employees are struggling to meet the 15-minute average response KPI due to the volume of enquiries, perhaps he needs to consider increasing the number of staff per shift to meet the demand. This will ensure prospective customers remain happy when their enquiries are responded to quickly, as well as ensure his staff don't burn out.

When it comes to setting goals and KPIs in your own business environment, ensure that they're specific, measurable, attainable, relevant and have the forward thinking to help you achieve your long-term plan. Take some time now to think about the KPIs you would set, and how you could measure these to get closer to your goals.

Check your knowledge 4.5

That's right, great work! The KPIs you've selected are: - Specific - Measurable - Attainable - Relevant - Time bound Think about how you could improve the remaining two KPIs that were not quite right. Do they need to be more specific or time bound?

Question 1 of 4

Ensure 80% of clients use the gym's online system to book personal training appointments

True / False

Question 2 of 4

Increase how much money customers spend in the gym's juice bar

True / False

Question 3 of 4

A score of 85% or more in the annual survey for the question 'Would you recommend this gym to a friend?'

True / False

Question 4 of 4

Ensure 90% of new gym members book an induction session within the first two weeks of joining

True / False

(answer: F, F, T, T)

Activity 4.5

When you consider your business, or the business you work for, remember that a KPI can be anything that gets you closer to achieving your goals.

Have a think about the types of KPIs you could introduce.

Come up with five goals, and then five KPIs that measure how close you are to achieving those goals.

Ask yourself:

- Is this KPI specific to the goal you want to achieve?
- Can this KPI be measured?
- Is this KPI actually achievable?
- Is it relevant to what you want to achieve?
- Is the KPI time bound?

- When should you measure it?
- Weekly?
- Monthly?

Check your knowledge 4.A

Question 1 of 5

What is the first step in creating an online business strategy?

1. Identifying business goals
2. Understanding what the competition is doing
3. Knowing the market
4. Aligning goals to the strategy

Question 2 of 5

What is the purpose of the 'See, Think, Do, Care' framework?

1. To help determine a marketing strategy
2. To help a business understand the customer journey online
3. To help a business reach a global audience
4. To give insight into specific customer groups

Question 3 of 5

Why is optimising customer touchpoints online beneficial for businesses?

1. It allows brands to add pop-up ads at every point of the customer journey, ensuring high visibility
2. It gives businesses the opportunity to save money on online advertising
3. It provides customers with value every time they come into contact with a brand, helping build trust

4. It gives businesses an opportunity to collect more data from potential customers

Question 4 of 5

Once you've worked out your Unique Selling Point (USP), how would you use it in a long-term online strategy?

1. Incorporate it within marketing materials across all channels to help raise customer awareness

2. Create an email campaign letting your customers know why you are unique

3. Film a video explaining your unique selling point and send it to employees

4. Create a press release and distribute it through your channels

Question 5 of 5

What type of information can KPIs provide?

1. Audience segmentation

2. Long-term projections

3. Financial viability

4. Board decisions

(answer: 1, 2, 3, 1, 2)

Module – 05: Get Started with Search

Search engines make it simple to find what you're looking for with a click of a button. But how do they work, and how can you improve your visibility on them? Learn the difference between organic and paid search results and why advertising on search engines is so effective.

Lesson 5.1
Search Engine Basics

Key learning

Search engines catalogue the Internet to help connect searchers with exactly what they're looking for. That makes them a great marketing tool. This video covers:

- a brief history of search engines
- how search engines changed business
- why search is a good place to start.

Knowledge:

In this video, we'll talk through some of the history behind search engines. We'll explain how search engines have changed business, and tell you why they're a great place to market your business on.

OK, so where did search engines come from? One of the earliest search engines was a program called Archie, which debuted in 1990 and allowed people to access and search file names-basically the names of the web pages. But Archie couldn't tell you what was on those pages.

Fast forward a few decades, and search engines like Google, Bing, Yahoo!, Ask.com, AOL, Baidu, and Yandex have come a long way. These search engines use incredibly sophisticated computer programs to sort through a massive number of web pages.

Most search engines basically work in the same way. When a person wants to find something, they type in a word or phrase, called a search query.

Then, the search engine compares that query to its catalogue of web pages, pulling out the best matches to show the searcher. These are displayed on a search results page.

Their goal is to create the most relevant list of results possible, to help searchers find what they are looking for. The results page includes links to websites, but you might also see local business listings, items for sale, advertisements, images, maps, videos and more.

So how does this apply to you?

Well, imagine you own a coffee shop. If someone searches for coffee shop Cotswolds- that's you! -this is the perfect opportunity to appear on the search results page.

In the same way, if you're a technician who repairs air conditioning units, or a local takeaway ready to deliver dinner, you want to show up when people search for related words and phrases.

Why? Because the words entered into the search engine indicate the searcher is interested in your products and services, right now.

See why search is such a great place to be? It's a way to target people who are already looking for you.

Don't just take our word for it. Many marketers will tell you that search is essential to their online marketing strategy, and the numbers back this up.

Does this mean you should ignore other ways of advertising online? Of course not! Your plan can and should include lots of different ways to promote your business, like social media, email marketing, and display advertising.

But, if you're a business interested in promoting products and services online, being on search is a pretty safe bet.

Check your knowledge 5.1

Search engines allow people to look for the product or service they want, at the precise time they want it. They can also help businesses to target the customers who are most interested in what they're offering. The mix of these benefits is what makes advertising in search engines so relevant for most businesses – they can appear exactly when potential customers are looking for what those businesses offer.

Question 1 of 1

Seth is opening a coffee shop and is looking to attract new customers.

Take a look at the list of benefits Seth sees in using search engines.

One statement is not true. Can you cross it out?

1. Customers can locate Seth's products and services when they search for them online
2. Search engines can help to get the word out locally about Seth's new business
3. Search engines can help Seth to target customers who are already looking for his business
4. Customers will see advertisements for Seth's business whenever they use a search engine

(answer: 4)

Activity 5.1

Think of something you'd like to research and try searching on a few different search engines.

Compare the results.

Can you find different types of information using different search engines?

Lesson 5.2
How Search Engines Work

Key learning

Search engines examine all the pages on the World Wide Web, categorise them and put them into a logical order when you search for something. Understanding how this works can help your business. This video will cover:

- how search engines find web pages
- what they do with the web pages they find
- how they decide what to show on search results pages.

Knowledge:

Welcome to our course explaining how search engines work. We'll give you the basics on how search engines find web pages, what they do with the pages they find, and how they decide what results to show.

When you're using a search engine to find the closest coffee shop, you're probably not thinking about search engine technology. But later you might wonder, how did it do that? How did it sort through the entire Internet so quickly, and choose the results you saw on the page?

Each search engine uses their own software programs, but the way they work is pretty similar. They all perform three tasks:

First, they examine content they learn about and have permission to see (that's called crawling).

Second, they categorise each piece of content (that's called indexing).

And third, they decide which content is most useful to searchers (that's called ranking).

Let's take a closer look at how these work.

Search engines "crawl" the Internet to discover content, like web pages, images and videos. Each search engine uses computer programs called "bots" (short for robot), "crawlers" or "spiders" to make their way through the pages.

The bots hop from page to page by following links to other pages. These bots never stop; their sole purpose is to visit and revisit pages looking for new links and new content to include in the index.

Indexing is the second part of the process. The index is a gigantic list of all the web pages and content found by the bots. The search engine uses this index as the source of information displayed on the search results pages.

But not everything the bots find makes it into a search engine's index.

For example, search engines may find multiple copies of the exact same piece of content, located on different websites.

How is that possible? Well, imagine you're not searching for a coffee shop, but a coffeemaker. You might notice that the top-of-the-line CoffeeKing2000 has the same word-for-word description on the websites of many major retailers. The description might have been provided by the manufacturer... but now the search engine has decisions to make: which version to keep in the index? There's no need for hundreds of duplicates, so it's unlikely that every page will be added.

So, if you own a website that's selling coffeemakers, you're likely better off writing your own description of the CoffeeKing2000.

Make sense?

That covers crawling and indexing, which just leaves us with ranking. When you type in a search, the engine compares the words and phrases you use to its index, looking for matching results. Let's say, for example, the search engine finds 230 million matching results. Now it's time for the last part of the search engine's task: ranking.

The way search engines rank pages is top secret-it's their 'special sauce.' There are hundreds of ways search engines determine rank, including things like the words on the page, the number of other websites linking to it, and the freshness of the content.

But no matter what formula they use to determine rank, the goal remains the same: to try to connect the searcher with what they are looking for.

Say you've read about an Australian-style cappuccino called a flat white and you want to try it. If you search for "flat white coffee near me" the search engine will show you nearby shops selling the drink, because your search indicated your location. You might even see a map to help you find them.

So, what have we learnt? Search engines are constantly working to scour the web for content, organise it and then display the most relevant results to searchers. Understanding this process will help you make your website the best it can be.

Check your knowledge 5.2

They're all good ways of making Seth's website relevant, apart from pasting in content from another site. If lots of sites use the same content then it will be hard for any one of them to stand out in the search list. How search engines rank sites is their 'special sauce' – the details of exactly how this works is a closely guarded secret. However, it's safe to assume that Seth's ideas above (apart from the one that suggests pasting content) are all likely to have a positive effect on his search visibility.

Question 1 of 5

Point out unique aspects of his business

True / False

Question 2 of 5

Write a blog to sing the praises of his Peruvian beans

True / False

Question 3 of 5

Make sure his shop appears on Google maps

True / False

Question 4 of 5

Paste in a product description of his Peruvian beans that he found on another website

True / False

Question 5 of 5

Try to get other coffee-enthusiasts to review his business/website

True / False

(answer: T, T, T, F, T)

Activity 5.2

Search for a few terms that interest you, or for the products and services that you sell.

What types of results do you see on the search engine results pages?

Do you notice things on top-ranked sites that might explain why they appear in such prominent positions?

Make a wish list of content you might add to your website, so you'll have more opportunities to be in the index, and rank well on search results pages.

Lesson 5.3
How Search Engines See the Web

Key learning

If you want to make sure your website turns up in more search engine results, stay tuned for this video, which includes:

- how search engines understand what's on a web page
- which parts of a web page help search engines do this
- how to make your web pages more visible to search engines.

Knowledge:

welcome to our course looking at how search engines see web pages.

We'll go over how search engines understand what's on a web page, which parts of a web page specifically help them, and how you can make your pages more visible to search engines.

In simple terms, when you ask a search engine to find something, it looks through a huge list of previously indexed pages, called "the index," and pulls out relevant results based on what you're looking for.

Pages make it into "the index" only after the search engine has determined what they're about. That way, it can file them in exactly the right place amongst the other pages, and find them the next time a search relates to their content.

By knowing how a search engine decides what a page is about, you can optimise your pages to make sure they show up in the search results of people looking for websites just like yours.

Let's say you own a coffee shop, and you've got a website to promote it. When you look at a page on the site you see this.

But when a search engine looks at the same page, in addition to seeing what you see on your screen, it also sees the code behind it, called HTML.

Specific parts of this code help the search engine understand what the web page is all about. And knowing which parts are important can help you to optimise your site.

First, the title of the page in the code.

In this example, you can see the title in the tab at the top: "Cotswolds Coffee Shop." The search engine sees the title enclosed in a piece of code called a title tag. It looks like this:

Many websites can be edited using tools that handle all the HTML coding for you - that's called a content management system, or CMS. If you use a CMS to make changes to your website, there's probably a place to add this title, too.

You can help the search engine index your page properly by making sure your page title accurately describes its content. That way it can show up in relevant searches.

The next thing you'll want to think about is the page's text. Think about who you want to visit your page, and what words they're using to describe your products and services. Do they talk about fair trade coffee? Do they use the term cappuccino instead of macchiato? These are probably the terms they're also using to search.

Try to speak the language of your customers when you write your content. Because this can help ensure they'll find your pages when they search.

Finally, let's talk about the page's images.

Search engines won't see the mouth-watering photos of your coffee creations in the same way we do - which is a shame. But what they will see is the code behind it.

To help search engines identify the image, give it a descriptive name.

For example, image.jpg is not a great file name for search engines. Whereas, something that describes exactly what's in the picture, like iced-peppermint-mocha.jpg, is.

You can even take it one step further by adding "alternative text" in the code with your image. Known as an "Alt tag," it describes the image, which is useful for people using web browsers that don't display images, or for people with visual impairments who use software to listen to the content of web pages.

In the HTML, the ALT tag will appear something like this:

src=http://www.example.com.com/iced-peppermint-mocha.jpg alt=" Iced Peppermint Mocha">

Again, if you use a content management system to update your website there's probably a place to add an Alt tag, too.

So, remember: Use descriptive, unique titles for each page on your site. Write for your customers, but remember to include important words and phrases that can help search engines understand what your pages are all about. And don't forget to name image files with descriptive words and include alternative text.

Together, all of these tips can help search engines understand your pages and put them in front of the people that matter - your potential customers.

Check your knowledge 5.3

Using accurate labels for images helps search engines to pick them up when people make relevant searches. Using generic file names, like image3.jpg, can be counterproductive as they're unlikely to appear in a specific search. In the same way, using accurate page titles can also help websites appear in relevant search results. Lastly, using the kinds of keywords that interested people might be searching for – such as 'fair trade' or 'cappuccino' – will mean that Seth's website is more likely to be displayed in their search results.

Question 1 of 4

Image file names

True / False

Question 2 of 4

Page titles

True / False

Question 3 of 4

Key words in the content

True / False

Question 4 of 4

Keyword meta tags

True / False

(answer: T, T, T, F)

Activity 5.3

If you have a website, open a web page and view the source code for the page.

How?

If you're using Google's Chrome browser, you can find this by navigating to a web page, clicking "View" in Chrome's top navigation, then selecting "Developer", then "View Source".

Can you find your page titles, meta descriptions and images?

Are there areas that need improvement?

Lesson 5.4
Organic Search Explained

Key learning

When a person types in a word or phrase on a search engine, a list of results appears with links to web pages and other content related to the search. This video covers the content found in the organic results. You'll learn:

- what organic results are
- what search engine optimisation (SEO) is
- how good website content affects the organic search results.

Knowledge:

Are you ready to dive into the world of organic search? In this lesson, we'll explain what organic - or unpaid - results are. We'll find out what search engine optimisation means. And discover how good website content affects the organic search results.

OK, let's get started. Back to the coffee shop, and imagine that you've just started offering authentic French macarons, using an old family recipe.

You know there must be other people in your city who would enjoy this international treat. Someone might even be searching for it right now. So, how do you help them find you?

Well, when someone searches for something using a search engine, the results page they see contains a list of organic, or unpaid results.

Organic results typically appear in the centre of the page, and are the results the search engine decides are the best match for the search query, or words, that were typed in.

Results pages will also display advertisements, or paid results, though they'll be separate and labeled as ads. Although organic results and ads appear on the same page, there's one big difference: there's no cost to appear in the organic results.

Websites do not-and cannot-pay to appear here.

So how can you improve your website's chances of appearing in the unpaid results?

It all comes down to quality.

Think of it this way. The search engines' primary goal is to help people find what they are looking for. If you can help the search engine decide that your website is what people are searching for, you're in good shape.

Making improvements to your website to help it appear in the organic results is called search engine optimisation, or SEO. Good SEO involves helping a search engine find and understand your site.

So, what do search engines like? Good, relevant content. Think about exactly what your coffee shop's potential customers might be searching for.

If they want a macaron, they might search for those words. But that's a pretty broad search and could also mean a searcher's looking for a recipe, or an image, or the history of the pastry.

Understanding that, it would probably be more useful for you to focus on appearing on searches for homemade macarons, in your city. So your focus might be to create relevant, original content that reinforces the "how"-that all your macarons are made from scratch at your location, and the "where"-that your macarons are available at your bakery, or delivered to certain areas. This can help your website appear on searches for "macaron bakery", or related searches like "the best macaron in Cotswolds" or "readymade macaron for pick-up now."

That's organic search results. Showing up in them is a great way to help customers find you-and it won't cost you a thing.

All you have to do is make sure that your content is relevant to the people searching, so they'll click and stay for a visit. We have a whole lesson coming up on this, so stay tuned!

Check your knowledge 5.4

Question 1 of 1

Select the SEO activity that won't cost you:

1. Organic
2. PPC

(answer: 1)

Activity 5.4

Think of some words and phrases you're interested in, then try a few searches for them to see what appears in the organic results.

If you have a website, try searching for related keywords to see if you appear.

You can also use a search operator to see if your pages are in the organic index.

Search for this, replacing the bracketed text with your URL, to see what shows up: site: [your-website.com]

Lesson 5.5
Paid Search Explained

Key learnings

When a person types in a word or phrase on a search engine, a list of results appears with links to web pages and other content related to the search. This results page is organised into different sections; this video covers the adverts. You'll learn:

- a bit about advertising on search engines
- why advertising on search engines is so effective
- how advertisers compete for an opportunity to show ads on the search results page.

Knowledge:

Are you ready to learn a bit about advertising on search engines? We'll cover how advertising on search engines works-that's called SEM, or search engine marketing. We'll explain why it's so effective, and how businesses compete to show ads.

Imagine you live in the Cotswolds, you're out running errands and are desperate for a coffee. You pull out your mobile and search for 'coffee shop Cotswolds'.

Now you have a page full of options to consider. Every section on the page -the map, the ads, and the search results - presents options. Who knew there would be so many?

Some of these results are selected by the search engine's organic formula. These pages are considered the most relevant web pages the search engine can find for this search. The other sections are ads.

If you take a moment to compare the ads you see to those in a print magazine, you might notice one big difference - every ad is for a coffee shop.

You don't see ads for unrelated things, and interestingly enough, the adverts seem quite similar to the organic results.

This is by design, and it's what makes paid search advertising so effective. A search engine's most important job is to show people the results they are looking for, and this extends to the ads. The ads you see complement the search results page, with the ultimate goal of helping a searcher find what they're looking for.

So how exactly does search engine advertising work? There are several models. Let's take a look at one popular option, the text ads you see on search engine results pages.

Every time someone searches advertisers compete for the opportunity to display ads. It happens in milliseconds and the searcher won't see the details, only the winners: the ads that appear on the page.

So, how do search engines decide who wins? The primary components are the bid and the quality.

The bid is the maximum amount an advertiser is willing to pay for a click on an ad. If someone clicks the ad, the advertiser is charged an amount equal to-or sometimes less than-the bid.

So, if an advertiser bids £2 for a keyword, that's the most they would pay for a single ad click. If an ad shows on the page but no one clicks, it doesn't cost the advertiser anything at all.

Ideally, bids correspond to the value of the keywords to the business but the amount is up to each advertiser. Some advertisers may be willing to bid 50p for a keyword; others may be willing to bid £10.

Bid averages vary industry-by-industry, and keyword-by-keyword.

Bids are important, but so is quality.

Winning the auction doesn't always hinge on having the highest bid. Search engines reward ads and keywords with strong relevance to the search. In fact, it's possible that relevant ads can "win" higher spots on the search results page, even with lower bids. In some cases, no matter how high a bid, a search engine will not display the ad if it's irrelevant.

To summarise, paid ads offer another way to promote your products and services on search engine results pages.

With a well-constructed search advertising campaign, you can reach customers at the very moment they're looking for what you offer.

Want to learn more about SEM? Check out the search advertising lessons.

Check your knowledge 5.5

Paid search ad results are targeted at people who are already looking for a particular kind of product or service. This means Seth's marketing will be seen by people who are already very likely to make a visit to his shop. Although they contain the same content as organic search results, paid ad results have a different position on the page. In addition, it's usually made clear to people that these are adverts or paid results, so users are aware they are clicking on an ad, and there's no trickery involved. A great benefit for Seth is that he's only charged if users click on the ad, not by how many times it appears in the search results.

Question 1 of 4

Seth's adverts are shown to people who are already interested in his type of business.

True / False

Question 2 of 4

Seth will only be charged for advertising when his ad appears in the search results.

True / False

Question 3 of 4

The paid search results are given a more prominent position on the search results page.

True / False

Question 4 of 4

Seth will be charged for advertising only when someone clicks on his ad.

True / False

Activity 5.5

The next time you search, take a moment to study the results page.

Do you notice any ads?

Can you see the correlation between your search and the ads you see on the page?

Lesson 5.6
Google Search Console

Key learning

When it comes to your website, the more information you have, the better. In this video you'll learn:

- what Search Console is, and how it can help
- some of its useful features
- how to set it up.

Knowledge:

Want a great tool to get your website more traffic? Then this is the video for you. We're going to tell you all about a free Google service called Search Console. And show how it can help you, and how you can get it set up.

So, what exactly is Google Search Console? Well, it's a service that gives you feedback about how your website is doing in Google search results.

It has two primary functions. It monitors your performance in Google Search results. And it also shows you how Google "sees" your site.

Say you own a coffee shop, and your website needs some updating. Let's take a closer look at a few ways Search Console might be able to help you out.

One way is through its "Search Analytics" reports. This can help you answer a few important questions like which searches bring people to your site. Or tell you when searchers click on your links. They can even let you know which other sites link to yours.

Why is this important?

Well, the "Search Analytics" report shows lots of things, including the most common searches bringing people to your site. Ideally, you'd see words and phrases relevant to your business, like:

'Coffee shop Cotswolds', 'Coffeehouse near me', 'Pastries near Cotswolds', or 'Fair trade coffee near me'.

If you review the report and see unrelated or irrelevant words and phrases, it's a hint that the text on your website needs some attention.

Another thing to look for is the number of clicks. You'll want to know how often your site appears but gets no clicks-that's a sign your content doesn't match what people are looking for.

The "Links to your site" report shows websites that link to your site. Think of these as "referrals." The list should include websites relevant to coffee.

More and more people use mobile devices to access the Internet, so while you're in Google Search Console you should also check out the "Mobile Usability Report". This'll point out pages on your site that don't work well on mobile phones, which you can then fix to improve your website performance when people search on mobile.

There are two more really handy features within Search Console to know about: "Crawl" reports, and "Google Index" reports.

"Crawl" reports let you monitor whether Google can visit your web pages. This is important because if Google can't access your web pages, your content can't be included in Google's search results.

The "Google Index" reports show what information Google recorded about your site and tells you if your pages are accessible.

It's easy to get started with Search Console.

Go to www.google.com/webmasters.

Once signed in, add your website and complete the verification to prove you own the website.

Now Search Console can generate reports for your site-for free! It might take a few days before you see useful information because it must first gather and process the data. If you see a "No data yet" message, check back later.

Now that your site's set up in Google Search Console, you can use the reports to figure out how to improve your presence on Google. Using the reports, you can make changes to help Google better understand your web pages and as a result make your website perform better.

Check your knowledge 5.6

Google Search Console can help Seth to figure out if the keywords he's using on his website are helping it appear in the search results for the kinds of searches his customers are making. It can also show him whether appearing in these results is translating into visits to his website from potential customers. Google Search Console can recommend better page titles, but it can't recommend more effective content for Seth to use, or show him the type of people who usually search for businesses like his. Google Search Console presents information for Seth to review, and in some cases like mobile usability will give specific recommendations on how to fix issues.

Question 1 of 3

It can help show whether he's using proper keywords in his content 16179795

True / False

Question 2 of 3

It can recommend better page titles for Seth to use 16179795

True / False

Question 3 of 3

It can recommend content that will drive more traffic to his site 16179795

True / False

(answer: T, T, F)

Activity 5.6

Visit Google Search Central and set up Google Search Console for your website.

If you've already done that, review your reports to do a check-up on your website's health and visibility in Google Search.

Check your knowledge 5.A

Question 1 of 6

Why are search engines a great place for a business to be found?

1. People pay to use search engines, so there is a wealthy customer base there
2. People who search are actively looking for information, products or services
3. Search engines are a big trend these days
4. Search engines guarantee new customers

Question 2 of 6

What technology do search engines use to 'crawl' websites?

1. Androids
2. Interns
3. Automatons
4. Bots

Question 3 of 6

Which of the following can help a search engine understand what your page is about?

1. The date it was published
2. The number of images used
3. The total number of words
4. The title tag

Question 4 of 6

Fill in the blank: Spending money on search advertising influences how your website appears in _____.

1. Organic search results
2. The search results page
3. Business directories
4. Display advertising networks

Question 5 of 6

Which of these is an important factor in the paid search auction system?

1. How famous your brand name is
2. How cool your logo is
3. How long your business has been around
4. How relevant your ads are

Question 6 of 6

Which of these can Google Search Console help you to do?

1. It helps you increase your social media following
2. It helps you optimise your Google Business Profile listing

3. It helps you understand which keywords people are searching for on Google
4. It helps you run A/B tests on your home page

(answer: 2,4,4,2,4,3)

Module – 06: Get Discovered with Search

Search Engine Optimisation might sound like a mouthful, but once you understand how search engines work, you'll be on your way to becoming SEO confident. Learn how to develop an adaptable SEO plan, identify the most effective keywords, and which tools can help you measure what matters.

Lesson 6.1
Intro To Search Engine Optimisation (SEO)

Key learning

Understanding how search engines work can help your business improve its online presence. This video explains:

- what search engine optimisation is
- how search engines understand your website
- what they value most.

Knowledge:

Welcome to our introduction to search engine optimisation, also known as SEO.

In this video we'll explain what SEO is, how search engines understand your website, and what they value most. Because when search engines understand your content, it will be shown to many more potential customers.

Every day, millions of people search online, for everything from airline tickets to zoos. That means there are millions of opportunities for businesses to appear in front of potential customers.

Let's say you own a small farm and want to expand by selling your produce online. SEO helps search engines understand better what you have to offer. That means, when someone searches using a word or phrase related to your business, like, say, heirloom tomatoes, you're more likely to appear in their results.

When a search engine returns results some of them are paid advertisements. The rest are unpaid results that the search engines believe are relevant to the phrase entered into the search box. These are referred to as "organic results."

Search engines have formulas, or algorithms, that help them order the list of results. The search engines constantly scour the web for new content and try to make sense of it.

Where your website appears in these results is affected by the words you use on your site (fresh farm produce, for example) as well as other factors-such as how many websites link to yours.

Does this seem confusing? How's this: Think of a search engine like a matchmaker. The goal? To find the searcher exactly what she is looking for on the web.

But how does this work?

To present the best possible results, the engines look for as much information as possible about websites.

They might look at how popular sites are, or what other people or sites are saying about them.

They might consider words on web pages or keywords in the code of a page to better understand the topic.

Each of these components will help search engines find the best match for your search.

Search engines can now also consider the searcher's geographic location. A search from the UK will display a localised set of search results.

Chances are, the same search originating from France will show different results.

And, with the explosion of mobile usage, search engines now consider the devices people use when they perform a search.

But just like a matchmaker who's been in business for years gets better and better, search formulas evolve and add more and more information along the way.

Are you wondering what you can do to make your site attractive to search engines? We'll touch more on this in other videos, but here's a good starting point.

What search engines value most is unique, engaging, relevant content because their job is to find and show the most useful stuff.

So, there we have it. Search is a simple thing to use, and many of us use it every day. But what's happening behind the scenes is constantly changing. To effectively promote your website online, you've got to keep tabs on what search engines value most-and make sure your website gives it to them.

As we move along, we'll tell you more about how search engines work and help you create a strategy for improving SEO in order to achieve your business goals.

Check your knowledge 6.1

Question 1 of 1

Select the right option to make the search engine work as expected

1. Put all the information in the Picture and Video
2. Put all the information as Text in the content

(answer: 2)

Activity 6.1

Search for a word or phrase in a few search engines and identify the paid and organic search results.

Take a look at the top organic results.

Why do you think those websites appear higher than the others?

Lesson 6.2
The Importance of An SEO Plan

Key learning

In this step-by-step process to create an SEO plan for your website, you'll learn how to:

- develop
- prioritise
- adjust the plan to best suit your goals.

Knowledge:

Once you have a good grasp of search engine optimisation (SEO), you are ready to optimise your website. Just follow this step-by-step process to create an SEO plan, and learn how to develop, prioritise and adjust the plan to best suit your goals.

Let's say you want to reach new customers for your fresh-from-the-farm fruit and veg online delivery service.

Your first step should be keyword research-that means finding out what your potential customers are searching for.

Are they looking for organic produce? Weekly fresh vegetable deliveries?

By the way, if you want to learn more about keyword research, check out our lesson about choosing keywords to focus on.

Next, consider related topics. Are vegetarian diets popular? Do requests for gazpacho recipes come up?

This will help make your keywords more specific and a better match to what your customers are looking for. You should do this at least once a year as part of your SEO plan.

Once you've identified good keywords, take a look at how you're doing in search results for those words.

How many of these words and phrases bring up your website on a search engine? Are there specific topics that don't bring much traffic to your site?

This info will help you figure out what's working for you and what's not. If a popular phrase like "fresh farm vegetables" isn't pointing customers to your site, you can address those missing pieces in your SEO plan.

Once you've discovered gaps in your SEO performance, your next step is to think about how to fix them. Maybe none of the content on your site mentions that you can arrange regular seasonal deliveries.

Is no one linking to your site? Perhaps you can invite food bloggers to check out your farm in the hopes that they'll mention you in a future blog post. Make a list of anything you think might improve your SEO performance.

OK, so now you have quite a to-do list. Don't worry. It's just time to prioritise.

It's natural to want to tackle the items that will give you the biggest bang first, but be realistic. Adding an entire section about sustainable farming methods to your site might require hiring a programmer to help, which might cost a fair bit. In the short term, you could post a quick article about the topic on your blog.

The next step? Give yourself a deadline for each task so you're working through your SEO plan steadily throughout the year.

OK, once you've set this plan in motion, don't just forget about it.

Your SEO plan will change over time. But how do you know when it needs updating? One easy way is to check in when you're making other changes in your business, like introducing a new product or redesigning your website.

Also remember that search engines release new features and improve their algorithms. For example, many have made adjustments because so many people now search on mobiles.

Finally, adjust your plan when something isn't working. Is there a web page that's not getting much organic traffic? It may need a refresher.

Are you attracting visitors to your site but not making sales? Perhaps you need stronger calls to action.

Review your results regularly and shift focus to the areas that need help.

And that's how you build an SEO plan.

Let's recap. Start with keyword research to understand what your customers are looking for, then use that info to assess your successes and failures.

Brainstorm solutions to improve your weak spots, and prioritise them.

And never be afraid to redo your SEO plan based on changes in your world and the world of search engines.

Be sure to check out our lesson explaining the SEO process. That has more helpful information to get your plan in motion.

Check your knowledge 6.2

There are four steps to creating an SEO plan. First, Eric should do some keyword research and consider related topics. That way he'll know what people are searching for. Next, he should see where he appears in the search results for those keywords. If there are gaps where keywords aren't bringing traffic to his site, Eric should plan ways to fix these gaps and improve SEO performance.

Question 1 of 1

Eric is keen to improve his search engine results and he wants to use SEO to do it.

He's written the step-by-step process for his SEO plan, but it's currently in the wrong order. Can you reorder it?

Arrange the items into the right order, then select Submit.

1. Look for gaps in my SEO performance
2. Do keyword research

3. See where I appear in search results for specific keywords
4. Review results and adjust plan

(answer: 2,3,1,4)

Activity 6.2

Start creating an SEO plan by considering how to perform better in organic search for your most popular product or service.

Which keywords seem important but aren't sending you much traffic?

How could you fix that?

You can use Google Trends to research keywords.

Lesson 6.3
The SEO Processes

Key learning

This video explains the SEO process and the steps you need to take in order to optimise your website, including:

- discovering what words or phrases people use to search for your products or services
- improving the content on your site.

Knowledge:

In this video we'll explain why search engine optimisation is an ongoing process, and the steps you'll need to take to reach your goals. Such as discovering what words and phrases people use to search for your products or services, and improving the content on your site.

There is no shortcut for search engine optimisation (SEO), which helps you improve your website's visibility to people who are searching for products or services like yours.

The first step is called keyword research: discovering what words or phrases people are looking for when they are searching for products and services related to your business.

Let's say you have a small farm and have begun a fresh fruit and veg delivery service. Once you know what people are searching for-maybe vegetarian recipes or sustainable produce-you can optimise your content and offerings to better match what they are looking for.

That might mean posting a weekly recipe or writing a blog about life on the farm.

The work of SEO is never done, because trends come and go, users can change their behavior, and search engines evolve over time. Your job is to consider how changes will impact your site and what you need to do to continue to attract unpaid (organic) traffic.

Here are 4 quick tips on how to stay up-to-date on search.

1: Learn how search engines work.

Many have blogs that offer updates on new features, algorithm changes and suggestions on how to better optimise your website.

2: Keep an eye on changes and monitor how they affect your website.

For instance, you might read that the major search engines made a change that improves users' experience on mobile search results. If your website isn't optimized for mobile devices you'd probably want to update your website to be more mobile-friendly.

3: Find inspiration from other websites.

Do they offer free shipping? Are they active on social networks? Do they regularly update their website with photos? Adopt the practices that will work for your own business.

And finally, 4: Talk to your customers. They have the best insights on what content your site is missing, features that are needed, or products they are looking for. Even the way your customers describe your products can be a form of keyword research-they likely use those same terms to search.

And there you have it: the ongoing SEO process. It's simply understanding what visitors want, creating and sharing the content they're searching for and being willing to change tactics when necessary.

Check your knowledge 6.3

SEO work is never finished – search engines evolve and so do trends. That means you should refine your keywords over time and don't assume that if something works you can keep doing the same thing forever. Instead, keep up with how search engines work and how they're changing. Get inspiration from other websites and don't forget to get feedback from your customers. Remember, no agency can grant you top organic search positions. If someone does offer you this then it's probably a scam.

Question 1 of 1

Eric sells fruit and veg online and is using SEO to improve where he ranks in search engine results. He's researched what people search for to get to his website, and he's created content to match it.

Eric's SEO work doesn't stop there though. He's been talking to some friends and they've all offered him advice about how he should keep up with SEO over time.

Which advice should he not take?

1. Contract an agency offering top organic search positions
2. Don't change your keywords as it confuses search engines
3. Stay up to date with search engine changes
4. Read about the trends in your industry and use them to create content for your page
5. Get opinions from your customers on what might be missing from your site

(answer: 1, 2)

Activity 6.3

Many search engines use blogs to publish information about important changes they've made recently.

Take some time to research recent changes that might affect how you optimise your site.

Is anything coming down the line you should know about?

You can use Google Trends to research keywords.

Lesson 6.4
How To Choose Keywords

Key learning

Choosing keywords is the cornerstone of successful search engine optimisation. In this video, we'll discuss:

- why you need to do keyword research
- the difference between short tail and long tail keywords
- what to consider when selecting keywords.

Knowledge:

In this lesson we'll discuss what to consider when selecting keywords, so that you can reach your SEO goals and benefit your business.

Choosing keywords is the foundation of successful search engine optimisation. Why do you need to do keyword research? Here's an example:

Suppose someone is looking for fresh berries. What might they search for? It could be simply berries, or it could be strawberries, blackberries, blueberries or raspberries.

If you sell fresh berries, you need to know the terms people use most often when searching. Ideally, you'll match your website content to what people are actually looking for. If you don't, there could be a disconnect: visitors to your site could be looking for one thing while you are talking about another.

There are three things you should consider when choosing the keywords for your SEO plan.

First, frequency, or the number of times a word is searched for. Obviously, you want to include the terms that people search for most often in relation to your products. Just keep in mind that it may be difficult to differentiate your business on highly searched-for terms.

That brings us to our second consideration: Competition. If you have a large, established website, you may be able to appear on the search engine results for high-volume, highly competitive keywords, like fruit and veg.

But new sites have big opportunities too: if you're just getting started, look for keywords that have a bit less competition.

Only a small number of keywords have very high search volume. But there's a large number that have low search volume.

This is what's called the "long tail" of SEO.

While the keyword strawberries might have a lot of competition, a term like get organic strawberries delivered in Cornwall would be an example of a long tail keyword that might give you more immediate SEO results.

For a small business, the long tail is often where you will find your SEO opportunities. It typically takes a website lots of time and focused efforts to appear in the results on searches for popular generic keywords. However, smaller websites may get good rankings for long tail keywords with less effort.

Finally, and most importantly, the third consideration is relevance. The keywords you select should closely match what you actually offer. If someone comes to your site looking for strawberries but you only sell raspberries, they're just going to leave.

Make sure your chosen keywords match the intent of the people who are searching.

How? One option is to use Google Search Console to see which pages appear in search and get clicks. (Stay tuned for our Google Search Console video.)

Through all your SEO efforts, remember the golden rule: Your site's content should be made for your human visitors, not for search engines.

Don't add extra keywords or variations of keywords to your pages. Repeating them unnecessarily is called "keyword stuffing" and is against search engines' guidelines.

So that's what you need to consider when selecting keywords: frequency, competition and relevance. Keeping these things in mind will set you on the right track for successful SEO.

Check your knowledge 6.4

The long tail of SEO means longer keyword phrases that are very specific to whatever you're selling. These have a low search volume, which means there's less competition, so it's more likely to be relevant to a user's queries.

Question 1 of 1

Eric is optimising his fruit and veg website for SEO and would like to improve his 'long tail' keywords.

Which of these sets of words contains an example of long tail keywords?

1. Maris piper potatoes
2. Potato, potatoes, farm potatoes, organic potatoes
3. Buy organic potatoes from a family farm

(answer: 3)

Activity 6.4

Brainstorm a list of keywords for your most popular product or service.

Research the search volume for each keyword.

What are the most specific long tail keywords that apply to your product or service?

Lesson 6.5
Setting Realistic SEO Goals

Key learning

Setting realistic goals for organic traffic and assessing them with measurements that matter will help you strengthen your SEO strategy. In this video, you'll learn:

- how to define success
- how to select measurements that matter
- what tools can help.

Knowledge:

Does search engine optimisation seem intimidating to you? One way to tackle SEO is to set clear goals, then measure your progress each step of the way.

In this video we'll talk about why it's important to set SEO goals. We'll look at how you should define success, how to decide what to measure, and what tools can help.

When you set SEO goals, you can measure, track and report on the results. You'll know which efforts are succeeding-and which aren't. And then you can adjust things to make it work better.

Let's start by identifying your SEO goals. What are you trying to achieve online? How do you define success?

Imagine you own a small farm. You probably want to sell fruits and vegetables to as many new customers as possible. And you'd like to build relationships with existing customers through good content-and hope they eventually return to buy more fruits and vegetables.

You've just identified three business goals:

Conversions: Turning website visitors into paying customers.

Engagement: Persuading people to interact with the content on your site.

Acquisition: Getting new customers.

Setting SEO goals gives you something to measure to help you better understand how your site is-or isn't-performing.

So how do you find out if you're hitting the mark? Some measurements matter more than others.

For example, it's exciting to be number one in search engine rankings, but it's not a guarantee of success.

Here's why: Let's say your farm website is the first result when someone searches "vegetable gardens." You're getting a lot of visitors to your site-but not an increase in sales.

Maybe that's because people searching for "vegetable gardens" want to plant a garden, not buy your fruits and veg. The lesson? Don't waste effort on keywords that aren't relevant to what you do.

So, if being number one isn't your goal, what is? Let's come up with a few other ways you might measure success. Remember those goals you set above? Look at those.

You can measure conversions by tracking the number of visitors who come to your website and buy fruits and vegetables; or tracking a smaller action that can lead to a sale, like signing up for your email newsletter.

You can measure acquisition and reach by tracking the number of times your business appears in search results-your "impressions"-and how often people click through to visit your site.

And, you can measure engagement by tracking what content your visitors read and interact with, such as leaving comments, or how many visitors become your fans on social media networks.

So how do you track all these things?

Analytics tools and webmaster tools provided by search engines can give you this information-often for free. Most major search engines like Bing,

Google or Yandex offer tools like these. They're basically a collection of reports and services that help you track and monitor your website's visibility in search.

Tools like these tell you which keywords bring up your website in the search results, which web pages they link to, and how many visitors click the links to visit your site. This is valuable information if your goal is to attract customers searching for certain terms.

Analytics tools can also be used to better understand visitor behavior. They can answer questions like:

How many organic visitors become customers?

Which web pages or content on your site turn visitors into paying customers?

Which content isn't performing well?

Armed with this information you can adjust your SEO strategy to do better (or evaluate the performance of an SEO agency, if you've hired one to help you).

To sum up:

To understand how your site is performing in organic search results and how it benefits your business, set SEO goals.

To measure the success-or see where you need improvement-track your performance in various areas. Once your goals are clear and you have tracking tools in place, you're well on your way to success with SEO.

Check your knowledge 6.5

Analytics tools are a great way to get information about how content is performing, who visits the site and turns into a customer, and what content they interact with. It will give Eric most of this information, but won't tell him whether customers enjoy the fruit and veg they buy from his store.

Question 1 of 1

Eric has been selling fruit and veg online for a while.

He's chosen the keywords that he feels will drive the right people to his website; now he needs to track the progress of these keywords with analytics tools.

What information will analytics give him?

1. Where website visitors are located
2. Which website visitors turn into paying customers
3. What content visitors interact with
4. Whether customers enjoy the fruit and veg they buy

(answer: 1,2,3)

Activity 6.5

List your business goals.

Do you want to increase revenue?

Expand your customer base?

Now list the things you want visitors to do on your site that contribute to these goals. For instance, more visitors who order fresh fruits and vegetables contribute to your revenue goal.

Check your knowledge 6.A

Question 1 of 5

Which of the following factors should you consider when optimising your website for search engines?

1. Colour scheme
2. Recycled content
3. Inspiring business name
4. Site popularity

Question 2 of 5

What should be the first step of a structured SEO plan?

1. Identifying your ad budget
2. Buying an analytics software
3. Setting up your presence on social media sites
4. Keyword research

Question 3 of 5

When it comes to search ads, which of the following could dictate how an ad will perform against a competitor?

1. Social media following
2. Bid value
3. Domain authority
4. Average number of visitors to the company's website

Question 4 of 5

Fill in the blank: short strings of specific keywords with low search volume are called _____.

1. Long-hair keywords
2. Long-tail keywords
3. High-relevance keywords
4. Top-tail keywords

Question 5 of 5

Which of the following would be an ideal goal for an SEO plan?

1. Increasing social media likes and follows
2. Increasing how many relevant people visit your website

3. Showing your website to as many people as possible
4. Being in first place in SERP for any keyword

(answer: 4,4,2,2,2)

Module – 07: Make Search Work for You

Optimising web pages correctly means more people can find your content faster. There are lots of ways to achieve this, so choosing the most effective methods will save you time and resources. In this topic you'll learn how to master meta tags, backlinks, international SEO and more.

Lesson 7.1
Making Your Web Pages Search Friendly

Key learning

Get started in search engine optimisation by improving the pages on your website. This video explains the elements that you can tweak to make your website easier for search engines to understand. We'll cover:

- title and description meta tags
- heading elements
- page copy.

Knowledge:

In this lesson we'll talk about the simple things you can do to optimise the pages of your website so search engines can find you more easily. Because if they can, so can potential customers.

On-page optimisation, or changes you can make on your website's individual pages, can quickly help search engines better understand your content.

Let's say you run a small farm called Blake Produce and are looking to optimise a page about your fruits and vegetables selection.

There are several elements on your page that can tell the search engine that the page is about fresh fruits and vegetables. These include: meta tags and title, headings and the page copy itself.

Let's start with meta tags and title. These aren't something you would see on a web page unless you were looking at its code. They're embedded messages that help the search engine determine what's on the page. In particular, there's the title and the meta description.

The title and meta description are important because they both are used by the search engine to generate the actual search result for the specific page. The title is used to generate the first line shown; the meta description is used to generate the few short sentences that follow.

For a page about fruits and vegetables, you'll want to make sure that the phrase "fruits and vegetables" is in both the title and meta description. A good title would be: "Blake Produce - Fresh Fruits and Vegetables." This describes what the page is about and also highlights your company name.

A good meta description is usually two short sentences. It should also reinforce the title by using the keyword or phrase again. A good description would be: "Blake's Produce delivers organic fresh fruit & veg to your home, as often as you need it. Order your customisable box online."

A title should be short and sweet; a description should match what the page is about.

You should also consider what's on the page itself-what people who visit your site - not just search engines - actually see. There are two things you can optimise here to help search engines categorise your content correctly: headings and page copy.

Like meta tags, headings are embedded in the HTML code of your page, but they're also visible to people. Often, they're displayed at the top of a page. A great heading would be "fresh fruits and vegetables," which clearly tells a person what the page is about but works well for the search engines, too.

Finally, if you're writing a piece of content about fresh fruits and vegetables, you'll naturally want to use that phrase in the copy. Don't go overboard and repeat the phrase over and over because search engines may see that as spam. Remember that you're writing primarily for people, so be sure your message is clear.

So, let's recap what you've done to optimise the farm's web pages. You've looked at each of the major elements used by search engines and, in each instance, told them, "This page is about fresh fruits and vegetables."

No matter where search engines look, they'll see consistent and clear information about what's on the page. And that might help improve your search engine rankings.

Check your knowledge 7.1

The title and meta description are used by the search engine to generate the actual search result, so they'd appear in the search results page. In this case, Eric should use the phrase 'fruit and vegetables' in both his title and his meta data description. A good title shows the company name and highlights what the page would be about, like 'Blake's Produce: Fresh Fruit and Vegetables'. A good meta description is two short sentences that just summarise the page.

Question 1 of 2

Click to select title

1. Blake's Produce: Fresh Fruit and Vegetables
2. Blake's Produce
3. Blake's Produce: Local to you

Question 2 of 2

Click to select meta description

1. Produce grown locally and delivered to you
2. Fresh fruit and vegetables grown locally and delivered straight to your door
3. Farm fresh produce grown by local farmer Eric and delivered straight to your door

(answer: 1,2)

Activity 7.1

Do a search for one of the products or services you offer.

Take a look at the results with a close eye on how other businesses optimise title tags and meta descriptions.

Lesson 7.2
How Other Websites Can Work for You

Key learning

You can improve your search visibility across the web by thinking about off-site optimisation; that is, using what happens on other websites to promote yours. This video will show you some ways to start, including:

- encouraging links to your website
- engaging with your audience through good content
- promoting your site with social media.

Knowledge:

In this lesson we'll show you how to improve your website's visibility on search across the web by encouraging links to your site, engaging with your customers through good content, and promoting your site with social media.

Your search engine optimisation, or SEO results are influenced by things you do on your site and things that happen off your site. The latter involves what other sites are saying about yours.

Two of your best chances to control this are "backlinks" and social media.

Let's start with backlinks. This is the term for a link from another website to your site. Think of links like votes-if you have a lot of links to your site, it means many different people on the web believe your site has good content. It's a vote of confidence.

Search engines might see these links as a sign that you have a high-quality site, and are perhaps a good option to show searchers.

So, we've established that links to your site are important-but how do you get them?

The key is to think quality, not quantity.

In the past, people creating websites focused on getting large numbers of links to promote their position in search engine results. In some cases, these links were irrelevant to their products and services, or came from low-quality sites (by low quality, we mean websites with minimal content that exist only to link to other sites).

Search engines caught onto this and responded by giving less value to sites that tried to manipulate the search results, which resulted in a drop in their search ranking.

What does this mean for you? Links to your site are great, as long as they are legitimate links from good websites.

So how can you get more of these good links? The best way is to create great content on your own site. Then, others may link to you because they think their audience should see your content. You can also encourage others to write about you, and share links to your website. In the SEO industry, this is called content marketing.

So, what's good content? If you have a small farm that sells fresh fruit and vegetables, it could be a list of Top 10 Summer Fruits or the 5 Best Dishes with Broccoli. To create good content, you have to understand who your potential customers are, what they are looking for, and how you can provide it.

OK, let's touch quickly on the other way you can optimise off-site, social media.

Search engines will crawl any page they can access, including social media sites. But they generally don't place special significance on your popularity within a social media site. For example, you won't get more credit for having more "likes" or "followers."

But using social media is still a great way to reach a bigger audience. It promotes your site-and your business-because it helps people discover your content and encourages them to interact with you.

By the way, if you want to learn more about using social media for your business, we have an entire lesson about it.

To sum up: off-site optimisation is a valuable way to potentially increase your search engine rankings.

The best way to support off-site optimisation is by creating good content that establishes your site as a quality resource, attracting visitors who then share it across social media.

Check your knowledge 7.2

Eric needs to work hard to get backlinks – that means links to his site from other websites. To do that he needs to produce quality content, such as writing recipes. He can also encourage people to write about his business. Social media is a great way to improve his visibility, but search engines don't recognise the number of likes or followers an account has, so this won't help the search rankings. Eric should avoid creating artificial links to his website.

Question 1 of 4

Write recipes that use vegetables that he sells

True / False

Question 2 of 4

Get lots of likes or followers on social media

True / False

Question 3 of 4

Encourage others to write about his website

True / False

Question 4 of 4

Add lots of links to the website

True / False

(answer: T, F, T, F)

Activity 7.2

Visit a social media page of a company you admire.

What kind of information are they sharing?

What type of content gets the best response from customers?

Think about this as you create your own content strategy.

Lesson 7.3
Cross Borders With SEO

Key learning

Different countries require different marketing tactics, and international search engine optimisation is no different. In this lesson, you'll learn about changes to make when your website crosses international borders, including:

- language
- localisation
- country targeting.

Knowledge:

In this lesson, we'll explain how search engine optimisation (SEO) strategy can help your business reach international prospects and customers.

If your potential customers are in different countries or speak multiple languages, there are many aspects to consider. We'll go over the most important ones: language, localisation and country targeting.

First things first: you need to speak your customers' language-literally.

There are some SEO guidelines for websites that offer content in multiple languages. The first is to make sure that each page in a different language has its own unique web page.

Why is that important? Let's say you grow avocados in the U.K. and you want to sell your prime product to other countries.

Web design technology makes it possible to have English language content on a web page-say www.example.com/avocado.html-but allow visitors to click a button to view the same page written in French. Sounds great, right? The problem is that humans can click that button, but search engines can't.

A better approach is to separate each translated version on its own web page. In this example, it would be much better to place the French version on its own page, with a separate URL: www.example.com/avocat.html

The second thing to keep in mind: mixing languages on the same page. This is a big no-no. For example, when half your content is in French and the other half is in English, search engines can't decide what language your content is in. It's better to use different pages for different languages.

Next: Avoid using automated services to translate your content. Have a piece of content about organic produce that needs to be in French? Get a real live person to translate it for you.

Why is this necessary? Search engines don't value content generated from automated translation tools. Even worse, the page might be considered spam. Translation service may cost you a bit more upfront, but you'll likely have higher quality content that can drive better results for your business.

If you've taken the time to translate content, some search engines allow you to add language annotations to your web pages. These annotations help search engines serve the right content to the right person based on his or her country or language.

Let's imagine you are a farmer who ships delicious fruits and vegetables across borders. You have created some great content for your U.K. clientele, but you have also had the same content carefully translated into German for your market in Germany. One such page is about your avocados.

As a farmer, you'd expect your German avocado page to show up on a search results page for your prospects in Germany, and your U.K. page for customers in the U.K. To help search engines discover this alternate content, in this case you'd be able to add an annotation to each English and German page.

These tags will mark your pages so search engines can serve up the right version of your content to viewers in their respective countries.

When you explore annotations a bit further, you'll see that they can be great tools for more advanced multilingual and multinational setups.

That covers some of the structural considerations for adding different languages to your website. But even if you don't add multiple languages, there are other considerations for customers in different countries and markets.

Start by thinking about what information would be useful to them.

Do you need to provide product prices in different currencies?

Do they use a different system of measurement-metric versus imperial? For example, would customers weigh your avocados in kilos or pounds?

Did you include local addresses and phone numbers so they can contact you?

Do you need to list your business hours in different time zones?

These are all small things you can do to make sure your website remains useful to potential customers in different countries. They are also signals to help search engines understand your content is relevant to international markets.

Beyond language and localisation, you can help search engines understand the country (or countries!) you are targeting.

For instance, if your website has a country code top level domain name-ccTLD for short-it's a strong indication that your site targets a specific country. An example of a U.K. site with a ccTLD would be www.avocadofarm.co.uk. For Germany, that site might be www.avocadofarm.de.

And if it doesn't? What if you have a generic domain such as www.example.com?

Search engines may use a number of factors including where your website is hosted, its IP address, and information on your web pages. You can still help your site and its content be more visible to international prospects by using country targeting tools such as those found in Google Search Console.

And there you have it. As you start promoting your website in other countries, keep three things in mind: language, localisation and country targeting.

If you do, you can adjust your website and SEO strategy to make your website an international success. Want to learn more? Be sure to check out our lessons about International Marketing and Export.

Check your knowledge 7.3

Search engine best practise is to create individual pages for each language that you wish to support on your website. Doing this will help ensure that Eric's website is correctly indexed by search engines. He should also avoid different languages on the same page as the search engine won't be able to decide what language the content is in. Using an automated translator is sometimes seen as spam, so he should avoid that too. Language annotations are useful as they help the search engines serve up the correct content to the correct user in a particular country.

Question 1 of 1

Eric's farm produce business started locally in the UK, but he's started getting orders from overseas as well.

Not wanting to miss this opportunity, Eric decides to optimise his website to an international audience. What should he avoid doing?

Select the things Eric should avoid then select Submit to remove them.

1. Separating out each language into different pages
2. Having different languages on the same page
3. Adding language annotations to his webpage
4. Using automated services to translate content

(answer: 2,4)

Activity 7.3

Find three companies in your industry or business niche that target other languages or countries.

How do you feel about their localisation approaches?

Do they translate all content on the pages?

Customise content such as currencies and navigation?

Which options do you prefer for your internationalisation plan?

Check your knowledge 7.A

Question 1 of 3

Which of the following page titles would be most suitable for a website page describing a store's return policy?

1. How to Send Stuff Back
2. [Company Name's] Return Policy
3. Return Policy
4. Company Policies

Question 2 of 3

Which of the following is a good way to get other websites to link to your site?

1. Keep linking to them until they link to you
2. Send them emails until they link to you
3. Building relationships with similar sites
4. Use as many relevant keywords on the page you'd like them to link to

Question 3 of 3

When expanding a business internationally, which of the following is most important to provide on your website?

1. Products and delivery details in the correct currency
2. Time and dates written in the local format
3. Exchange rate information
4. Free giveaways for local customers

(answer: 2,3,1)

Module – 08: Be Noticed with Search Ads

Search Engine Marketing (SEM) can open up a world of opportunities when it comes to promoting your service or product. By specifically targeting people interested in your website, you can use online advertising to directly connect with future customers. Learn how an SEM auction works and which elements are important to master so you can create ads that stand out from the crowd.

Lesson 8.1
Introduction To Search Engine Marketing (SEM)

Key learning

Traditional advertising broadcasts a message to the world at large. But search engine marketing targets a very specific group of people – those actively looking for your products and services. In this video, you'll learn:

- what SEM is
- how it works
- why it works so well.

Knowledge:

Welcome to our introduction to search engine marketing, or SEM. In this video we're going to be talking about how SEM works, and more importantly, what makes it unique in marketing, and why it's so effective.

You're probably already familiar with search engine marketing, even if you don't know how it works. Let's say you do a search for something like wedding photos. You'll get lots of options on the search engine results page. Now we're going to take a closer look at those results.

The links you see in the main part of the page are called "organic" results. It costs nothing to appear here. This is where search engines show sites they think have the most relevant content.

Now look at the right column and across the top of the page. See those results? These listings are paid advertisements.

SEM lets you use this space to advertise to potential customers when they search for certain words and phrases relevant to your business. These are known as keywords.

Another really unique thing to know about SEM is the advertiser only pays when someone clicks on their ad. So if your ad appears, but no one clicks on it, you won't be charged.

Yes, you heard that right! That's why it's called "pay-per-click" advertising.

Let's say you're a wedding photographer. You may want your ads to show when someone searches for wedding photographer Cardiff. But you'll only pay if the searcher clicks on your advert.

That's the big difference when comparing SEM to traditional forms of advertising, like ads in newspapers and magazines, or billboard posters. If you advertise wedding photography using those, the ad is shown to a bunch of people… whether or not they want wedding photos. And you pay no matter what.

With SEM, it's very likely that people who clicked your ad are interested in what you have to offer, because they told you so. Or rather, they told the search engine when they searched for wedding photographer Cardiff, saw your ad and clicked on it.

Unlike traditional marketing, SEM targets people actively looking for products and services. This is different from broadcasting a message to people that they may-or may not-have any interest in.

Makes sense, right? Now you know why SEM works so well.

Let's sum up. Search engine marketing is a uniquely powerful option for your business. It's simple, but effective: People search for things they want. And advertisers target specific searches, but only pay if someone clicks to learn more. That's search engine marketing.

If you stay tuned we'll cover lots more about SEM. We'll explain how it works, how to identify effective keywords, how to write ads people will click on, and much more.

Check your knowledge 8.1

Question 1 of 1

SEM targets people actively looking for products and services

True / False

(answer: T)

Activity 8.1

Do a search for a product or service you're interested in buying.

Take a look at the paid ads that appear - who do they seem to be targeting?

Are they similar to what you searched for?

Lesson 8.2
The SEM Auctions

Key learning

When advertisers compete to show ads on the same search results page, search engines use an auction to determine which ads appear and in what order. But there's more to consider than just the price. In this video, we'll talk through:

- how an SEM auction works
- factors that influence the outcome
- a detailed example.

Knowledge:

By now, you probably know that search engine marketing is a great way to advertise to people at just the right moment - when they're looking for your products or services. But do you know how it actually works?

Search engine marketing is based on an auction system. So in this video, we'll discuss how the auction works, and look at an example to help you figure out how to use SEM in the best way for your business.

Let's start with a search for a common service-say, wedding photography. Take a look at the results page.

In the centre you'll see organic listings - listings that weren't paid for. And at the top and down the right column you'll see the paid ads.

Search engines limit the number of slots adverts can appear in on an individual page. Advertisers then compete in an auction for those slots.

So, after you search for wedding photography, you see the outcome of the auction. The adverts that "win" appear in more desirable slots on the results page - usually that means near the top. The "runners-up" appear in lower slots.

Alright, you're probably wondering: how does the auction work? Well, like most auctions, you place a bid, which influences your performance in the auction. But it's not all about your bid. In this auction, the relevance of your adverts is crucial as well. So, success in the auction means having a competitive bid, as well as strong relevance. Getting both of these right is the recipe for success in SEM.

Let's look at both of these factors, starting with the bids in the auction. Say you're willing to pay up to £2 when people click on your ad after searching for wedding photography. This price is often called your maximum cost per click, or Max CPC. If your competitor's only got a Max CPC of, let's say, £1, you'll have a higher bid, meaning you'll be "ahead" in the auction. Keep in mind: businesses can change their Max CPCs at any time, so you'll need to keep an eye on your bids regularly to ensure you're getting the performance you want.

But as I said earlier, there's more to the auction than just the bids.

The other big factor is relevance. This is a measure-normally rated from 1 to 10-of how closely your ad relates to what a person searched for. Search engines such as Google and Bing refer to this as your Quality Score.

For example, if someone searches for wedding photography, and your ad's headline is Wedding Photography in Cardiff, the search engine probably considers your ad highly relevant. That means you'd likely get a high-Quality Score.

But what if your advert's headline is Wedding Services Cardiff? Both adverts refer to weddings, but this one is less relevant, because it's talking about wedding services instead of wedding photography. In this case, your relevance wouldn't be as good, so you'd probably have a lower Quality Score.

Think of it this way. When two competing businesses have equal bid prices, the business with a higher Quality Score will appear higher on the search results page. One of the best ways you can improve your performance in SEM is to consistently review your campaigns to find ways to become more relevant.

With us so far? The price you're willing to pay for a click - the max CPC- and your Quality Score are the main things that determine your performance the auction.

Now, let's push our example scenario one step further.

Say two different businesses compete on the same keyword: wedding photography.

Richard bids £4, but his advert is deemed not very relevant, a 3 out of 10. Claire bids £3, and her relevance is a full 10. If we look closely, we can take all this info and figure out what will happen in the auction.

Multiplied out, Richard's auction score - called ad rank - is 12. Claire scores an impressive 30, even with a lower Max CPC.

So, what does that mean? Although her bid was a pound less than Richard's, Claire's advert wins the auction, and she gets a higher position on the page than Richard.

And that pretty much covers SEM Auctions. As you can see, you can't simply "buy your way to the top." This is to ensure the most relevant adverts win the auction, not simply the ones with the highest bids. If your ads lack relevance and get a low-Quality Score, it'll be difficult to compete. In fact, if relevance is too low, the search engines may not display your ads at all.

To improve your performance, stay focused on improving the relevance of all your adverts. Make sure that your adverts always closely match the terms that people have just searched for. By doing this, you can win better positions for your ads, without having to pay more money.

Check your knowledge 8.2

When you're advertising on a search engine, the 'quality' of your advert heading is all-important. It needs to be very aligned to the keywords you're targeting. Here 'Cardiff wedding photographer – 25% discount' is most aligned with the target keywords, so it will have the best quality rating.

Question 1 of 1

Michelle has created some adverts to promote her wedding photography business in Cardiff.

She wants her adverts to align with the keywords 'wedding photographer Cardiff discount', as she's offering 25% off at the moment.

Can you order the following advert headings from best to worst in terms of how well they align with the keywords?

1. Click and hold to drag the items into the right order, then select Submit.
2. Cardiff wedding photographer
3. Discount wedding
4. Wedding
5. Cardiff wedding photographer – 25% discount

(answer: 4,1,2,3)

Activity 8.2

Search for a handful of keywords relevant to your business.

What do you notice about the advertisers for these keywords?

Which ads appear at the top of the page?

Which ads appear lower?

Can you see a correlation between relevance and ad position?

Jot down your observations for future reference.

Lesson 8.3
What Makes A Good Keyword

Key learning

When you're starting a new search engine marketing (SEM) campaign, it's important to understand what makes a keyword "good". In this video, you'll learn which factors to consider before bidding on keywords, including:

- relevance
- traffic
- competition.

Knowledge:

Today we're here to talk about search engine marketing. This video will explain what exactly makes a keyword "good."

We're also going to touch on three important factors to consider when choosing keywords. These are relevance, traffic and competition.

In search engine marketing (SEM), you pay every time someone clicks on your ad. So naturally you want to make sure you're getting your money's worth.

Let's go back to our wedding photographer in Cardiff, and we're going to imagine you're the business owner. You've just updated your website, and now you want to attract new visitors.

You find that on average, the keyword wedding photographer Cardiff costs you about £2 per click. By the way, a "keyword" doesn't have to be just one word - it can be a phrase as well.

Now, without knowing more about what these clicks are worth to your business, you can't really know whether this is a good keyword or not.

For example, if you discover that the average value of these clicks to your business is £40, it's safe to say that this is a good keyword. On the other hand, if the average value is £1, then you might want to make some adjustments.

Measuring the value of your ad clicks will help you know if keywords are "good" or not. But before you start a campaign, you won't be able to measure the value your keywords are generating. So how can you research keywords before adding them to your campaign? Well, you have a few different options here.

The first thing to ask yourself is: is this keyword relevant? Or in other words, does this keyword closely describe your products or services?

Keywords that indicate a person looking to hire a wedding photographer in Cardiff are clearly relevant. However, keywords that suggest a person looking to do their own wedding photography, or that suggest digital photography when you only shoot in film, are far less relevant.

Try to focus solely on keywords that are relevant to your business, and you'll have more success going forward.

Another factor to consider is how much traffic a given keyword is likely to get.

In other words, you might compile a list of highly relevant keywords… but what if nobody searches for them?

In this case, we have to go back to the drawing board.

Take, for example, the keyword:

Cardiff photographer specialising in photography for outdoor weddings

This might describe your business exactly… but with so much specific detail it's unlikely that many people will search for it. Bidding on this keyword probably won't result in many people finding your business.

On the other hand, the shorter keyword:

Cardiff wedding photography is still relevant to your business, and may result in more exposure.

Keyword research tools can provide traffic estimates to help you get a handle on this. But in reality, you'll probably have to use a bit of trial and error to figure out which keywords are relevant and get sufficient traffic.

Now you know how important relevance and traffic are to finding good keywords, let's move on to one more important factor to consider when determining if your keywords are good.

Quite simply, you're going to want to consider what your competition are up to. Think about it: if a keyword is relevant, and gets quite a bit of traffic, your competitors are more likely to be using it too.

For instance, when it comes to the keyword Cardiff wedding photography, there's a good chance that every photographer in Cardiff is bidding on that keyword.

That doesn't mean that you shouldn't include it. But you should look for keywords where the relevance and traffic is high, and competition relatively low.

Perhaps a keyword like Cardiff film wedding photography would be less competitive, because it's more unique to your business.

So, when you're thinking about which keywords you want to include in your ad campaigns you're going to want to remember relevance, traffic potential and competition.

It's a bit of a balancing act, but weighing these three factors can set your ad campaign off to the right start. Be sure to monitor your keywords closely - if you do, you'll quickly learn about what's working, and then you can make adjustments as you move forward.

Check your knowledge 8.3

Question 1 of 1

Measuring the value of your ad clicks is irrelevant in deciding the keywords to be "good" or not.

True / False

(answer: F)

Activity 8.3

Make a list of keywords you think are relevant to your business.

Now, have a look at them with keyword research tools like Google Keyword Planner.

How much traffic can you expect?

What's the estimated cost?

Can you find other keywords you hadn't thought of?

Lesson 8.4
Make Your Ads Stand Out

Key learning

Take a look at any search engine results page. It's full of text! How do you make your business's adverts jump out in this jumble of words? In this video, you'll learn how to:

- attract more traffic with adverts that catch the searcher's eye
- write headlines that make a connection
- write a clear, compelling call to action.

Knowledge:

Have you ever noticed when you search for something online, most of the adverts that you see in the search results look similar? In this video, we'll help your business stand out by showing you how how to write eye-catching ads, compelling headlines and clear calls to action.

Let's start by doing a search for 'hire wedding photographer' and having a look through the ads that appear.

The first thing you might notice is: there are a lot of wedding photographers online, and the ads all seem to get a bit lost in the fray. That's because they aren't particularly relevant to our search, and don't seem to be offering anything unique.

There are also lots of organic search engine results-the results in the centre of the page- competing for your attention.

You can imagine how easy it is for your ad to get lost here, which is why it's really important to create something unique that stands out from the competition.

So how can you take your ad to the next level, and make it "jump off the page?"

There are a few simple guidelines you can follow to turn a plain advert into something attention grabbing.

Let's start with relevance. Relevance is the name of the game in search engine marketing. Try and write your advert's headline to match the searcher's words as closely as possible.

Remember our example search for hire wedding photographer?

If you want to be sure to show up in search results for that search, just use it for the ad's headline:

Hire Wedding Photographer

Now, when someone searches for this keyword, your advert will perfectly match what they're searching for.

So what other ways can you make your advert stand out from the crowd? How about some kind of unique, timely offer or promotion?

If you're running a sale, or have a special benefit the customer can take advantage of, that's a really easy way to attract attention. Let's take your first description line, which said Photos for All Weddings, and update it with a special offer.

How about this: Get 25% Off Your Photo Collage.

This already looks a lot more exciting, and gives the customer a clear reason to visit your website. Similarly, you could try something like: Free Shipping on Purchases over £25.

The last thing you want is a strong, clear "call to action" in your advert. In other words, tell visitors what you want them to do when they get to your site. You could say "Browse Our Portfolio!" or "Buy!" or "Make a Reservation!" Research shows that people respond when you direct them to do something specific.

It's a good idea to include this as the second line of your advert, so the searcher knows exactly what to do after they click on your ad.

Let's say your advert's call to action is Book online today. That's alright, but it's not very exciting. Let's try something a bit more compelling. How about:

View our Wedding Photo Gallery!

This is much better. It tells the customer what they should do when they visit your website. And it also reinforces the fact that your business is highly relevant to the customer's need, because you've got a wide selection of wedding photography.

Right, now let's go back to our original advert to compare the before and after. Looks better doesn't it? The advert's new headline is far more relevant to the search. We have an exciting special offer, and a clear call to action. This new advert is much more likely to attract customers to your website.

So, what have we learned? Using a few simple guidelines can help your adverts stand out from the competition. First, you want to customise your advert headline to the search. Then include a special or timely offer. And finally, give a compelling call to action.

These techniques can help improve your ads across the board. Just remember that writing great adverts is an ongoing process - just like researching keywords or monitoring your bid prices. Focus on these tips over the long run, and you're likely to see success.

Check your knowledge 8.4

Ads need to stand out from the crowd. The best option works because the headline is similar to what the customer would be searching for, the 25% off discount grabs people's attention, and there's a clear and compelling call to action.

Question 1 of 1

Michelle is writing her search ad for her wedding photography business. She wants to make sure it stands out.

Which of these text statements would work best as an ad?

**Cardiff wedding photography. ** Get 25% off your first order. Make your reservation now.

**Wedding photographer. ** Cardiff based photographer specialises in outdoor weddings and scenic locations. Book now!

**Welsh wedding pics. ** Want great wedding pics? Cardiff based photographer, Michelle, available for hire.

(answer : 1)

Activity 8.4

Does your business have any offers or promotions that you can use in your adverts?

Brainstorm a few calls to action that will help potential customers understand what they should do when they reach your website.

Check your knowledge 8.A

Question 1 of 4

Search engine marketing can also be called what?

1. Pay-per-click advertising
2. Organic advertising
3. Search box marketing
4. One-click advertising

Question 2 of 4

In an SEM auction, your Quality Score is based on which aspect of your ad?

1. Bid
2. Relevance
3. Wit
4. Length

Question 3 of 4

Fill in the blank: It's possible to determine how well a/an _____ will perform without bidding on it.

1. Auction
2. Website
3. Keyword
4. Advert

Question 4 of 4

What should your search ad have in order to promote more clicks?

1. A call to action
2. A catchy headline
3. A close-up photo
4. A social media link

Module – 09: Improve Your Search Campaigns

The world of Search Engine Marketing (SEM) is full of opportunities, but to benefit you'll first need to master research tools and keyword selection. From there, you can improve and optimise your search campaigns to ensure you get maximum value for what you spend.

Lesson 9.1
Achieve Relevance with Good Structure

Key learning

To succeed as an advertiser, you need to create adverts that help searchers find what they're looking for – and when you do, search engines may reward you. In this video, you'll learn:

- how SEM campaigns are structured
- how to use that structure to achieve relevance
- the benefits you'll get by focusing on relevance.

Knowledge:

In this lesson, you'll learn why relevance is so important for SEM campaigns. We're also going to look at the structure of SEM campaigns, and show you how to build your campaigns in a way that helps you achieve that relevance. Ready to be one step closer to SEM success? Alright, let's get started.

'Relevance' sounds like a tricksy sort of word, but it's easy to understand if you think about it as someone who uses search engines. For example, let's do a search for 'wedding photographer', and take a look at some of the adverts that appear.

Here we have three.

The first headline says Wedding Photographer, followed by information about pricing and selection. This ad is extremely relevant, because the headline matches our search, plus it has plenty of useful information.

The second headline says Candid Wedding Photoshoot. It includes some information about the types of wedding photo packages this business offers. This ad is fairly relevant, but less than the first because the headline doesn't precisely reflect the search. As a whole, search engines might consider this advert less relevant.

The third headline says Wedding Photograph, but appears to be an ad for a site that sells posters. That's not relevant to what we were searching for.

When it comes to relevance, search engines also consider the first web page people see after they click on an ad. This is called the landing page. So what does this mean for you? Well, just as your advert should be relevant to the words a person just searched for, your landing page should be relevant to the advert a person clicks on.

Makes sense, right? Great, let's move on.

Relevance is important to search engines - After all, it's their job to find relevant results for searches, and this includes finding relevant adverts. Relevance is also really important to businesses who advertise on search engines.

For starters, search engines reward relevant adverts with higher positions on the search results page.

What's more, if your adverts are more relevant than your competitors', you might be able to get the same amount of traffic for a lower price.

So, it makes a lot of sense to pay attention to relevance.

Now let's look at ways you can structure your SEM campaigns to achieve greater relevance.

Think of your SEM plan as an upside-down tree. At the top is your account, which you create with Google Ads, Bing Ads, or another search engine.

Within the account are campaigns. Each campaign controls important decisions, like the daily budget, the areas or countries where ads can appear, and the advertising networks you want to use.

Within each campaign, you can create multiple ad groups. These are collections of keywords and the ads that go with them.

Structuring your account in this organised way helps ensure you show the most relevant ads.

Let's go through another example with the photographer to bring this to life.

Imagine you're the photographer, and you specialise in various types of photography. Let's say weddings, baby photos and family portraits. Each of these specialities contain different products, so you decide to split them into separate campaigns.

Within each campaign, your next move is to create ad groups for each type of product. For example, within your wedding photographer campaign, you might create ad groups for engagement photos, bridal portraits, candid wedding photos, and more.

Within your baby photos ad group, you add keywords that someone would search for. For example, keywords like baby photography or newborn photos. Now you can write an ad that corresponds to the keywords, like:

Baby Photography

We Take Beautiful Newborn Photos

Affordable Rates, Book Now!

If someone searched for your keyword baby photography, this would be a relevant ad!

To sum up: No matter what type of business you have, your SEM campaigns should have a solid, well-thought-out structure.

By dividing your products or services into separate campaigns and ad groups, you can show ads that help customers find exactly what they're searching for- which is win-win for everyone.

Check your knowledge 9.1

Grouping keywords and ads this way means that Anna can show ads that are relevant to what customers are searching for. If someone searches for 'candid wedding photos' they see the ad specifically for her wedding photography services. Anna can run different campaigns for these ads and keep track of them separately.

Question 1 of 1

Anna is a commercial photographer.

She's setting up SEM campaigns to draw more traffic to her site. She needs to make sure her ads are relevant, and she's doing this by creating ad groups for each type of product.

Take a look at the ad below:

Wedding photography

Capture your special day with beautiful photographs

Call to book your date now!

Can you help Anna by eliminating the keywords that wouldn't be relevant to her ad?

1. Bridal party photos
2. Candid wedding photos
3. Baby photoshoot
4. Newborn baby photography
5. Professional website photos

(answer: 1,3,4,5)

Activity 9.1

Use a spreadsheet, a document, or even pen and paper to create 3–4 ad groups for the Wedding Photography and Baby Photography campaigns that you saw during the lesson. Need a hint to get started?

Think about the types of products that might belong to these two categories.

Lesson 9.2
Get the Most from Your Keywords

Key learning

Search engines, like Google and Bing, offer tools that take the guesswork out of choosing the right keywords, and can help potential customers find you online. We'll talk about:

- research tools
- related searches
- negative keywords.

Knowledge:

By now you should have a pretty good idea of how people use lots of keywords to search for your products or services. Now let's talk about making your keywords as effective as possible.

In this video, we'll be looking at research tools, like the ones provided by search engines like Google and Bing. We'll see how using these tools can take some of the guesswork out of choosing keywords, and help more potential customers find you online.

Let's put this into practice. Imagine you already have one SEM campaign promoting your wedding photography business. The clients are coming in, but now let's say you want to build a new campaign advertising your pet portraits.

A tool like Google's Keyword Planner or Bing's Keyword Research Tool can help you find out which keywords are most relevant and will work best for your new campaign.

For example, if you type in "pet portraits," the tool will show you other related searches.

Let's look at which of these keywords might also be a good fit for your new campaign.

We can see that people search for terms like [pictures of dogs], [animal artists], and [dog portraits].

The results also show how many searches each term tends to get. And other useful information, like suggested "bid prices" and "competition levels."

Knowing this, you can create several groups, called ad groups. One for terms related to pet portraits, one for [pictures of dogs], one for [dog portraits] and one for [animal artists].

By organising these terms into ad groups, you can write relevant ads for each group of keywords.

That takes care of the relevant keywords, but what about the ones that didn't seem so relevant?

For example, we can see lots of people are also searching for [pet portraits pencil], which suggests they're looking for something else.

There are also many who are searching for watercolour pet portraits, and horse portraits, neither of which you offer.

In situations like these, you should use "negative keywords" to prevent your ads from appearing when people search for things that aren't relevant to your business. For example, [-pencil], [-pastel] and [-horse].

These negative keywords will block your ads any time a search contains one or all of them.

This is useful, because preventing adverts from appearing for irrelevant searches, is going to save you money, and make sure that only your ideal customer sees your ads.

So, to recap, keyword research tools can help you find keywords that attract customers... but they also help you discover keywords to avoid. It's also a good idea to try and revisit these tools regularly. People's search behavior tends to change over time, and if you let your campaigns sit untouched for too long, their performance could start to dip.

Check your knowledge 9.2

Anna can choose these 'negative keywords' to avoid people seeing her ad when they search using those keywords. For example, if someone were to search for 'Watercolour family portrait' Anna wouldn't want her ad to appear as her portraits are photographs. Similarly, if someone were to search for 'Buy landscape photo' Anna's portraits wouldn't be relevant either. Identifying negative keywords means when people see Anna's ad it's because it's relevant to what they are looking for.

Question 1 of 5

Photographer

True / False

Question 2 of 5

Portrait

True / False

Question 3 of 5

Landscape

True / False

Question 4 of 5

Family photo

True / False

Question 5 of 5

Watercolour

True / False

(answer: F, F, T, F, T)

Activity 9.2

Use one of the research tools linked on the right.

See if you can find five keywords that are relevant to your business.

Then, see if you can find three irrelevant keywords that you can use as negative keywords.

Lesson 9.3
Fine-Tune With Keyword Match Types

Key learning

Search engine marketing (SEM) is great for letting you choose specific searches to trigger your ads. But search engines often show your ads for keywords that are slightly different from the ones you're targeting. The solution: keyword match types. This video explains:

- what match types are and why they're useful
- the different kinds of match types
- how to control which searches may trigger ads.

Knowledge:

Want to make your search engine marketing efforts even more successful? Of course you do!

In this video, we'll be exploring a feature called keyword match types. And learning about how using different match types can increase your control over which searches trigger your ads.

Did you know that search engines might also show your ads when people search for other terms-terms you didn't specifically choose?

That's because search engines can show your ads when people search for variations of your keywords. This is called broad matching.

Most of the time, broad match is useful. It means that you don't have to add every variation of the keyword you'd like to target, like singulars, plurals and misspellings.

But this flexibility also means that sometimes, search engines show your ads for keywords that aren't relevant to your business. Using keyword match types can help.

Let's say you're a portrait photographer. As you brainstorm keywords for your ad campaign, you might consider "London photographer".

If you include this keyword, a search for "London photographer" could trigger one of your ads even though the person making the search might not be looking for exactly what you're offering.

What if they're actually looking to buy prints of photographs of the city of London? Or someone to photograph an event in London? Or do a commercial magazine shoot? Any of these searches could potentially trigger your ad, but the searchers are not likely customers.

One way to prevent ads from appearing on these searches is to choose more specific keywords, since your target customer is probably searching for things like "London portrait photographer" or "London family portraits."

On top of that, you can add match type to further refine the results. How do you do that? Let's take a look.

Keywords are broad match by default. Aside from broad match, the other primary match types are phrase match and exact match. To change broad match to phrase, simply place quotations around the keyword. So, the keyword London portrait photographer becomes "London portrait photographer."

Phrase match tells Google Ads or Bing Ads that adverts can't be displayed unless the search includes the entire phrase. So if someone searches for "London portrait photographer" that's great-your ads can show up! Minor variations, like plurals, are included. This means that a search for "London portrait photographers" can also trigger your ad.

But, if someone searches for the more generic London photographer, your ad won't show up, because the word portrait is missing.

With phrase match, the searcher can include words before and after the phrase, so "East London portrait photographer" could also trigger an ad.

To get even more specific, exact match keywords are distinguished by enclosing the word or phrase in square brackets. So, the keyword London portrait photographer becomes [London portrait photographer].

Now, if someone searches for portrait photographer, your ad can't appear because it doesn't match the keyword exactly. Along the same lines, a search for London photographer also won't trigger your ad.

Unlike phrase match, the ad can't display if the searcher includes additional words. But minor variations, like plurals, can still trigger the ad.

As you change keywords from broad match, to phrase, to exact, it restricts the opportunities for ads to display. Your best bet is to try to find a match type balance, allowing ads to show to likely prospects, but blocking ads when you think success is unlikely.

As you add restrictive match types for keywords, you'll probably notice that your traffic quantity goes down... but traffic quality should improve. And that's what matters here.

Check your knowledge 9.3

Refining keywords by changing them from 'broad match' to 'phrase match' and 'exact match' means that Anna will probably notice a decrease in traffic, but the quality of the traffic she gets will increase. That's because when her ad appears to a customer, it's likely to be relevant to what the customer is looking for. 'Photography, portraits' is a broad match and also a plural, so may have nothing to do with Anna's business. It could also be someone looking for tips on how to set up their own camera for a portrait, for example. If they click on Anna's ad, it costs Anna if her ad is in the paid ads. By narrowing keywords to exact matches like 'Film themed portrait photography, low cost' Anna is more likely to get traffic for her more niche business, and therefore paying customers.

Question 1 of 1

Anna has a themed portrait photography studio. She offers competitive prices and reaches and engages with visitors to her site through her online presence. However, not many of them become paying customers.

Anna has a range of keywords and wants to fine-tune them to best target potentially paying customers.

Put the keywords in order of the broadest to the most restrictive.

Click and hold to drag the items into the right order, then select Submit.

1. Movie themed portrait photography
2. Photography, portraits
3. Portrait photography studio
4. Film themed portrait photography, low cost

(answer: 2, 3, 1, 4)

Activity 9.3

Use one of the research tools linked below to see how your estimated traffic and costs change if you restrict the keyword match types from broad to phrase or exact.

Use the tool to help find the right balance between relevance and traffic.

Think of it as the story of Goldilocks: not too hot, not too cold, just right.

Google Keyword Planner

Bing Keyword Research Tool

Google Trends

Search engine marketing jargon buster

Lesson 9.4
How To Know What's Working and What Isn't

Key learning

One of the best ways to measure how well your search engine marketing is working is by tracking conversions, or actions you'd like website visitors to take. In this video, we'll cover:

- what conversions are
- how to choose the ones you want to measure
- what tools you can use to track them.

Knowledge:

So, you've got some online advertising campaigns up and running and you want to find out how they're doing?

In this video, we'll explain how to do just that by tracking conversions. We'll cover what they are, how to choose the ones you want to measure and what technology to use to track them.

One of the best things about SEM is that you can measure the value you're getting from your campaigns. To do this, you track conversions - the key actions you want website visitors to take-using tools that search engines like Google or Bing provide. We'll get to those in just a minute.

Let's start with how you choose which conversions to track.

Say you're a nature photographer who sells prints online. What kinds of actions might count as "conversions" on your website?

Obviously, placing an order is an important one. But what else might you want people to do?

Well, your website should have a Contact form so potential customers can ask you questions like what other prints you have for sale, or if you're available to photograph special events. When someone submits an inquiry through this form, that's a conversion, too.

What if you don't sell prints online? Instead, you're a wedding photographer and the bulk of your site is a portfolio of your work. You might have references in downloadable PDF form, so when people download it you can track that as a conversion.

You could also have a link people can click to receive your rates via email. That's another way potential customers can become paying customers, so you should track that as a conversion as well.

In these two examples, we've mentioned a handful of different conversions: successful transactions, contact form submissions, and downloads. And there are plenty of other possibilities. Can you think of what conversions you'd want to track for your own business?

So how can you actually track these conversions? Well, you can use tools provided by search engines. These allow you, or whoever is managing your website for you, to place a small piece of code on certain pages of your website. That sounds complicated, especially if you don't have any technical support, but don't worry, we'll walk you through it.

Let's go back to the nature photography business. You want to track a completed order, so you need to figure out the proper place for the conversion tracking code. You wouldn't want to put the code on your homepage-if you do that, you'll be counting conversions every time someone visits your site.

Instead, you would install the conversion tracking code on the order confirmation page. That's the page customers see after they complete an order. That way, you know a conversion happened.

Next, you decide to track online inquiries. Just like the previous example, you need to install the conversion tracking code on a page the visitor sees only after they submit an inquiry. For example, on the page that thanks the customer after they've placed an order.

Make sense? In order to properly track conversions, you need to attach the code to pages someone will only see after they've taken the action you want.

Once you install the code, you'll start getting reports that tell you how many conversions you got. That's valuable information in figuring out if your online ad campaigns are working.

To sum up: By using online tools from search engines like Bing or Google, you can measure online conversions and set yourself up for success.

Check your knowledge 9.4

Anna should place the code on the enquiry confirmation page. If she places the conversion tracking code on the page that appears when a customer has sent their enquiry, she'll know when a customer has actually sent an enquiry. Her data won't get mixed up with people who have visited the enquiries page but decided not to send an enquiry. When Anna installs the code, she'll get reports telling her how many conversions she got.

Question 1 of 1

Anna is a photographer. She's previously focused on wedding photography, but she now takes requests to photograph other events as well.

Customers can contact her through the site's enquiry page to make requests. They can also look at her gallery and sign up to an email newsletter.

Anna wants to track how many people request photography for events that aren't weddings.

1. Where should she place the conversion tracking code?
2. Homepage
3. Enquiry page
4. Enquiry confirmation page

5. Newsletter sign-up page

(answer : 3)

Activity 9.4

Review your website and brainstorm at least one conversion that you want to track.

Then, search for "conversion tracking" tools that are offered by the search engine marketing service you're using, like Google or Bing.

Check your knowledge 9.A

Question 1 of 4

Which of the following is a benefit of using relevant ads and landing pages?

1. Increased cost for ad placements
2. Higher ad positions on the search results page
3. Higher cost per clicks on your ads
4. Ads that will ensure more purchases

Question 2 of 4

When it comes to search ads, which description best describes 'negative keywords'?

1. Keywords with no association to your site
2. Keywords with a poor search volume
3. Keywords that are excluded from a campaign
4. Keywords that are typed incorrectly

Question 3 of 4

Fill in the blank: If you use _____ keywords when building your search ads, minor variations, like plurals, can still trigger the ad.

1. Exact Match
2. Random Match
3. Direct match
4. Close match

Question 4 of 4

What can conversion tracking in search help you measure?

1. How many transactions are completed on your site overall
2. How many people click on your SEM ad and end up browsing your site
3. How many people visiting your site from a search ad end up completing a purchase
4. How many customers your ad has converted into brand ambassadors

(answer: 2, 3, 1, 3)

Module – 10: Get Noticed Locally

If you have a physical storefront, you'll need to harness local online marketing in order to reach customers. Ensure you're visible to people close to your store by creating a listing in local directories, engaging in mobile marketing and building a local search presence.

Lesson 10.1
Marketing To the Locals

Key learning

The Internet connects businesses and customers worldwide. But if you're a local business, you'll want to reach people nearby. Let's learn a bit about:

- what local means in digital
- how your business can build a local search presence
- and a perfect pair: local marketing and mobiles.

Knowledge:

If you run a business where local customers are its lifeblood, stay tuned. We'll cover what "local" means online, how your business can be found by people that are physically near you, and why local marketing and mobile are a match made in heaven.

But first, here's Mike of Cotswold Balloon Safaris to tell us a bit about his approach to local marketing.

[A real small business owner talks about how local marketing helped him attract more customers from his neighbourhood and grow his business.]

You may dream of growing your company into a global brand... or your goal might be to become a big fish in your neighbourhood pond. Either way, the web can help.

So what do we mean by local, exactly? We're talking about businesses with a shop-like a bicycle shop, or a hair salon. But we're also talking about a service area business that goes out to meet with customers-like a lawn care service, or a plumber.

These businesses usually sell products and services to people who live nearby... and people who are visiting from other places. For example, a potential customer might live hundred of miles away, but she's coming to your town on holiday and looking for a place to rent a bicycle while she's there.

These types of local businesses used to rely on tools like The Phone Book to connect with customers looking for their products and services. If a person wanted to buy something, like a bicycle, he might look up stores nearby, and then visit a few to see what was available.

Nowadays, people hunt for stuff from their sofas via laptops and tablets, or browse the Internet on mobiles to pass time standing in a queue.

If they're searching for a product or service you offer, and they're in your neighbourhood, it's the perfect opportunity to get on their radar.

So how does a local search work? Let's take an example.

A man wants to find a bicycle shop near his flat. He does a search for a bike shop, including his city or neighbourhood as one of the terms. Next, he'll get a list of local businesses, including the address, phone number and the working hours.

If he's on a mobile, he can click to ring the shop, or he might even use the mapping functionality of the smartphone to can help him navigate his way to the shop, a great perk if he's already out and about.

So how can you build a local online presence for your business?

First and foremost, be sure your location details are on your website. If you have a shop, be sure to include your address, and maybe even an interactive map so a customer can get directions, plus your telephone number, and your working hours.

And if you have a service area business, be sure your website explains what areas you serve, and how people can get in touch with you.

But there are some very specific things you can do to help local people become your local customers, and in the lessons that follow, we'll cover the importance of local search listings like Google My Business, Bing Local and Yahoo! Local that can help lead searchers to your local business, local advertising opportunities on review sites, social networks and search engines, some unique things you can do with local customers and mobile devices, and finally some tips around search engine optimisation to help you find your local audience.

Local businesses need to be seen by searchers in the neighbourhood, on any device. Someone looking to buy in a specific location is usually ready to pull out his wallet-and you want to be his go-to shop. If you stick with us, you'll learn how you can build and promote an online presence that ensures that's just what happens.

Check your knowledge 10.1

The better way to attract tourists would be for Jim to tailor his website for local search. These days people are used to using their phones when they're out and about to get information quickly. That's why it's so important to create a local online presence for your business.

Question 1 of 1

Jim is running a bike shop in a popular tourist city and he's started a bike hire service.

1. What would be the better way for Jim to attract more tourists – a map feature or a social media page?
2. A website showing a map feature for local search with times for car, bike, public transport and on foot.
3. A social media page for Jim's shop.

(answer: 1)

Activity 10.1

Using your favourite search engine, type in a term such as "bicycle shop near me".

Take note of the various features that we have reviewed in this lesson.

Do you see bicycle shops that are near your physical location?

Does the search result list reviews?

An address?

Directions?

Lesson 10.2
The Power of Local Directories

Key learning

One of the best ways to connect with customers online is to get listed in local directories. In this lesson we'll show you:

- where to start
- how to list your business
- how to manage your local profiles.

Knowledge:

If you're a business that operates out of a physical, brick and mortar storefront, then the odds are you want to attract and serve customers that are nearby - or local - to you.

In this lesson we'll be explaining the ins and outs of one of the best ways to connect with local customers: local directories. By the time it's done you'll know how to get started, where to list your business and how to manage your "local" profile.

Local directories are a great way for local businesses to connect with potential customers in their area. The first step is to create a listing in local directories.

These online listings include your key information, like your business name, your address and your telephone number.

Many local directories require that your business has four walls or a local service area in order to be listed, so virtual businesses that don't meet with customers directly are usually ineligible.

To get started, you'll need to pull together the name of your business as you want it to appear everywhere online, your street address, or where you receive mail in the post, and your phone number.

The name of your business seems straightforward, right? But consistency is key. If the sign in front of your shop says Mike's Bikes, then you don't want to list your shop like that in one directory and as Michael's Bicycles in another.

For the address, you'll need a physical address or location. Post office boxes and shared locations usually won't be accepted.

Just like with your business name, enter your address in the same exact way for every directory.

Telephone numbers should be local as well, including area and country code, so generally you won't want to use a freephone number.

You've got to have these three things-name, address, telephone number- to land local customers.

Now that you know what to list, it's time to find out where to list it. There are loads of online directories to choose from, but we'll start with the obvious ones.

First, you want your business and all those great local details to show up on the most popular search engines, like Yahoo!, Bing and Google-and all of these have local versions and local business listings for you to use.

You should also explore options on major local directories, social networks and review sites, and some of these might be industry specific. Not sure where to find them? Try searching for a business that's similar to yours to see where they appear.

Every local listing site has its own registration and verification process, but most work essentially the same way.

You need to include those three key pieces-name, address and phone number-plus additional business details like your working hours, photos of all those beautiful bikes, videos of your shop, and anything else they'll let you list. You may be asked to choose one or more categories to describe your business, and while you might not find the perfect category, you should always try to choose the closest fit.

Sometimes the directories will ask you to prove that you are, in fact, the owner of the business you're verifying. It makes sense, and every directory is different, but most will verify you by doing things like mailing you a postcard with a special code on it, leaving a voice or text message for you with a code, or sending you an email with verification instructions.

Once you're approved, you can update and manage your listing any time. That just means regularly reviewing and changing the particulars as needed.

If you're listed on a bunch of directories-and you should be-you'll want to keep track of what you've got where, maybe by making a spreadsheet.

You always want to keep your local listings consistent and up-to-date. Remember if your name, address or phone number change, you need to update all those listings immediately.

To sum up, you want to connect with your local customers, and that means taking advantage of the major search engines' local business listings and creating profiles on business directory websites, review sites and more.

Being there gives you the best shot of connecting with local customers.

Check your knowledge 10.2

At a minimum, Jim needs to include a business name, address, telephone number and opening hours to have a listing in a local directory. He can also add other optional information such as photos of his products, depending on the listing site he's using.

Question 1 of 5

Jim's Bikes

True / False

Question 2 of 5

10 Bird Way, Cowseld, West Sussex, RH11 5XN

True / False

Question 3 of 5

Phone number 01269 559632

True / False

Question 4 of 5

Open 9–5 Mon–Sat

True / False

Question 5 of 5

Image of a bike

True / False

(answer: T, T, T, T, F)

Activity 10.2

Visit one of the major local directories, such as Google's, Yahoo's or Bing's.

Search for your business to see if it is already listed and follow the steps to claim your listing.

If you have already claimed the listing, make sure it's optimised so that your listings are consistent, current and are placed in proper categories.

Check your knowledge 10.A

Question 1 of 4

How can you improve a business's visibility to people located near you geographically?

1. Translate your website into at least two more languages
2. Offer free phone support during business hours
3. Ensure you have good analytics on your website
4. Make sure your phone number, address and business hours are easy to find

Question 2 of 4

Which of the following is an example of a local search?

1. "bike shop near me"
2. "bike shop in UK"
3. "local bicycle shop"
4. "bike shops"

Question 3 of 4

Which of the following is a benefit of registering your business in online local listings?

1. Discounted pricing on your search advertising campaigns
2. Increased likelihood of being discovered through search engines
3. More mentions on social media platforms
4. Guaranteed sales to local customers

Question 4 of 4

Which three pieces of information are essential to include first in your local directory listing?

1. Business address, website, telephone numbers
2. Business name, business address, telephone numbers
3. Website, telephone numbers, email address
4. Business name, email address, website

(answer: 4,1,2,2)

Module – 11: Help People Nearby Find You Online

Thanks to search engines, local directories and social networks, reaching customers who are physically close to a store is a relatively easy task. Learn some ways to take advantage of that unique opportunity to attract new customers, by mastering local advertising, mobile marketing and more.

Lesson 11.1
Using Digital to Advertise Locally

Key learning

Local advertising is a great, affordable (sometimes even free) way to connect with customers who are close at hand. In this lesson we'll talk about:

- why local advertising is important
- where you can advertise online to local customers
- some special features of "local" ads.

Knowledge:

Advertising on the web has changed how buyers and sellers meet up: what used to be the phone book has now evolved to almost exclusively search engines, online directories, review sites and social networks. And while all of these digital mediums are available to anyone, anywhere in the world, many of these offer ways to advertise to your local audience.

In this lesson we'll cover the basics of local advertising for your business. We'll explore why local advertising is important, the different places you'll be able to buy local ads, and the things you can do to limit your reach to a local audience.

First, you have to remember that the Internet is everywhere. That means that if you're a bicycle shop in East London, people in West London are going to be able to find you online... and people from Sydney to New York City as well. But assuming that someone in New York City isn't very likely to hop over the pond to buy something from you, it's probably not going to be a good idea for you to waste your advertising money on people in New York.

And that's what makes local advertising different - it's limited to showing your ads to people who are local to you and likely to be - or become - your customers.

You can accomplish local advertising online through a lot of different channels, and search engines, local directories, review sites, and social networks are great places to start.

On search engines, you can bid to show your ad when people type in certain search terms, and all of the major search engines allow you to limit your ads showing to only people in certain locations and geographies. For example, if you were bidding on a keyword like "bicycle repair," you could set up your campaign to only bid if the person that typed it in was within, say, 10 miles of your bicycle shop.

So, what else? Well, social networks like Facebook and LinkedIn offer business pages, as well as paid advertising to target local customers. The social networks can figure out where people are, and just like with search engines, you can specify your ads to show only to people who are nearby with a really relevant, local message.

And of course, the local directory and review websites offer advertising opportunities as well. Over and above your listing, which is usually free, you can often pay a little more to get your ad shown in premium locations like search results or even on your competitors' listings!

And there are some pretty neat things you can do with local ads that can take advantage of someone being nearby when they see those ads. First, your message can be really tailored to someone that's physically close to your shop. And lots of local advertising channels offer some unique features. You might be able to list your hours of operation, or only show your ads when you're open. Or you might be able to let people get directions right to your storefront on a smartphone or mobile device, let them ring your phone number with a single tap, or let them browse all your great reviews.

Local advertising can help you find customers that are close to where you do business, and there are lots of options for running local ads.

Whether you choose to use search engines, social networks, directories or review sites, limiting your advertising budgets to people near you and taking advantage of the special local advertising features can help boost your business in the neighbourhood.

Check your knowledge 11.1

Esmeralda can target local customers in a number of different ways. She can set up her ad campaigns to only bid if the customer doing the search is within 10 miles of her shop. She can also set it to only bid during the hours that she's open. With local ads, Esmeralda can tailor her messages to people who are close to her shop. These are all ways that she can make her searches more specific to locals.

Question 1 of 1

Esmeralda runs a local bike shop.

If she advertises her shop using the internet, Esmeralda could reach people in many different countries.

But she doesn't want to do that. She wants to target her online ads to local customers.

How can she do this effectively?

1. Show ads to people within 10 miles of her shop
2. Display the ad during the shop's opening hours
3. Tailor her ads for people who live locally
4. Hand out flyers and business cards to local shops

(answer: 1,2,3)

Activity 11.1

Look for the advertising options that would make sense for your business.

Start by entering the names of businesses similar to yours into a search engine and take notes.

What directories do they appear in?

Are they using paid advertising?

These are the options you will want to think about. Also, ask your customers where they hang out on social media.

This will give you other ideas about where you can connect with new customers online.

Lesson 11.2
Reaching Locals on Their Mobiles

Key learning

Take advantage of the ways that mobile and local complement each other to connect with customers closest to you. In this lesson we'll explore:

- the importance of being found in local search results
- making the most of mobile features, like GPS and applications (apps)
- using paid advertising to reach a local audience on the go.

Knowledge:

Let's chat about mobile devices, and how they can help your business connect with customers nearby.

We'll show how mobile phone technology-from maps to apps to paid advertising that targets people nearby-can help bring more customers to your door.

Today, many people walk around with a smartphone in their pocket. As a business, you can take advantage of this to reach nearby customers.

First, let's take a look at how local and mobile work together.

We've all used our mobile to find, say, the closest shop to where we happen to be. Say you're riding your bike around town when suddenly your chain breaks. If you've got your mobile on you, you're probably about to do a search for a bike shop that's really close.

So if you own that bike shop, or any other kind of business, what can you do to improve your chances of showing up when people need you?

Of course you'll want to make sure your business is listed in local directories, review sites and search engines, and you might want to take advantage of some local advertising opportunities, but let's talk about how you can harness the power of mobile devices for local customers.

The first thing you need to do is make sure your site looks good on mobile devices and includes contact information.

Next, you can take advantage of some things that only mobile devices tend to have. For example, many people allow websites and mobile apps to use a GPS function that can detect where they are and direct them to where they want to go (like that bike shop).

Or, if the bike shop has an app that people install on their smartphones, it could use that GPS functionality to send messages-like sales alerts-when potential customers are within a certain distance of the shop.

Depending on the capabilities of the app, it could allow customers to schedule appointments for repairs, find answers to common questions or even order accessories. The app could also send reminders of cool events taking place at the shop, like a monthly group ride or free tune-up clinic.

Another common way GPS-enabled devices work with mobile is in local advertising. Paid advertising programs help you target the right customer, at the right time, and now, in the right place.

Say someone who hasn't downloaded your app-or might not even know you exist-happens to be nearby searching for bicycles on her mobile. With local search, your ad could appear high in the search results because your shop is nearby, and a relevant result for what she's looking for.

And remember, local advertising opportunities can be found in other places too, not just major search engines. Local advertising through social networks, directories, review sites and more can be a really cost-effective way to reach local customers.

Think about your business. How do you marry mobile with local?

To get started, make sure your customers can find you online, using any device, and have a good experience whether they're on a laptop, desktop, smartphone or tablet.

Then, think about using mobile specific technology like GPS and apps to motivate customers with local features and promotions.

And finally, if you're advertising locally, you can target people nearby and on the go with your campaigns.

Check your knowledge 11.2

GPS is a great feature that Esmeralda can take advantage of. Depending on the capabilities of the app she uses, Esmeralda can send sales alerts when customers are near the shop or simply use maps to navigate them to it. The app can also help Esmeralda to remind people of events in her shop, send personalised coupons or let customers schedule appointments, but all this can work without GPS technology.

Question 1 of 1

Esmeralda runs a local bike shop.

She knows a lot of her customers use smartphones with GPS, so she invested in a mobile app that can utilise this technology.

She has a couple of ideas how to use the app to engage her customers.

Can you remove the ideas that do not need GPS?

1. Send sales alerts when customers are near the shop
2. Notify people of promotional events like a free tune-up
3. Direct customers to Esmeralda's shop
4. Send personalised coupons to repeat customers
5. Let customers schedule appointments for repairs

(answer: 2,4,5)

Activity 11.2

Search for a nearby business on your mobile.

Note the number of businesses you recognise.

Next, click on a few results and browse the websites from your mobile.

Are they easy to navigate? Are the layouts appropriate for a smaller screen?

Lastly, see if you can find a local business that offers an app.

What sort of functionality is being offered?

What could you offer in an app for your business?

Lesson 11.3
SEO For Local Businesses

Key learning

If you want to increase the chance of local customers finding your business, you need to know a bit about:

- including key information on your website
- how search engines choose local results
- the importance of mobile.

Knowledge:

Let's talk about search engines and local businesses.

You probably already know that search engines are powerful tools for connecting potential customers with businesses. But did you know that they can prioritise your business in the search results if a searcher is nearby or wants options in your geographic area?

Let's head back to our bicycle shop example to see how this works.

You've got a website where customers can order products online... but they often need to buy replacement parts ASAP, which means they won't be waiting around for delivery. You need to make sure those customers find your shop, so they can buy what they need, on-the-spot.

So, how can you help your bicycle website show up in 'local' search results? First, you have to let the search engines know where "local" is, for you!

Start with the basics, and make sure your website includes information like your business name, your business address or your service area, if you meet with customers at their location, your phone number and your working hours.

Another way to help? Add relevant content that also helps identify your geographic location.

Content goes a long way in helping customers and prospects connect with your business. For a bike shop, content might include a blog about bike repairs and maintenance, and details about the bike clinics you host at your shop.

It could include descriptions, photos and videos of local bicycle races or popular biking trails in your area.

It might include how-to articles about choosing the correct bike frame size with an offer for local customers to visit the shop for help.

As you add more local information to your website, and search engines recognise its relevance to local searchers, the chances of appearing in the local results may increase, too.

Remember: the role of a search engine is to provide the right result, at the right time and in the right place for the searcher. In order to do this, search engines may use the proximity of the searcher to your business, or the geographic area they type in as part of their search.

And it's important to recognise this: you can't expect your bike shop to appear in the search results when someone wants to find a bike shop in another country.

Just how well your business is known may also be a factor. Just like in the offline world, some businesses are just more established than others. In the online world, businesses that may have had websites around for a longer period of time or have built up a lot of references and content over time can be rewarded by search engines in the results pages.

And don't forget to take advantage of the local offerings of the search engines themselves. Making sure that you're using services like Yahoo! Local, Google My Business or Bing Local will help the search engines know more about your business and when to list you in their results.

Once your business is listed and the physical location or service area confirmed, these local search listings become another way local searchers can find you online.

Let's do a quick recap. What do you think a result for a search on "bike shop in the town where you live" would include?

If you said "a list of shops in your town that sell bicycles," you'd be correct.

And if you take a look at the businesses that are showing up, you'll probably find that they have lots of local listings and websites with lots of relevant content along with detailed information about their business locations.

Last but not least, don't forget that many searchers are on the go, looking for local results on smartphones.

If your website can be found in the mobile search results it can be an important way to connect with customers, so make sure that you've got a mobile friendly, quick loading website that search engines can understand and visitors love.

And that's it: local SEO 101. Remember, following these steps can help search engines understand if your business is local:

Add location details to your website,

Continually add quality content that's relevant to your audience and highlights the location of your business,

Check your business listings on search engine and local business directories, and

Ensure your site is mobile-friendly and easy for both search engines and visitors to understand.

It may take some work to get found locally, especially for a new business, but if you take the time to add clear business information to your website, build great content, and promote your site in local directories, your customers can start finding you on the other side of their local searches.

Check your knowledge 11.3

For Esmeralda's content to be geared to local searches, it needs to focus on relevant content that identifies her shop's location. Although the post about famous cyclists would be interesting, it doesn't have a local angle. However, the post about popular bike trails in the area does, so it would draw local interest. This would make it more likely for search engines to pick up Esmeralda's website. Once search engines recognise the relevance of these posts to local searchers, her shop will be more likely to appear in local results.

Question 1 of 1

Esmeralda owns a bike shop and wants to make her website interesting for local customers.

She's currently planning blog content that will help her show up on searches for local shops.

She's had an idea for a post about famous cyclists and one about popular bike trails in the area.

Which one do you think Esmeralda should start with?

1. A post about famous cyclists.
2. Popular bike trails in the area.

(answer: 2)

Activity 11.3

If you already have a website, let's see how mobile friendly it is. Visit the mobile-friendly testing tool and run some of your key web pages through the tool.

Did you pass?

If so, congratulations! Your site is on its way to optimisation for local prospects.

Did the tool discover any errors? Not to worry - you can use the recommendations to prioritise and address any mobile usability issues.

Check your knowledge 11.A

Question 1 of 3

Which of the following factors help search engines determine if your business is local?

1. Location details on the website, quality content and how mobile friendly the website is
2. Location details on the website, list of shops local to you and a contact form
3. Quality content, list of local suppliers and location details
4. Location GPS tags on photos, quality content and how mobile friendly the website is

Question 2 of 3

When looking to attract a local audience, why it is important to optimise your website and content for mobile users?

1. Because local users tend to use their mobile devices when they're out of the house
2. Because mobiles will replace desktop computers
3. Because all online users browse on mobile devices these days
4. Because marketing for mobile is more cost effective

Question 3 of 3

Which of the following can help you gain visibility in search engines?

1. Adding relevant content that highlights the location of your business
2. Including your address on your Twitter account

3. Optimising your site for desktop devices only
4. Adding a list of shops local to you on your website

(answer: 1,1,1)

Module – 12: Get Noticed With Social Media

Everyone's on social media, so it makes sense for your business to be there too. Take advantage of popular social media networks by understanding why you need to be there, joining the right social media sites and growing your presence by engaging with your networks.

Lesson 12.1
Social Media Basics

Key learning

Social media is everywhere, and people engage with it every day. Learn what it is and how you can take advantage of these networks by:

- understanding why you need to be there
- joining the right social media sites
- growing your presence and engaging with your networks.

Knowledge:

Eat, sleep, Tweet, repeat. Social media is now a given in our daily lives. As a business, it can be a big opportunity for you.

Online networks, or "social media" as we call it, allow people to link, interact, share and exchange information. They've quickly become something we can't seem to live without. Literally millions of people connect and share on social media every single day.

But it can also be a great tool for businesses. Social media can be a platform that lets you talk directly to your customers and prospective customers alike, share content, get involved in conversations, build trust, reach more people, grow your sphere of influence, and ultimately understand your customers better.

Imagine you own a vintage clothing shop. Your customers might already be using social media to talk about you. They might be sharing their amazing finds, asking for advice about alterations or even to post photos of celebs in retro outfits.

When you join these social networks, you can join these conversations and start new ones. Maybe you'll start by sharing photos when you get new items in stock, and this will help you stay "top-of-mind". It also give people a reason to visit, again and again.

This way your network can grow quickly. Those people might see your posts and share them with other fashionistas, which can score you new followers and new connections. These are people who just might become your next customers.

Social media can also help you build trust with your audience. Imagine a potential customer reading reviews, or watching videos of real people- not models-wearing and raving about your clothes.

Social media provides an opportunity for your customers and fans to promote your products, and when this happens, you earn trust. Why? When someone else says how great you are, it carries more weight. You're not promoting yourself-your customers are doing it for you.

And, there's one last benefit of social media for your business: You can learn by watching how people interact with your brand online.

Maybe no one's interested in a blog post about the history of brocade, but a video showing 20 ways to tie a silk scarf gets tons of shares. Figure out what people like-both online and in your shop-and give them more of it.

Sound good? Right, let's talk about how you can make social media really pay off for your business by joining the right social media sites, sharing content and participating in lively conversations and growing your networks.

You can't tap into the power of social media unless you're there. First, you'll want to get to know the different networks. Which ones are your customers using most?

This will help you decide if you need a Facebook page, a YouTube channel, a Pinterest account, a Twitter handle, a Google+ page, a LinkedIn company page, or some combination of these and others.

Then, you'll need to create your profile, or what usually ends up being your "home page" on each of the sites you're going to participate in.

Each social network is different, but whenever possible, you'll want to add particulars about your business, like your location and contact information. Some let you add more information about your business or even photos and video.

Once you "move in" to a social network, it's time to get to know the neighbours. Making friends takes time and effort, but if they can help get the word out about your business, it's an investment that really pays off.

It's important to know that while you may be using social media for business gains, it's a very different medium than your typical advertising channels. The people you interact with on social media don't want to just to be "talked at." Think of it more as a conversation - a give-and-take relationship that ebbs and flows. Treat this network as you would your friends and colleagues in the real world.

Making friends on social media won't happen overnight, and it can't be forced. Start by recruiting existing customers, maybe with a sign in your shop that says "Follow us here" or-even better-a 10% discount if they connect with you online.

Follow that up with other ways to grow your network: contests, special events, members-only offers, entertaining content, or even real, face-to-face meet-ups for members of your social circles.

And remember, every member of your social network has a network of their own. Social media is all about sharing, so as you add posts and photos and get involved in conversations, it's easy for people to connect with you. And that means more eyeballs on you and your business.

Social media is a great way to start a conversation with people and ultimately grow your customer base. And just like anything else in the online space, you'll need a plan.

If you follow along with the rest of our videos, we're going to cover what kinds of social networks are out there, and how to build your presence on them. Then we'll talk about creating and managing a plan for social media. And if you're really into social, we'll even talk about paid advertising on social sites, and how to measure your success with social.

Check your knowledge 12.1

Social media is all about connecting with your customers; starting a conversation with people can help customers get to know you and your company. Posting regularly keeps the conversation going, although make sure you don't overload your followers with posts. Naming and shaming competitors and deleting all negative posts could reflect badly on you and put followers off. The same could be said of commenting too much on followers' personal posts.

Question 1 of 5

Start a conversation with your followers

True / False

Question 2 of 5

Comment on all of your followers' personal posts

True / False

Question 3 of 5

Delete all negative comments

True / False

Question 4 of 5

Post regularly

True / False

Question 5 of 5

Name and shame competitors

True / False

(answer: T, F, F, T, F)

Activity 12.1

Explore some of the popular social media sites you think your customers use, like Facebook, Twitter or Google+.

As you do, write down the kinds of posts you could make there.

What would this audience find interesting, funny or valuable... and want to share?

Lesson 12.2
The Right Social Media Sites For You

Key learning

New social media sites pop up constantly. Here's an overview of what's out there and how to figure out which ones might be important to you. We'll go over:

- different types of networks
- understanding their contexts
- the best ways to get involved.

Knowledge:

In this lesson we'll get a "lay of the land" in the realm of social media. There are some really big social networks that are important to know about, but there are also smaller, more niche networks that can be really valuable to your business, too. This video will help you understand what's out there, and how to figure out which social networks you need to be a part of.

When getting started with social media, it helps to sort all the different networks into categories so that you can understand where you need to focus your attention.

Let's start with some of the biggest social networks out there. For example, Facebook, Twitter, Google+ and LinkedIn have some very big audiences. Did you know that Facebook alone has more than a billion users across the globe? This means that your existing and future customers are likely participating in these huge networks, so if you're a business, you should probably consider having a presence on these large networks so you can find them there.

But beyond the big ones, you'll also find niche, or industry-specific players that cater to specific topics or specific audiences who really know their stuff and are looking for more detailed or insider content. Think about sites like TripAdvisor for social travel reviews, or Opentable in the restaurant space. There are lots of different sites out there dedicated to lots of different industries, and you should search around to find the most important ones for your business.

And although membership on these sites might be smaller, those members can be exactly the kinds of people you're looking to attract.

Another thing to think about when you're deciding where you should participate, is the purpose of each social network. For example, some social networks are mostly used for personal relationships. Some are more focused on sharing content, and some are used more for professional networking.

Let's dig into that a bit more. Personal networks are one way that people keep in touch with friends and family online, but that doesn't mean that you can't participate as a business: people discuss products and services all the time. You just need to be aware of the context. That means your updates should be light, interesting and useful - not salesy. For example, a vintage clothing shop could post photos of a customer carrying a fabulous vintage handbag, and that might get referenced or shared by people on the network, exposing the business to more people.

Content sharing networks give potential customers information they can sink their teeth into: facts, figures, graphics, reviews, and things like that. For example, YouTube, where that same vintage clothing store could publish videos that show "how to wear it," or Pinterest, where beautiful photos of 'street style' outfits could be featured.

Professional networks tend to be aimed at the business world and attract people looking to network, find jobs or hire people. Again, it's important to know your context here: you're not likely to get much of a response by trying to sell vintage clothing here, but you might be able to locate your next employee.

On the other hand, if you're a business that sells to other businesses, this might be exactly where you want to advertise your products and services to other professionals in very specific industries or job roles.

In the end, it's all about understanding the objectives of each network, and the people hanging out there that you want to connect with.

The big networks like Facebook, Twitter, LinkedIn, Google+, YouTube, and others have lots of users, so you're likely to find lots of people there. But beyond that, you might find smaller networks dedicated to exactly what you do, filled with people who are super-interested in the types of products or services you offer.

With each network, spend some time looking around to see how people are using it. This will help you better understand how you can participate in the conversations, or what kinds of content you might share.

Check your knowledge 12.2

It's important that the tone of a post matches the purpose of the network. These posts might be best placed on the following: - A professional post looking for a contractor would be best positioned on LinkedIn, which is designed for professional networking. - Professional-looking photos can be shared in multiple places by Instagram, a network designed for photo sharing. - The post announcing her first late-night fashion show would be well positioned on Facebook where Lily could set up an event for customers to RSVP to.

Question 1 of 3

Vintage Lily is looking for a carpenter to create a bespoke counter top for our vintage clothing shop; contact me for details

1. Instagram
2. Linkedin
3. Facebook

Question 2 of 3

Loving these recent photos of the new range by my fantastic photographer friend Rae

1. Instagram
2. Linkedin
3. Facebook

Question 3 of 3

So excited about our first ever after-hours vintage fashion show on Thursday at 7 p.m. – join us?

1. Instagram
2. Linkedin
3. Facebook

(answer: 2,1,3)

Activity 12.2

Make a list of at least four social networks.

Which category do you think each falls under: personal, content sharing or professional?

Lesson 12.3
Setting Your Goals For Social Media

Key learning

Once you've learned the lay of the land when it comes to social media, it's time to figure out what you're trying to accomplish. Let's talk about:

- setting specific goals for your social media efforts
- focusing your efforts on those goals
- putting your plan into action.

Knowledge:

Social media offers some great opportunities for businesses, but it can also be overwhelming. To help you formulate your social media plan, you'll need to start with your business goals.

Are you ready to figure out what you're going to get out of social media?

There are lots of social networks out there, and lots of ways to use them, to achieve lots of different objectives. But before you start signing up and posting all over the place, start with a simpler question. What are you hoping to accomplish with social media?

Maybe you're looking for a faster way to respond to customer inquiries. Maybe social media's a way for you to reach your existing customers and encourage them to buy from you more often. Or maybe you're looking to grow your business by finding new people who could become new customers.

These are all good examples of goals that social media can help you achieve, and there are plenty more.

Remember our vintage clothing shop? Let's use that example to see how this plays out. Say you've just opened your shop. You want to get more customers through the door, but in order to do that, you need to generate some buzz and get in front of as many people as you can. So that's your first goal: raising awareness about your business.

Keeping this goal in mind will help you map out your next social media move.

For starters, you'll need to have something interesting to say, and you need to find people to say it to. Since you know you're trying to find people who haven't heard of you before, think about what they would be interested in or likely to respond to. Maybe you just got in a new line of hats or you're having a big grand opening sale.

Once you've got something to say, it's time to figure out how you'll find people to say it to.

Because you're looking to grow your network, you'll probably want to start with some of the big networks. So maybe you've decided to join Facebook and Twitter. Once you've established yourself there, you can reach out to a group of your loyal customers or even your friends and family and ask them to connect with you. As you share with them and they share with their own networks, you'll start to grow your own connections, and you'll be achieving your business objective!

Remember, social media isn't a one-way street. You also have to participate and give back to your new network of friends and followers.

Engage with the network by re-sharing some of their content, or maybe you can spark some discussion by commenting on other people's content around current fashion trends, or a celebrity who put together an amazing vintage look.

The last thing you'll need to plan is how you're going to speak to the different audiences in the different networks you're using.

This will depend in part on the function of the networks themselves, but it's worth thinking through the tone of voice you want to use, and the interactions you want to pursue.

Are you going to be professional and authoritative? That might work well if your target audience is formal and professional, or for specific networks like LinkedIn.

Or are you going to be light and friendly? That might work better in less formal or personal networks, where you're interacting with a more casual consumer.

And again, don't forget your business goals. If you're looking to attract more people to your networks and your business, then make sure to use an engaging and inviting tone. And if you're trying to engage your existing customers, make sure you speak to them with gratitude for being your loyal customers.

The world of social media can be broad and complex, but starting out with clearly defined goals will help you figure out which networks to participate in, how to use them, and ultimately, how they'll help you achieve your objectives.

Check your knowledge 12.3

Social media can help Lily raise the profile of her business, and grow her customer base with new customers by getting followers to share her content with their friends. While budgeting is important for the business, it's unlikely social media will be able to help. Financial planning tools would help support this goal, which could be found online. Lily wouldn't be able to control her flow of stock via social media, although she could host flash sales online to clear some old stock.

Question 1 of 2

Lily has had fun experimenting with the various social media networks but it's time to get a little more serious. Which of Lily's business goals can she achieve with social media?

1. Raise the profile of the business
2. Keep expenditure within the stated budgets
3. Attract new customers and grow the customer base
4. Control the flow of stock

5. Discuss new products with customers

Question 2 of 2

Lily is setting up a Twitter profile for her business. She's put together a list of the key things she'll need to get her profile up and running. Can you check her list and cross off any items she doesn't need to include in her Twitter business profile?

1. A business email account
2. Annual membership fee
3. A company logo or photo
4. Business description and contact details
5. Number of employees in the business

(answer: 1 3 5, 2 5)

Activity 12.3

Consider your social media goals.

Are you trying to build awareness?

Are you looking for a way to communicate more with your customers?

If you had to choose one goal to start, what would it be?

How can you begin to put it into motion?

Lesson 12.4
Getting on Social Media

Key learning

Joining a social network usually starts with opening an account and creating a profile. In this video we'll explore:

- the basics of getting started with a social media site
- the difference between business and individual accounts
- the importance of your profile.

Knowledge:

There are lots of different social networks out there, and knowing your business goals, and how you want to incorporate social into your strategy, will help you decide which ones are right for you.

Once you decide, you'll need to join and establish your presence in your chosen networks. Each one is different, but there are some common elements.

First, social networks for businesses can be a little different than social networks for individuals. For example, you might have a personal Facebook account where you connect and share with your personal friends and family, but the platform also offers pages specifically designed for businesses.

Other networks don't look all that different whether you're a business or an individual.

Before you sign up, check into whether the network you're joining distinguishes between businesses and individuals, and make sure you set up the right one.

Once you've got this figured out, it's time to sign up. This usually means creating an account. Generally, it's best to use your business email address to do this so you can keep your personal and professional accounts separate.

Next, start loading up information. Now, every social network is going to be different, but there are some universal things, like your business name, a description of who you are and what you do, your address, your email address, and your phone number. These are all pretty standard, and you may even be able to upload an image of your business's logo.

Many networks will use this information to create a profile page for you, which is kind of like your homepage within the network itself.

Different social networks offer different things, so take some time to explore your options, not forgetting your plan.

Remember the tone of voice you decided to use and the business goals you want to support. This will help you as you write the descriptions of your business, as you list your products, choose the images or videos you want to showcase, and even personalise your profile page with background images.

Your profile page is often the place where you'll be sharing your content, having conversations, and displaying your activity. Generally, all that information you've entered about yourself will be accessible to people when they visit this page, and all the things you're posting and sharing, along with the comments and activity on those posts, will show up here as well. This creates a kind of living history of your business's virtual life in the network.

Also, don't forget many of these profile pages are also accessible by search engines, so the more great content you provide here, the better the chances that your social pages might even show up when people are searching on search engines!

Whether people find you through search or by seeing something they're interested in that you shared, they'll likely click over to this profile page, and it can give them a great overview of who you are and what you offer. Even better, they'll be able to easily interact with you, and hopefully become your next customer!

Finally, many social networks offer advertising opportunities, or special features for a price. For example, you may be able to pay for the right to see who else in the network has been looking at you, or you may be able to pay to put the content you're sharing in front of specific groups of people on those networks. Have a look at the paid programs offered by your social networks, and see if they're valuable to you.

Creating your business's presence on the networks you'll be using, always keeping your goals in mind, is an essential step on the path to social success!

Check your knowledge 12.4

Most social network profiles require similar information including a business description, image and contact information. For Twitter, a membership fee and detailed business information (such as number of employees in a company) isn't needed. This kind of information might be required on LinkedIn, which is more focused on business structures and offers Premium (paid for) accounts.

Question 1 of 1

Lily is setting up a Twitter profile for her business. She's put together a list of the key things she'll need to get her profile up and running. Can you check her list and cross off any items she doesn't need to include in her Twitter business profile?

1. A business email account
2. Annual membership fee
3. A company logo or photo
4. Business description and contact details
5. Number of employees in the business

(answer: 2,5)

Activity 12.4

Get your business signed up for a social media network.

Think about your customers, and which social networks they might already be using.

Then, open an account and start building your profile.

Check your knowledge 12.A

Question 1 of 4

Which of the following can businesses achieve by using social media?

1. Attract new audiences
2. Build a good reputation with customers
3. Meet sales goals
4. Increase traffic to their website

Question 2 of 4

Fill in the blank: Businesses should focus on social media platforms with _____.

1. The biggest reputation
2. The most expected engagement
3. A relevant audience
4. The most users

Question 3 of 4

Which of the following is an example of a social media goal?

1. Acquire genuine reviews on products
2. Drive more traffic to your store
3. Develop one-way communication with customers

4. Mimic your competition's approach

Question 1 of 4

Which details should you look to include on a business profile page on social media?

1. Details about the CEO
2. Link to a local listing site you're on
3. Description of the business
4. Cost of products and services

(answer: 1,3,2,3)

Module – 13: Deep Dive into Social Media

An organised social media plan and strategy will go a long way in saving you time and energy. Become familiar with what social content works best, why advertising on social can be a powerful addition to your strategy, and how to measure success so that you can optimise future social content.

Lesson 13.1
Your Long-Term Social Media Plan

Key learning

Once you start engaging with social media, you'll realise pretty quickly: it helps to get organised. Putting together a serious plan for how you want to invest in social media will really help. In this video, we'll cover:

- the benefits of creating a plan for social media
- what a social media plan might look like
- tools to help you put your plan into action.

Knowledge:

Getting serious with social media means a lot of work, and you can find yourself lost pretty quickly if you don't have a plan. This video will give you all the details you need to put a plan on paper, and show you some tools that can help you put it into action.

Let's jump straight in. If you've already started to dabble in social media, you've probably noticed how much work it takes to do things well.

It's not easy to keep everything up to date, reply and interact with all your connections, or come up with a steady stream of ideas for unique, interesting things to be posting all the time across a number of different networks. Don't worry.

The key is to sit down and sketch out a formal plan for what you want to post, when you want to post it, where it makes sense to post, and even who at your business should be posting.

Why is that so helpful?

Well, if you just assume that you'll have enough free time to come up with creative, compelling posts "on the spot," the odds are that you'll end up disappointed. Life gets in the way, other things take priority and, without a plan, your social pages might end up being silent for too long, or your posts might be lower quality, because you're feeling pinched for time.

It's understandable. This stuff is challenging and you've got a lot going on. But the truth is, a good social media strategy deserves just as much careful thought and planning as any other type of marketing.

Alright, so what should a social media plan look like? Consider the next 6 to 12 months, and start creating a calendar. Sketch out details like what topics it makes sense for you to post about? What's your audience interested in?

Then take it a step further. When does it make sense to post about those topics?

If we go back to our vintage clothing shop, think about when there might be major fashion shows, special shopping seasons like back to school or the holidays, or other timely events that you can "piggy-back" on. Whether you post daily, hourly, or weekly, laying out your calendar will help make sure you're consistent in your sharing.

What and when is a great start, but you also have to consider where you should be posting. For example, if you're sharing some awesome pictures of the new line of dresses that just came into the shop, that might be a great update to share on social sites like Instagram or Pinterest. On the other hand, if you want to share a special offer for your biggest fans, you might share that with your connections on Facebook or Google+ instead.

Next, don't forget to think about who's going to be doing all of this posting and sharing. Are you going to do it all yourself or are you going to share the work? Writing down who's responsible for what in your plan will help make sure you can follow through.

And finally, don't forget about the why. Why are you posting all of these updates? Which business goals are these posts meant to support? If social media is all about raising awareness for you, make sure your posts are designed to do that. On the other hand, if social media is more of a way for you to deepen relationships with your existing fans and customers, your posts are going to look quite different. There's no right or wrong approach, but again: make sure you know why you're sharing what you're sharing.

So that's a social media plan. Once you've got all these tasks spread out across a calendar for the next several months, all of a sudden, it's much easier to see how you're going to tackle the brave new world of social media.

You might be thinking "wow, that's a lot of work! How am I going to actually do it?"

Well, wouldn't it be great if you could block out a day in your calendar, write up all the things you'd like to post for the next six months, and then queue them up so they automatically get shared when you're ready?

The good news is there are tools out there that can help you do that and more. With social media management tools like Hootsuite, Buffer, and Every post, you can create the things you want to post and share in advance. You can decide which networks you want to share them on, and you can collaborate with your co-workers to let them help you along the road to social media success.

On top of that, you can use tools like these to listen to what people are saying back to you on social media. You didn't forget, did you? Social media is a two-way conversation, not just a megaphone for you to use to broadcast your message.

So what have we learned? Social media takes some work and dedication if you want to have real success. Putting together a detailed plan will help you take your efforts to the next level, and there are lots of tools available to help you. Now you're well on your way to conquering social media!

Check your knowledge 13.1

The first thing Lily needs to do is create a social media plan. This will help her define her strategy, plan how she will engage with social media in the coming months and identify how she will measure her results. Then, she can create profiles on the social media sites that best suit her business, and set up a social media management tool to keep track of her activity on those sites. Finally, she can prepare posts in advance that will be automatically posted to coincide with key events in her plan. For example, she might set up some festive posts to promote her products in the lead up to Christmas.

Question 1 of 1

Lily runs a vintage clothing shop and wants to engage more with her customers online.

She currently posts to two social media networks but wants to develop a full social media strategy.

Review the possible options. Can you place them into the right order, starting with what Lily should do first?

1. Create a social media plan
2. Set up accounts on appropriate social media sites
3. Sign up to a social media management tool
4. Create a list of posts to be automatically posted in the coming weeks

(answer: 1,2,3,4)

Activity 13.1

Keeping your overall business goals in mind, start to build your social media plan.

Don't forget to cover the what, the where, the when, the who… and the why.

Lesson 13.2
Advertising On Social Media

Key learning

If you want to reach specific audiences online, advertising on social media sites is a great option. In this video we'll talk about:

- how to get your message in front of specific audiences
- how advertising on social networks can complement your other social efforts.

Knowledge:

Wondering if there's anything more you can be doing now you have your social media plan up and running? Well, the answer is often yes, and many social networks offer paid advertising opportunities that can give you access to very specific audiences and get your message out there.

Let's jump into it. We'll use the vintage clothing store as our example. Perhaps you've noticed that your best customers seem to come from certain demographics... let's say women, aged about 20 to 35. Wouldn't it be great if you could focus your advertising on people who fit this profile and are more likely to become your customer?

Well, social media sites can help you do this and more. That's because social media sites often know a lot about their users. Think about your Facebook or Google+ page, for example. Have you included your age or gender on your personal social media pages? Many people do, and that's why social media sites are able to offer businesses the ability to reach such specific groups.

Sounds pretty good so far, right? Well, it gets better. Not all women aged 20-35 are going to be interested in vintage clothing. So, if we can avoid spending money advertising to people who aren't interested in vintage clothing, that's a win.

Luckily, social media sites can help you narrow down your audience even more. For example, you could target women aged 20-35 who are interested in a certain fashion designer. Or who have posted about vintage fashion in the past. That would be a great way to focus your advertising only on the people who are most likely to be interested in your shop.

And we can take that even further. Like other online advertising channels, you can also target your ads to a specific geographic area. That means, you could use social networks to advertise to women, aged 20-35, within 25 miles of your shop, who are interested a specific fashion designer that you care about. Pretty cool, right?

Social media sites provide great options for targeting ads or content to very specific audiences, and that's a great way to make sure we're investing our marketing budget wisely. Now, let's talk about how paying to promote your messages to social network users can complement your other efforts on social.

Building up your presence on social networks is usually a gradual process. Over time, you post interesting, unique content, and gain more and more visibility. But what if you want to accelerate that process? That's another great reason to try paid advertising on social networks.

Say you've got a Twitter page with a few hundreds of "followers" so far. What if you wanted to reach a lot more people - people who aren't necessarily following you yet? You could try a "Promoted Tweet." This is a way for you to get your shop in front of potential customers - fast! For example, your Promoted Tweet could be shown to people who have "tweeted" about vintage fashion in the past, or people who follow an influential designer. All of a sudden, you're potentially reaching a lot more than your 200 followers, and hopefully growing your network with even more followers as a result.

So that's advertising with social media sites. You get the ability to do some really fancy targeting. And on top of that, you can ramp up your visibility on social networks very quickly... as long as you're willing to pay for it, of course.

Check your knowledge 13.2

There are lots of different types of Facebook users Lily could aim her ads at. As Lily's going for global reach, she doesn't need to limit her ads to a local audience. Advertising globally is much more likely to find potential customers than just staying within the home country. Combining a global reach with more appropriately targeted advertising means Lily can use her budget wisely, concentrating on people who have the biggest potential to turn into customers.

Question 1 of 1

Lily has decided to use some of her social media budget for targeted Facebook adverts. She's keen to take her vintage clothing business global and wants to reach a wider audience, so which groups should her advertisements be targeted at?

1. Users who have posted about buying vintage clothes
2. Users who have 'liked' vintage clothing
3. Users who live within 20 miles of Lily's shop
4. Users who live in countries that she'd be happy to mail her products to

(answer: 1,2,4)

Activity 13.2

Visit one or two social networks that you think your audience might be using.

What kinds of paid adverts do you see there?

Do they seem like something you could make use of?

Lesson 13.3
Measuring Success in Social Media

Key learning

Knowing how effective your social media efforts are is invaluable to your business. Here we'll explore how to:

- collect data from the networks themselves
- make the most of social management and monitoring tools
- see what social visitors are doing on your website.

Knowledge:

Tracking the impact of a social media campaign is really important, but it can get complicated. That's when analytics and tools can help.

In this video we'll cover how analytics and different tools can help you track the impact of your social media efforts and understand your customers a bit better.

Let's assume our vintage clothing business has established accounts on a few social networks - Facebook, Twitter, and maybe even some smaller, fashion-related social networks.

First, it's important to take a look at the social networks themselves. When you log in, many provide data about what's happening on those networks. For example, you might be able to get reports about how many people you're connected with and how that's been trending over time, which of your posts are getting shared or interacted with the most, or even who your biggest fans might be.

By looking at the data and reports available in many social networks, you can learn a lot about who your connections are, how they behave, and how they consume or interact with the content you're providing.

But logging into every single network and looking at the data and reports in each one separately can be time-consuming and tricky. Remember those tools that can help you schedule your posts and consolidate all of your logging in to just one place? Well, many of those tools can also track and provide data that can compare the different networks against each other, and give you all that reporting in one place.

Tools like these are really helpful, and you can investigate them by searching for 'social media management tools'. There's also another kind of tool that might help you: social media monitoring. There are lots of them out there and a wide range of features and pricing, but basically, these tools will scour all the social networks out there looking for mentions of you, your competitors, or even certain themes being talked about. These can help you identify new social networks you might want to participate in, and let you join conversations about your business or your industry.

But these reports and tools typically only measure what's happening on the social networks themselves. So, if you want to know what's happening after someone decides to click on a link you shared, or a piece of content you posted and ends up on your website?

For this, you'll need a separate tool dedicated to tracking what's happening on websites, like Google Analytics.

Web analytics tools will generally pick up the trail as soon as someone hits your website, and many of them will automatically track when visitors are coming from social media sites. That means that if you're tracking what people are doing on your website, you can see how many visitors from Facebook or Twitter are not just arriving on your website, but also submitting your contact form, buying items from your online store, or downloading your monthly PDF newsletter.

Now you'll really be able to see how your social media efforts are paying off!

Lots of web analytics tools also let you track not just what network visitors are coming from, but even the specific posts or pieces of content that got them to visit your website.

Each web analytics tool does this differently, but the end result is pretty cool: You'll be able to look at different reports and see things like which kinds of content from which networks tend to get people to visit your website, engage further with your pages, and eventually convert on your business goals!

So that covers how to measure the success of your social media efforts. Using the data and tools available from the social networks themselves, using social media management and monitoring tools, and using web analytics to see what social visitors are doing on your website will help you understand exactly how and where your efforts are paying off. That way you can keep improving your social media strategy.

Check your knowledge 13.3

Social media analytics can help businesses gain knowledge about how customers interact with their products and services and how they have accessed them. The knowledge gained through these tools can help Lily find out what she is doing right and which campaigns are the most effective at driving traffic to the shop's website. She will also be able to pinpoint what isn't working, and use this information to continually refine and improve her social media strategy.

Question 1 of 1

Lily is keen to use analytics to evaluate the results of her social media campaigns. Analytics can help with this question. Can you help her by crossing off the things that analytics won't be able to help her with?

1. Tell Lily how many visitors interact with her website
2. Show Lily how visitors found the site
3. Schedule content to be posted automatically at specified times
4. Send custom posts to specific visitors

(answer: 3,4)

Activity 13.3

Log in to some of the social networks you use and see what kinds of reports are available.

How can they help you improve your social media efforts?

What else would you want to see?

Lesson 13.4
Avoiding Social Media Pitfalls

Key learning

Social media can be a powerful tool, but it's also been known to cause some issues for businesses. We'll show you what not to do, like:

- bore people to tears
- put your posts on autopilot
- spread yourself too thin.

Knowledge:

Feel like you're getting the hang of social media? Now that you're up and running, this video will cover some of the pitfalls that could end up hurting your efforts and maybe even your business. Stuff like boring, repetitive sales messages, posting once every three months, or, the opposite, spreading yourself too thin with far too many posts.

Ready to look at some no-nos?

The first rule of social media: It's not all about you.

People go online to share news, how-to tips and funny cat videos. They're not there to hear your sales pitch-and brands that have nothing else to say tend to get boring and ignored fast.

If you're a business, remember that anyone who follows you on social media is already interested in you. There's no need to aggressively sell. Just focus on providing a good experience and keeping their attention.

So if you own that vintage clothing shop we've been talking about, let your followers know what's new, what's coming soon and how you do what you do. You don't have to recreate your product pages and try to push them down people's throats.

Building on that, people don't want one-way pushes crowding up their feeds. They want to be on a two-way street. They want to know that you're listening.

Make sure you 'man the phones' online to monitor when people are responding to you, and have a plan for answering comments.

Be understanding, be considerate, but most of all be consistent. Follow up on complaints, and give people the information they ask for. Negative feedback doesn't necessarily have to end in disaster. It can be an opportunity to show your customers - and everyone else who might be watching - that you truly want to help them.

The next pitfall: Don't spread yourself too thin on social media. With all the networks out there, there are almost unlimited opportunities to talk to customers, but those conversations take time.

If you're not careful, you'll get overwhelmed trying to juggle too many sites. Focus on the ones that matter most and branch out as it makes sense and as you can handle it.

Have you ever checked out the social media page for a brand or product you're interested in, only to find nothing's been updated for months? Another big mistake.

It might make people wonder if anything's stirring over there or if you're even in business anymore. Growing, innovative, exciting businesses have a lot to say. Stodgey, slow-moving ones might not say much.

Which would you rather be?

Finally, it can't be emphasised enough that you'll want to measure what your efforts are actually doing for you. Using social media and analytics tools, you can see firsthand how your social media efforts are contributing to your bottom line, and learn which are more valuable than others.

It's easy to sidestep a social media disaster.

Stay true to yourself, respond to comments, focus on the sites that make sense, be consistent and measure your results. Do all this and your social media efforts can thrive.

Check your knowledge 13.4

The big benefit of social media is being able to talk directly to customers and engage with them in a timely and appropriate way. Lily now has the opportunity to resolve this customer complaint by offering an apology or to replace the zip for free, thus showing her customers how important they are to her business.

Question 1 of 1

Lily sees a negative post on Twitter about her vintage clothing business:

"Received my #VintageLily dress today only to find the zip was broken! #lousyservice #vintagewoes"

How do you think she should respond?

1. "So sorry to hear that @sophie112 DM me so that we can get that dress fixed up as soon as possible."

2. "@sophie112 – We've never had our zips break before. Did you pull it too quickly?"

3. "@sophie112 That's a shame, sometimes the zips just break."

(answer : 1)

Activity 13.4

Pick out a few brands you like, and look back through a few weeks' worth of their social media posts.

What are they doing well?

Can you spot any of the mistakes mentioned in this video?

Check your knowledge 13.A

Question 1 of 4

A robust social media plan includes which of the following?

1. A list of content that mimics competitor content
2. All of your online business goals

3. A long-term schedule identifying when to post content
4. A list of friends who can post on the accounts

Question 2 of 4

What is the best way to put your social content in front of people who don't already follow you?

1. Increase your email marketing campaigns
2. Ask people to share your content to their networks
3. Use paid promotion to reach new audiences
4. Put links to your social on your website

Question 3 of 4

What can social media analytics tools help you measure when assessing campaign results?

1. Whether the campaign was more successful than your competitors
2. Whether the visitors liked the social campaigns or not
3. Whether a visitor called the store after seeing a social post
4. Whether the visitor clicked on a paid ad or organic listing

Question 4 of 4

Which of the following is a pitfall when using social media for business?

1. 2-way conversation with customers
2. Not being present on every social media platform
3. Not having the resources to respond to comments and questions in a timely manner
4. Spending too much time reviewing social media analytics

(answer: 3,3,4,3)

Module – 14: Discover the Possibilities of Mobile

Web browsing on-the-go is very much a part of everyday life - which is why a mobile presence is important for businesses to embrace. Learn about mobile SEO, the differences between mobile sites and mobile apps, and which type of mobile marketing is right for your goals.

Lesson 14.1
The Evolution of Mobile Devices

Key learning

Today, people have so many different ways to access the Internet. We use computers, smartphones, tablets and now even smartwatches. Mobile marketing is constantly evolving; embrace it and your business will stay well ahead of the curve. In this lesson, you'll learn:

- how mobile usage has changed in the last four decades
- what features are available on today's mobile devices
- what the explosive growth of mobile use means for you.

Knowledge:

Mobiles have radically changed the world we live in. And, it seems like mobile devices continue to evolve at lightning speed.

Let's talk about: How mobile usage has changed in the last four decades. The features now available on mobile devices. And, how the rapid growth of mobile is changing how you can market your business online.

Did you know that the first ever mobile phone call happened way back in 1973? It took another 11 years before the world's first truly portable commercial mobile phone went on sale in 1984. A Motorola, that cost a whopping 2,500 GBP!

Since then, mobile phones have evolved dramatically, shrinking in size while expanding in features. Now they're an essential part of our everyday lives.

No longer just a way to make phone calls, mobiles have become powerful multimedia devices. We can browse the Internet, check email, take pictures, navigate with GPS, post on social media, and much, much more.

Mobiles have changed so much in the last few decades, it seems that anything is possible in the future.

This year, adults in the U.K. will spend an average of 2 hours and 26 minutes a day on their mobile devices. That means, for the first time ever, we're now using these devices even more than our computers and laptops.

Today's mobile users tend to have their phones in one hand while they watch TV. And, they're more active than ever on social media.

What does all this mean for your business? Well, your marketing needs to reach customers where they are. And these days, that means on mobile.

So whether you want to increase brand awareness. Encourage customer loyalty. Or grow your revenues. Mobile devices can offer your business numerous opportunities to reach the right customers, in the right place, at the right time.

The place to start? A website that works well on mobiles.

Let's just imagine for a second that you're a local plumber who wants to increase your customer base. How might you use mobile to get new customers? Well…

You might run an ad in the local papers that directs viewers to your website.

Your mobile-optimised site could have a promo button on the homepage, that offers new customers 20% off their first service.

The phone number near the top of your page, when viewed on mobile, can be clicked to start a phone call.

Links can be shortened, so they can be easily shared on social media.

And that's just a few examples of the many, many ways your business can use mobile to grow.

Coming up, we'll cover how to have a great mobile website, discuss whether mobile apps are right for your business, and chat about mobile advertising. Stay tuned!

Check your knowledge 14.1

The first step for Phil would be to adjust his existing site to make it responsive. This would ensure it displays optimally to as many customers as possible across all devices. Creating a fully functional app is likely to be more time consuming and expensive than adjusting his existing site.

Question 1 of 1

Phil runs a local plumbing business. He has a website but it isn't mobile-optimised.

1. He's deciding whether to make his site responsive or create a customised app.
2. Help him to decide which route to take first.
3. Create a customised App
4. Make his website responsive

(answer: 2)

Activity 14.1

Keep track of the time you spend using your mobile device during one day.

Write down the activity (email, phone call, taking pictures, etc.) and time spent during each session.

Lesson 14.2
Understanding Mobile Web and Mobile Apps

Key learning

When people search for businesses, they are quite likely to be searching on a mobile device. Search engines are adapting to this new approach, and businesses need to adapt as well. In this video, you'll learn about:

- search engines and the mobile searcher
- ways to make your website mobile-friendly
- what you should consider for mobile SEO.

Knowledge:

In today's business world, it's no longer enough just to have a website. People today access the Internet on mobiles more often than computers. Bottom line: Your business website needs to be mobile-friendly. That is, it needs to work well on smaller screens.

In this video, we'll talk about how search engines have adapted to the way we now use mobiles. How to make your website mobile-friendly; and, some important things you should know about mobile SEO.

Ok. Imagine you're just heading out of the flat, when you suddenly notice the kitchen sink is blocked. Not good. You've got friends coming round later and so you need a plumber to come sort this out today. But you've got a taxi waiting outside to take you to the train station, and you need to go now.

So, you grab your mobile, jump in the cab, and search for 'plumber near me'. The search results show a few options, including several businesses just a few streets from your flat.

One of the options has a clickable phone number. You'll be at the station soon, so you click to make the call. And the plumber agrees to meet you at your flat by 5. Thank you, mobile!

This scenario is a perfect example of how many of your potential customers are using mobiles. They're often on the go, pressed for time, and using search engines to look for quick answers.

Search engines offer people results that match their search terms, and location. They can also tell if a site is mobile-friendly. So what does mobile-friendly mean, exactly?

Let's start with the technology used to build your site. There are many options available, but most search engines prefer something called "responsive design."

A responsive website adapts itself depending on the size of a viewer's screen. When you have a responsive site, you don't have to create separate sites for computers and mobiles. So you save yourself a lot of effort.

A well-designed mobile site is usable on the smallest mobile screen.

Fonts and buttons should be easy to read and click on. And the navigation should be clear and simple to use. Visitors should immediately understand their next possible steps, and how to take action. For example, in our plumber scenario, there was a clickable phone number.

Despite the smaller screen size, website visitors should be able to complete common, important tasks.

Once you've created a mobile-friendly site, you'll want to help search engines find it, understand it, and hopefully show it in the results. That's search engine optimisation, with a focus on mobile.

Mobile SEO includes the same factors you'd consider for standard websites, like relevant content. But what's crucial for mobile site optimisation, is performance and usability.

Performance is how quickly a site loads, and this can be impacted by many things, such as overly large images and file sizes.

Usability refers to a visitor's experience using your site. Generally speaking, if your site has a good mobile user experience, it will be more likely to appear in mobile search results.

Here's an example. Some video and content formats can't be viewed on mobiles. So, if that's how your site is built, it won't offer a great user experience, right?

You can do a quick mobile check-up of your site by visiting Google's Mobile Friendly Test.

So let's recap.

It's important to make sure your business's website works well on mobiles.

A mobile-friendly site can bring you more site visitors, give them a better experience, and bring in more business.

Check your knowledge 14.2

Question 1 of 1

Now that Phil has decided on a responsive website, he needs to select a great design. Have a look at these website layouts. Which do you think is best suited for mobile?

1. It has clear navigation, and concise, easily visible content: perfect for mobile
2. Website with attractive graphics
3. Website with pictures of celebrities.

(answer: 1)

Activity 14.2

Use one of the free performance tools listed on the right to test your site.

Note the recommended areas of improvement and make any necessary adjustments to your site.

Lesson 14.3
Understanding Mobile Apps

Key learning

People interact with businesses through both mobile websites and mobile apps. Mobile-friendly websites are now a necessity, and many businesses can also benefit from a mobile app. In this lesson, you'll learn:

- the difference between mobile websites and mobile apps
- the benefits unique to mobile apps
- how to determine whether an app is right for you.

Knowledge:

An effective mobile marketing approach includes more than just optimising your website to work well on mobile devices. More and more businesses are also investing in mobile apps to engage with customers on the go.

But what purposes do mobile apps serve? And how do you know if creating one can benefit your business?

We'll discuss what makes a mobile app different from a mobile website, the benefits of mobile apps, and how to determine whether a mobile app is right for you.

Your mobile website is pretty much a simpler version of your main site. Mobile-friendly sites offer most of the same things as your main site, but are just built to work well on smaller screens. Visitors access a mobile site on a mobile web browser, just as they would on a full-size computer browser.

Mobile apps, on the other hand, are applications that can be downloaded and installed onto a mobile.

The apps typically provide a specific function that's not as easily accomplished on a web browser. They are often integrated with common smartphone features, like the camera or GPS.

There are so many ways that apps can directly benefit your business. Let's look at some examples.

Ok. Imagine you own an independent movie theatre. And you've decided to create an app to help drive ticket sales.

One of the main benefits of apps is that they can send messages to a person's mobile, even when they're not using the app. These are called "push notifications". You could use them to send your customers reminders when the latest films are released, or announce special discounted showtimes.

Your app could also power a new loyalty program. Your customers could use the app to earn points for every movie they see in your theatre, and for popcorn purchased at the concession stand.

Simplified checkout on your app could allow customers to purchase movie tickets in just a few clicks. And then, your app can use their mobile's GPS to share directions to the theatre.

With so many possibilities for your business, you may decide to develop your own app.

So, how do you start? It helps to think about your business goals, and what you would like visitors to accomplish on a mobile. Perhaps you can achieve all these things on your mobile website. But you might identify a specific business goal that would be better served by an app. This might be your next step towards online success.

So, let's sum up. A mobile app can complement your mobile website, helping your customers accomplish specific, useful goals.

An app for your business can help increase customer loyalty. You can actively communicate with customers and help them make purchases easily on their mobile devices.

Can't wait to get started? Well, you've got a couple of options. You can find a professional app developer to work with. Or, check out one of the self-service tools out there, such as Appy Pie, Build Fire or Como.

Check your knowledge 14.3

A professional app developer or a self-service tool would be the best options here. Hiring a professional app developer is easier than you think and there are also plenty of options available to create one online yourself via a self-service tool. With limited technical knowledge, repurposing an old app, or creating one himself from scratch, would be very difficult.

Question 1 of 1

Phil has limited technical knowledge but he wants to create an app to simplify the booking process for his customers.

It's important to select the right approach when making an app.

Which of the following routes would you not recommend to Phil?

1. A professional app developer
2. An online self-service tool
3. Repurpose an existing app
4. Make the app himself

(answer: 3,4)

Activity 14.3

Does your business have a mobile-optimised website and app?

Access your site from your mobile device and see if it's easy to use.

If your business doesn't currently have an app for mobiles, list any actions customers complete on your mobile site that can be integrated into an app in order to streamline the process.

Check your knowledge 14.A

Question 1 of 4

When looking to ensure your website is easily accessible by mobile users, what should you focus on doing first?

1. Redesign your website colour scheme
2. Optimise your site
3. Create a mobile app
4. Shorten your website content

Question 2 of 4

What does responsive design mean?

1. Your visitors can manually adjust the size of your website
2. Your website will adapt to suit whichever device it is being viewed on
3. Your customers can provide feedback on the design of your site
4. Your website will respond to clicks faster

Question 3 of 4

When it comes to optimising your website's SEO for mobile users, which of the following is a crucial factor to keep in mind?

1. Short content and fewer images
2. Performance and usability
3. Usability and short content
4. Less video contents

Question 4 of 4

What can a business use to send messages to users who have already downloaded their app?

1. Text messages
2. Pull notifications
3. Push notifications
4. Email notifications

(answer: 2, 2, 2, 3)

Module – 15: Make Mobile Work for You

With mobile video consumption on the rise, it makes sense to include mobile in your advertising strategy. Understanding the options and tools available and how to choose the right keywords and ad formats will set you up to succeed in your first mobile marketing campaign.

Lesson 15.1
Introduction For Advertising on Mobile

Key learning

As people spend more and more time on their mobiles, businesses are increasing their mobile advertising in order to reach new customers. In this video, you'll learn about:

- benefits of mobile-specific marketing
- mobile opportunities available to advertisers
- challenges to effective mobile advertising.

Knowledge:

These days, people spend more time looking at their smartphones than they do computers. Mobile devices allow people to stay constantly connected. And are helping them become smarter, savvier shoppers.

Smart businesses are catching on and putting more effort into reaching these potential customers through mobile advertising.

In this video, we'll talk about the benefits of mobile-specific marketing, and its many opportunities. We'll also cover a few things you should consider when taking this approach to advertising.

Advertising to users on mobile devices can help you achieve a lot of different things. For example, mobile advertising can help you get more phone calls and inquiries. Or drive more people into your shop or website. It can also get more people to download your mobile app.

But here's where it really gets interesting. Mobile advertising gives you a lot of unique opportunities to connect with people, while they're using their mobiles. For instance, you can target potential customers based on their location. Or offer them useful tools like "click-to-call" ads.

Your business' approach to mobile advertising will depend a lot on your specific audience, and your overall business goals. Let's look at a few places where you can target your mobile audience.

First, your website can show up in search results. And you can also run ads that appear when people search key terms related to your business, or industry.

Say you're a plumber and you want to target homeowners who might need your services. Your search ads might appear when people search terms like: plumbers near me or kitchen sink clogged.

Try to focus on shorter keywords and phrases mobile users might search. Remember, many people are all thumbs when it comes to typing on their phone! They're not searching the same way they do on a computer. They're much less likely to search for detailed, long phrases.

You can also use display ads to target people who are browsing mobile sites. The ads can appear in text, image or video form, on those websites.

Since mobile ads are naturally small, they should present a strong, concise message with a clear call to action.

You can even advertise to people while they are using mobile apps. For example, if you wanted more people in your local area to know about your plumbing services, you could post ads inside apps like Yelp or Which? where customers leave reviews.

While there are many opportunities within mobile advertising, there's also a few important things you should consider before investing money.

Running brilliant ads is only half the battle. It's equally important to have a mobile-friendly website, or your impressive ads on Google or Facebook could still fall flat. Because your mobile ads will send people to a site that hasn't been optimised for their device. Leaving them with a less-than-stellar customer experience.

Also, remember that not all mobile devices are the same. So another useful trick is customising ads. That way, they'll work well across a variety of screens.

One way to do this is to use short, clear text in your ads. You can also use what are called "ad extensions". These are special features that will help people call you, or get directions to your shop's address. These features will automatically resize themselves to best fit any device.

So that's mobile advertising.

Just remember: these days, people are using their mobiles more than ever. So it's important to think about how you can reach them while they're using those devices. You can advertise on search results, other websites, social networks, or even within apps.

To get the most out of your ads, you'll want to have a well-considered overall approach to marketing on mobile devices. If you stick with us, we'll cover the world of mobile advertising in much more detail.

Check your knowledge 15.1

People are more likely to search for short keywords than for lengthy phrases when using mobile. By choosing the right keywords you are much more likely to bring people to your website. When people type on a mobile device they're usually using a touchpad keyboard, which is slower to use than a desktop. So make sure you keep your keywords short, snappy and easy to type with thumbs!

Question 1 of 1

Mo is a plumber in Glasgow.

He has a mobile-friendly website, and wants to make sure his site becomes more visible on the results page during a search.

Which keywords do you think would work well for his mobile SEO?

1. Leaky tap
2. Blocked sink
3. How to fix a burst pipe in your bathroom

4. Local plumber
5. Pressure has failed in boiler, how can I fix it myself?
6. Ubend fix
7. Why is my dishwasher making a gurgling sound?

(answer: 1,2,4,6)

Activity 15.1

Practise writing clear, concise ads that will appeal to mobile users on the go.

What do you need to emphasise?

What are some calls to action you can use?

Lesson 15.2
Search Campaigns for Mobile

Key learning

By running mobile search ads, you can get your business in front of potential customers right when they are looking for products or services you offer. This video will cover:

- the importance of having a mobile-friendly site
- getting your keywords and ads right
- special features for mobile search campaigns.

Knowledge:

Let's talk about search ads on mobile devices.

If you're interested in how search ads can help you reach people on their mobiles, you probably already know a bit about how search ads work. In this video, we'll show how this applies to mobile, and focus on some useful strategies and tips to help you along the way.

Right then - let's jump into it. Running search ads on mobile devices can help your business with many goals. Perhaps you want to get more leads, phone calls, or purchases? But before you get started, it's really important that your website is mobile-friendly. So, what exactly does that mean?

First, your loading speeds should be super-fast. Nobody likes to wait for a website to load. Especially people using mobile devices.

Next, make sure your website looks and works the way it should on all types of mobiles.

Last, your site should be really easy to use for people on mobiles. That means nice big buttons that are easy to see and click, minimizing typing, and clear navigation options.

If your website doesn't tick all these boxes, that's where you'll want to start. Because if you don't address these issues now, you'll be spending money to send people to a poor website experience. Which isn't great for anyone. Fortunately, there are lots of tools to help you make your website more mobile-friendly.

OK, so let's assume your site is mobile-friendly and ready to get more traffic. Just as with any search campaign, you'll need to pick out which keywords you want your ads to appear on. You could use the same keywords you're using in a regular search campaign. But, remember: users on mobiles don't always search the same way that they do on laptops, or desktops. They are more likely to type shorter, simpler terms.

Let's say you're a plumber in North London. People on their laptops might search for terms like 'plumbers in Kentish Town'. But the same people might search for things like leaky tap or clogged sink when they're using their mobiles.

So how can you figure out which search terms are common on mobile devices? There are great tools for this to help you. Such as Google's Keyword Planner or Bing's Keyword Research Tool. They can help you research a search term you're interested in, and tell you what percentage of those searches come from mobile devices. Spend some time researching here and you'll find the best keywords to use for mobile. Ones that are relevant to your business, and also commonly searched by mobile users.

Next, let's think about your actual ads. People who search on mobiles are often very focused on completing a specific task. A person searching for plumbing services on their mobile is probably not casually browsing. They need help, fast!

So, make sure that your ad is laser-focused to the specific task your customer is trying to accomplish. If someone searches leaking bathtub, don't show them an ad that says you can fix all kinds of plumbing issues.

Instead, show them an ad that says if you can fix any bathtub problem fast. They'll see it and know you're right for the job!

So far, we've covered mobile-friendly landing pages, researching keywords, and focusing your ads. Now, let's talk about a couple more tips and tricks you should know.

The first tip might seem obvious, but here it goes. If you've created search ads targeted to people on mobile devices, make sure people on mobile devices will see them. If you don't want your ads to also appear to people searching on computers, they don't have to.

Search engines like Google and Bing will allow you to specify certain ads as "mobile preferred." Which means that users on desktops won't see your mobile ads. And vice versa. That's a nice, quick way to make sure the work you've done on those mobile ads really pays off.

Here's one last tip. People on mobiles behave differently to people on computers, and how much you choose to pay for your ads can reflect this. Let's say you've been running a successful search advertising campaign. But you check your analytics and notice that people on mobiles are 10% less likely to fill out your contact form. Well, if that's the case, you can use something called a "bid adjustment" to bid a 10% lower price when your ads are appearing on mobile. Using bid adjustments can help you make sure you're spending your money wisely, and getting the best bang for your buck.

Alright, we've covered a lot of techniques for making your search ads work well on mobiles. Remember, having a mobile-friendly site is crucial. Research the types of keywords your customers tend to search for when they're on their mobiles. Keep your ads laser focused. And make sure you take advantage of special features for your ad campaigns.

Get all of those things sorted and you'll be well on your way to success.

Check your knowledge 15.2

Google Keyword Planner is the right tool to use here. It can tell you which search terms are most popular on mobile devices. Broader analytics will give detailed insights into how users are finding and interacting with a site, but they won't help with identifying search keywords. Hootsuite is a social media dashboard that lets you organise all your social media accounts from one place.

Question 1 of 1

Mo's a plumber with a responsive website. He wants to make sure he's using the right keywords for his mobile SEO. Which online tool could help him identify which keywords would be most effective?

1. Google Keyword Planner
2. Google Analytics
3. Hootsuite

(answer: 1)

Activity 15.2

Visit your website from a mobile device.

Are your landing pages optimised for mobile?

Are your calls to action front and centre?

Are text and buttons large so visitors can easily read them?

If not, what changes should you make to your mobile site?

Lesson 15.3
Display Campaigns for Mobile

Key learning

Whether you're focused on driving sales or building a brand, mobile is more important than ever. That's why a display ad approach that doesn't include mobile is incomplete. This video will cover:

- the importance of trying different ad formats
- tools to help you quickly develop ads
- targeting apps.

Knowledge:

Let's talk about display ads on mobile devices.

People spend a lot of time on their mobiles these days. So, it's important to think through how your display ads work on their devices.

Display advertising can help you achieve a lot of different goals. Like finding new customers, or building a brand name. No matter what you're trying to do, mobile is going to be a really important part of your display advertising approach.

Display advertisements are all about capturing the attention of people browsing content online. That holds true in the mobile world as well. But there are few important differences to consider.

Let's start with size. Think about all of the different types of mobile devices out there. You've got smartphones large and small, tablets, phablets and smartwatches. And who knows what new devices will be popular in a year or two?

With so many different devices being used, it's safe to say that a "one size fits all" approach to display ads isn't going to work. Just think about it. You might have an ad that is super engaging on a tablet, but is oversized, or awkward on a smaller mobile. Or an ad that's perfect for a mobile, but doesn't capture the attention of a tablet user.

So, if you want your display ads to be successful on mobile, you're going to need to experiment a bit.

Try to find the right combination of ad formats to fit the devices your audience are using. This will give you a really good opportunity to dramatically increase the reach of your display campaigns.

And here's some great news. If you're using the Google Ads platform to run your ads, you can use the free Google Ad Gallery to quickly create professional-looking display ads, in all shapes and sizes.

Just like normal display ad campaigns, mobile display campaigns can be targeted to the audience you're trying to reach, based on their interests. That's true whether you're using Google Ads or other mobile advertising networks like InMobi. For example, if you're a plumber, you might target people who are looking at websites that review plumbing services.

What's unique about the mobile world, is you aren't limited to showing your ads on websites. You can go a step further, and show your ads on mobile apps as well.

Apps have become a huge part of how people spend time on their mobiles. So, it's more important than ever to include mobile apps in your display ad approach.

If this seems complicated, don't worry. We're going to take you through it now.

Remember our plumbing example? We showed how your mobile display ads might target websites that offer reviews, right? Well, it's quite similar with apps. You can target specific apps that are relevant to your plumbing business. Perhaps ones that provide reviews, how-to information, or DIY content.

So, when people are using those kinds of apps, your ads can appear. By including apps in your mobile display approach, you can reach even more potential customers.

Let's do a bit of a recap.

Display ads on mobile are evolving rapidly, as new technologies reshape the landscape. There are multiple mobile ad networks that you can use, such as Google Ads or InMobi.

A display strategy that doesn't include mobile is incomplete, because mobile is such a huge part of people's lives.

And a mobile display strategy that doesn't include apps is also incomplete, for the exact same reason.

Fortunately, it's easy to experiment with different ad formats and targeting options so that you can find out what works best for you.

Check your knowledge 15.3

Choosing an ad can't be a 'one size fits all' exercise. The design you've chosen works for this device, but it could be far too small or not eye catching enough for another device such as a tablet. Remember, designs will display differently depending on the device they're being viewed on. Good mobile ads need to be readable and clear on even the smallest smartphone screen and should contain a clear call to action.

Question 1 of 1

Mo is keen to advertise his plumbing business. He needs to find the display advert design that will display optimally on a large smartphone device, as that's what most of his customers use. Which of the designs would work best on smartphones?

1. A text only advert.
2. An ad with an image, limited text and a button.

(answer: 2)

Activity 15.3

Read about how to use Google's Display Planner to find ways to target your audience on the Display Network:

https://www.thinkwithgoogle.com/products/display-planner.html

Then, use the Display Planner to make a list of five mobile sites or apps where your audience might be on the Display Network.

Lesson 15.4
Social Media Campaigns for Mobile

Key learning

As a business owner, you want to make your brand visible to people who use social media on their mobile devices. This video will cover:

- how to create a mobile social media campaign
- targeting options available on social networks
- guidelines for creating mobile social ads.

Social media marketing is a great way to promote your business and achieve a variety of goals - everything from building a dedicated following to driving sales on your website. It can also provide valuable insights into your customers' social activity. And it can play a vital role in growing your business.

Now, let's talk about: How to create a mobile social media campaign. Which targeting options are available on social networks, and a few guidelines on creating mobile social ads.

There are three key steps to mobile social media advertising.

First, determine which social media sites you want to use. Social networks serve different purposes, like growing personal relationships, content sharing-some focused on particular types of content, like images or videos- and professional networking. Once you understand the objectives of a network, and the people who participate there, you can choose the places most relevant to your business.

Then, take advantage of audience targeting features. Social media advertising solutions like Twitter, LinkedIn and Facebook offer various targeting options to help you get your ads in front of the right people.

Finally, create ads with mobile in mind. People are more likely to visit social media sites on mobile devices. So your messages have to be optimised for viewing on small screens.

Let's say you own a plumbing company in London. You want to raise awareness of your business to people living in your area, by using targeted advertising on social media.

You decide to run mobile ads on Facebook to drive more traffic to your site. And you set your campaign to target people in London.

You also decide to target male homeowners. Because you know they make up the majority of your customers.

You also have the option to target people based on their interests, activities, and the pages they have liked on Facebook. So you refine your group to include men who have shown an interest in home improvement and plumbing problems.

Social media sites have lots of information about their users. Which allows you to target your audience in more meaningful ways. In our example, Facebook targeting has allowed your plumbing business to reach a very specific group of people, in a very specific area.

Your next step is to create eye-catching ads aimed at mobile Facebook users. Since mobile screens are much smaller than desktops, it's best to keep your messages short and simple. Or you might choose to make your ads image-based, rather than text-based. For example, a carousel ad to showcase your newest line of drains and pipes. People can scroll to see all of your products. And click on an image to be taken directly to your website.

So, let's recap. First, choose the right social media sites for your advertising. Then, target your ads for your intended audience. And finally, create impactful ads made for mobile devices.

As more people move towards using social media on their mobiles, a well-oiled social mobile marketing campaign could really help boost your advertising efforts.

Check your knowledge 15.4

Mo can target the right audience for his social media campaign by using parameters such as age, location and interests. This means his ads will be seen by those most likely to need his help. Hair colour, marital status, job title and internet speed, whilst fascinating, aren't relevant to the hunt for people with plumbing issues.

Question 1 of 1

After a lull in sales, Mo wants to use a social media campaign to launch some of his new plumbing services. He wants to make sure he's targeting the right audience. Which parameters should he use to decide who to target?

1. Age, interests, location
2. Internet speed, age, interests, hair colour, location, job title
3. Marital status, gender, interests, age

(answer: 1)

Activity 15.4

Write down the top two social media sites that would be best for your business's advertising efforts, and note the characteristics of your target audience.

Lesson 15.5
Video For Mobile

Key learning

Mobile video consumption is on the rise, which means businesses should be following the trend towards advertising with video. In this video, we'll review:

- the growth of mobile video
- how to create mobile video ads
- targeting mobile video ads to related content.

Knowledge:

Video advertising on mobile devices presents a valuable marketing opportunity for businesses. Video ads can be more engaging, and provide more information than traditional ad formats.

So, let's discuss the growth of mobile video, how to create mobile video ads, and targeting mobile video ads to related content.

Let's say you own a plumbing business in Glasgow. You've got a number of plumbers who work all over the city. Now, you're looking to grow your business even further, by running video advertisements.

So, let's take a look at ways you can create effective video advertising campaigns.

The first thing you'd want to do is create the actual videos you'll use. You don't have to have a huge budget to produce video anymore. In fact, many great high-quality videos can be recorded on a mobile.

When thinking about what video content to create, you should keep a few key things in mind.

First, make it relevant. You'll want to create content that your audience will be interested in.

Next, keep it short. Attention spans are limited, so you want to time your ads appropriately.

Finally, have a clear call to action in your video. Be sure to tell the audience what they should do next so they stay engaged.

So, let's say you decide to create a short video showing one of your best-rated plumbers laying pipe in a new construction.

From start to finish, the video demonstrates the skill and expertise of her plumbing crews.

The next step is to upload your video ad, and target it to your mobile audience.

When targeting video ads, consider the location of your audience. Think about the time of day they watch mobile videos, and what types of videos they watch.

Say you want to show your video to people within a 30-mile radius of Glasgow. Keeping the targeted area fairly small makes sense, because you know most people need plumbers who can reach their homes quickly.

She also wants to target her ad to run on home improvement videos. That way she can reach people who are more likely or want, or need, her services.

With video ads, you can choose keywords to target your ads to related content. You can even choose specific videos and websites where you want your ads to show.

If you know about a popular YouTube channel that shows videos of renovation projects on rundown homes, that could be a great channel to target. Now, people watching videos of plumbing disasters will see that your business offers solutions to any plumbing problem.

So now you see how mobile video advertising can help you interact with people in meaningful ways.

The more targeted and relevant your video ads are, the more engaged your customers will be.

Check your knowledge 15.5

The right answer in this case was 120 seconds, but when it comes to video every case and every industry is different. Most people prefer to watch short and snappy videos, but if you can present your material in a really engaging way you could probably hold the viewer's attention for longer. It all depends on the needs of your customers, so before you shoot the video, do some research into what will appeal to them most. Remember, video doesn't have to be expensive. Have you ever considered filming a short video advert on your mobile?

Question 1 of 1

Mo has a plumbing business. He's noticed that other service companies publish short videos to show off their expertise, products, and how they do things. This engages their customers and drives interest in their services. To help customers with common plumbing problems, he wants to create a Do-It-Yourself video on his website. How long should he make his video?

1. 30 Sec.
2. 60 Sec.
3. 90 Sec.
4. 120 Sec.
5. 150 Sec.
6. 180 Sec.

(answer: 4)

Activity 15.5

Create a storyline for a potential mobile video ad.

What's your call to action?

Remember to keep the mobile video ad short, but relevant.

Check your knowledge 15.A

Question 1 of 4

When considering how mobile users will search for your business, which types of keywords should you focus on?

1. Long tail keywords
2. Shorter keywords and phrases
3. Longer keywords and phrases
4. Exact match keywords

Question 1 of 4

Before running search ads, you should make sure your site is mobile-friendly. Which scenario best describes a mobile-friendly experience for a customer?

1. The business has a mobile app instead of a website
2. The site includes business phone numbers
3. The site works on different mobile devices
4. The site does not include any videos so it loads quickly

Question 1 of 4

Which of the following can be used to target an audience when using some social media ads?

1. People's names
2. People's address
3. People's pet names
4. People's relationship status

Question 1 of 4

When making video content for your display ads, what is most important to ensure?

1. Videos are entertaining, long and include a CTA
2. Videos are relevant, short and include a CTA
3. Videos are relevant, long and include a URL
4. Videos are short, informative and include a phone number

(answer: 2,3,4,2)

Module – 16: Get Started with Content Marketing

Content marketing is a great way to build trust and increase site traffic. In this topic, you'll learn how to write for online audiences, organise production and promotion, choose the right format based on your content, and track your content marketing success.

Lesson 16.1
Intro To Content Marketing

Key learning

With so many businesses and brands online, content marketing is a valuable tool in helping you to stand out. In this lesson, we'll explore:

- what content marketing is, and why it can add value to an online business
- best practices for creating your own content marketing strategy.

Knowledge:

With so many businesses operating online, standing out from the crowd is essential. Content marketing is a great way to help you attract your audience's attention.

In this lesson, we'll look at why content marketing is important, and how you can use it to engage with your audience. We'll also introduce some best practices to help you create your own content marketing campaigns.

Content marketing is based on the creation and sharing of online material, like videos, blogs, and social media posts. It's designed to generate interest in a company's products or services by capturing people's attention.

It can also help to increase sales by directing traffic to your website, boost awareness of your brand and build trust and recognition amongst your audience.

Let's journey back to the days before the web, when TV, print and radio dominated. Two-way interaction wasn't possible between brands and customers and audiences received advertising messages whether they wanted them or not. These days, people can pick and choose when they engage, and content marketing allows businesses to connect with their audiences like never before.

Imagine you run a dog walking business, and want to use content marketing to increase awareness of the company and drive more traffic to your website. To achieve this, you could publish engaging content about dogs on your website's blog, and promote it across the company's social media platforms to increase readership.

Great content campaigns are based on understanding who you're writing for. The more you know about your audience and share their passions, as well as their pains, the easier it will be to engage them on a personal level.

Try considering the challenges or pain points your customers face, and then tailor your content to these insights. For the dog walking business, for example, pain points for customers could include a lack of time, bad weather, or simply wanting to keep their pet happy.

Next, let's cover some effective content marketing practices. The key to success is creating a content marketing campaign that accomplishes three things: (1) answering your audience's questions, (2) providing something of value and (3) keeping them wanting more.

Here are a few best practices to keep in mind as you put together your own strategy:

- take the time to get to know your audience better. Look at which accounts they follow on social media to get a sense of their likes and interests
- experiment to find the best types of content for reaching your audience and don't be afraid to use multiple formats
- choose the right places to publish your content and make sure you're talking directly to your audience
- throw away the business speak and stock responses, and prioritise natural language to interact with your audience

> make your content unique, interesting and exciting. Use engaging headlines, eye-catching pictures and informative language to capture your audience's attention.

By keeping these pointers in mind when creating a content marketing strategy, you can boost your potential reach and strengthen your presence online.

When starting to write your own content marketing strategy remember the three keys to success mentioned earlier:

> focus on answering your audience's needs

> create content they'll find valuable

> keep them engaged so that they'll visit you in the future for more content.

Now, try brainstorming how content marketing can be used to engage your audience online, and consider what goals it could help you achieve.

Check your knowledge 16.1

Question 1 of 1

Angela opened her own beauty salon two years ago, and is now looking at how content marketing can help her boost the business's profile online. How could content marketing help her?

Answer: True or False

Could it help her find cheaper suppliers?

Could it help her develop a stronger brand identity?

Could it help her understand her customers' shopping preferences?

Could it help her connect with the right audience?

(answer F, T, F, T)

Activity 16.1

When it comes to producing great content, it's useful to try and define your values with regards to the content you're going to create.

A simple way to do this is to generate a content mission statement.

Complete the following: As a [insert business or brand description, e.g. 'A local pet shop] we aim to provide [insert service, e.g. 'top quality dog training toys and equipment] with [insert what makes you special, e.g. 'with expert knowledge'] with a view to [insert the desired outcome for your customers, e.g. 'to foster confidence in new pet owners'] Following this, your content mission statement could be something like: "As a local pet shop, we aim to provide expert content and quality dog training gear so that you can be the best pet owner you can be."

Lesson 16.2
Get To Know Your Online Customers

Key learning

Making sure you are saying the right thing, to the right people, and are connecting with them at the right time is critical when it comes to content marketing. In this lesson, we'll explore:

- what audience segmentation is and how it can benefit a business
- how to use audience segmentation to boost your content marketing efforts
- some of the tools and systems available to help you segment your audience correctly.

Knowledge:

Everyone is different, so when it comes to creating online content it's good to think about who your audience is, and what they want to know. This is where audience segmentation can help.

In this lesson, we'll explain what audience segmentation is and how it can be used to improve your content marketing campaigns.

Segmentation involves dividing your audience into groups of who they are and what they like. Rather than spending time and money targeting a wide range of people, segmentation helps to identify the groups most interested in your product or service. The result is a more cost effective and persuasive way to connect with potential customers.

By researching your audience and segmenting them into groups, you can then create specific content that excites, entertains and engages them.

For example, imagine a new dog walking business building its content marketing strategy. The first step would be to segment potential audiences and identify who would benefit from its service: this could be busy dog owners who don't have enough time to walk their dog, or people who want to socialise their pet with other dogs.

The next step would be to create content with that specific group in mind. For the busy dog owners' segment, this could include helpful content about puppy boredom busters, or a guide on how much daily exercise is ideal for certain breeds.

But why exactly is audience segmentation so important when creating and distributing content?

Understanding the habits and preferences of an audience can help you target content directly to that specific group of people.

For example, if you're looking to launch a new dog teeth-cleaning gadget, and your website analytics reveal that young men are statistically more interested in buying dog gadgets than other demographics, this would suggest you should target your content to this group.

Another benefit is being able to pinpoint audience behaviour and using this information to refine your marketing approach. Now that you know young men are interested in dog gadgets, you could research a step further and find out how often this segment walks their pets and at what time of day. Try to answer: What social channels does this group use? What do they do with their free time? For example, people who enjoy the visual nature of a social media platform like Pinterest are likely to prefer different content to those who like to read and contribute to forums. All this information can provide value when it comes to creating tailored content for this group.

To get insights into what people search for, try free online tools like Answer the Public and Keyword Planner. You also can utilise analytics features on social media platforms like Facebook and Twitter to get a glimpse of audience demographics and behaviours. Experiment with a number of tools and compare results to get a more complete picture of who your audience is, and how they behave online.

Finally, don't forget to talk to people. It may be easy to forget in this online world, but connecting with people face to face can yield some truly unique insights into who they are and what they need.

To wrap up, here are some questions for you to contemplate:

> why is audience segmentation so important in content marketing?

> how can it help brands when creating and distributing content?

> and which tools can you explore to better understand your audience?

Check your knowledge 16.2

You're right! Great job. Alex first needs to find out who his audience is, then segment this audience into groups before creating content targeted to them. Finally, he needs to publish his content and promote it to his defined audience segments.

Question 1 of 1

Alex is a mechanic who owns a small garage. He's also a keen blogger, and writes great posts about his passion: cars! He thought his blog would attract more car lovers to his garage, but so far his blog posts are not very popular and are rarely shared on social media. He has researched how to improve the blog and now has a number of actions he can take, but is unsure which should come first. Can you help him by arranging the following actions into the correct order?

1. Find out who his audience is
2. Segment his audience into groups
3. Create specific content targeted to these audience profiles
4. Publish the content and promote it to his audience

(answer: 1,2,3,4)

Activity 16.2

Use the tools mentioned in this lesson to start making profiles of your target audience.

Give each one a name, and then note jobs and other characteristics, such as: Who do they follow on Twitter?

Which newspaper do they read?

What TV shows do they watch?

This will help inform your content marketing strategy and allow you to make sure the content you create is aimed specifically at one of your audience profiles.

Lesson 16.3
Choosing The Right Format for Your Content

Key learning

Content is much more than just text on a screen. From entertaining GIFs to blog posts, whitepapers, and full-length videos, understanding which content format can make the most impact on your audience is critical. In this lesson, we'll explore:

- popular online content formats
- the four main purposes for content marketing
- how to match different formats to your content goals

Knowledge:

Online content can take lots of different forms: from case studies and ebooks, to infographics, images and video clips. Each of these different formats comes with its own benefits; whether it's to inspire, educate or entertain.

In this lesson, we will explore popular content formats and explain how to choose formats based on the specific needs of your audience.

Whatever format you choose, the purpose of content is always the same - to connect with an audience. This audience, in turn, will engage, share, learn, and perhaps even convert into customers.

Let's start by exploring some popular content formats.

Blogs are typically published as a subsection of an existing website, and can include original content or guest-authored content. Writing unique, quality blog posts can help increase publicity and give you interesting content to share across other channels, like social media.

Infographics are informative and a great way to present knowledge visually. They work well online thanks to their eye-catching format and can help present complex or unusual content in a creative way.

Ebooks are educational, easy-to-read guides focused on a specific topic. This format provides readers with practical content and will help you stand out as an expert in your field.

Videos can include anything from product demonstrations to tutorials and customer testimonials. They allow brands to create engaging, entertaining, and useful content that can be consumed on the go.

There are many other content formats to consider, including: press releases, webinars, reviews and case studies. To explore even more content formats, please check out the additional links provided at the end of this topic.

Successful content doesn't have to go viral or reach millions of people. Focus on the creating content should be tailored to your audience, and design it so that it moves customers towards a specific goal or action.

Now that you're familiar with different formats, the next step is to consider the main goal of your content. In content marketing, there are typically four main purposes of content, which are:

- to entertain
- to inspire
- to educate, and
- to convince.

Let's take a look at how to match different content formats to your content goals.

Meet Amber. Amber runs a dog grooming business, and is looking to create a content strategy to help boost her online presence.

To entertain her audience, she decides to publish funny video clips of dogs doing tricks over social media. To inspire, she plans to create a forum space on her website where people can post their questions and get insights from both her and other pet owners. To educate her audience, she shares blog posts including top tips on dog care and dog nutrition. To convince people to use her services, she'll share testimonials from happy customers, as well as ebooks to showcase her knowledge in specialist grooming skills.

In your own business scenario, consider how certain formats are best paired with specific content goals. For example, if your goal is to educate, then guides, ebooks and infographics would be the ideal formats–whereas if your goal was to entertain, a better format choice would be quizzes or competitions.

When assessing which content formats are the right fit for your goals, think about the ones you can easily produce yourself, and consider recruiting assistance for those you can't. Identify the purpose of your content, and then select the formats best suited to that goal. Finally, when designing your content, remember to consider your audience, and address their specific needs in a format that will wow them.

Check your knowledge 16.3

That's right, great work! If the aim is to engage with both existing customers and new customers, then a competition is a great way to grab people's attention and engage them with the brand.

Jamie is part of the content marketing team for Fitstuff, a sports shop. The content he's producing needs to appeal to new customers, as well as provide extra value to existing customers. Which of the following content would appeal best to both audiences?
List of the top 10 sports equipment outlets/shops

A competition inviting customers to submit photos of themselves wearing Fitstuff gear, with store gift vouchers up for grabs as prizes

1. 10% discount vouchers for all new customers
2. A blog about the store's recycling scheme for old trainers

(answer: 2)

Activity 16.3

Spend 20 minutes online researching the different formats content marketing can appear in.

What do you notice?

Which content types generate the most engagement or likes on social media platforms?

Try coming up with ways you could utilise these content types for your business or product.

Lesson 16.4
Writing For Online Audiences

Key learning

When it comes to writing for the web, there are key considerations to keep in mind which will help make online reading as enjoyable as possible. In this lesson, we'll explore:

- how online audiences and offline audiences differ in their the way they read content
- why it's important to adapt your writing style to an online audience
- tools and systems to help support writing copy for the web.

Knowledge:

When it comes to creating content, there are some key differences between writing for online audiences and offline audiences. In this lesson we'll cover some best practices for content copywriting, as well as explore tools to help you choose engaging topics for your audience.

Reading habits can vary a lot between online and offline content, with factors like style, length and structure all having a big impact when it comes to writing for different channels. To capture your online audience's attention, you'll need to adapt the way you approach writing. For example, while reading a long article in a newspaper could be enjoyable, reading multi-page articles online are more likely to be frustrating. This is because as online readers we are constantly flooded with information, so our need to multitask and consume online data quickly and efficiently has left us with shorter attention spans.

Keeping this in mind, here are a few best practices for successful content writing:

Start with a good hook that clearly explains to the reader what they can expect. A great hook or opening sentence is important to draw people in. This could be a statistic, like "60% of people say owning a dog makes them happier", or a question, like "are you up to date with the latest in puppy fashion?".

Make sure that as you're writing, you always keep your target audience in mind, and focus on what you can offer them. Try to read your content through their eyes, and don't be too salesy - you want to engage your audience, not bombard them with too many sales messages.

Another valuable tip is to incorporate a "call to action", or CTA. CTAs are short statements designed to entice a website visitor to take a specific action, so you should make them as creative and persuasive as possible. It could be 'start now' or 'sign up today'. Tailor your CTA to your strategy, and make sure it helps you achieve your objectives.

Creating content regularly means it can be tough to stay inspired, so here are a few ways to come up with engaging topics.

Try researching your competitors to see what topics they cover. As you research, keep a list of potential topics and refer back to it when it's time to brainstorm new content. In addition, tools like Answer the Public allow you to type in a specific subject or key term and receive a list of some of the most searched queries involving those words. This is great for creating content topics that respond to real user demand.

Other tools to help you get an idea of how popular a topic is include Search Console, which can help you see the terms people use to find your website, and Keyword Planner, which shows you how many people search for a specific term.

Finally, make sure you're consistent in your writing style, so that when readers read your content, they immediately associate your brand or business voice with it. A clear and recognisable tone of voice will help to establish a relationship with your audience and differentiate you from competitors. Try writing down the attributes you want readers to associate with your brand, such as honesty and enthusiasm, and always write with these qualities in mind.

To wrap up, consider how writing styles differ between online and offline, review our top tips for writing for an online audience, and consider how you can tap into online resources to get inspiration for new content ideas.

Check your knowledge 16.4

That's right, great work! Josh should remember to focus on his target audience and find a consistent style and tone of voice. He should always aim for quality writing over quantity, and remember to open each blog post with an engaging hook.

Question 1 of 1

Josh, an interior designer, has decided to create blog posts and share them on social media to promote his new business. He's made a list of all of the things he should remember when writing – however, not all points on his list are correct. Can you help him identify the points that are correct on this list?

Focus on your target audience

1. Only write about the products or services you offer
2. Be consistent in your writing style and tone of voice
3. Add the hook to the end of your blog post
4. The longer the post, the better

(answer : 1,3)

Activity 16.4

When writing for an online reader, it's crucial to keep in mind who you are writing for and to tailor your writing style based on the audience's needs.

Try this writing exercise to hone your skills: Come up with a concept for a blog article.

Think about writing on a topic you know will resonate with your readers- for example, if you're selling baking supplies, perhaps you could write about different meringue techniques.

Before you start writing, consider two distinct audience profiles.

Come up with characteristics for both audience profiles and detail the following:

Their age

Their job roles

What interests they have

What matters to them

How much they already know on the subject

Now, draft two different versions of the same blog article for the different audience types.

Do you alter your tone, depending on whether your audience is made up of professional patisserie chefs or amateur bakers?

Does the language you use change, based on the audience's existing knowledge level of baking terminology?

Lesson 16.5

Help Your Content Be Seen

Key learning

Once you've created content, knowing how to distribute and promote it online is key to getting the reaction that you want. In this lesson, we'll explore:

- the channels available to promote and distribute content effectively
- how a content calendar can help you organise your content marketing activities
- best practices that ensure your content gets the attention it deserves.

Let's face it, creating good content can be time consuming, so you want to make sure as many people as possible enjoy it.

In this lesson we'll look at different ways to promote your content, how to create a content marketing calendar, as well as ways to increase visibility through owned, earned and paid channels.

Did you know - some bloggers recommend you spend as much time promoting your content as you do writing it? With so many people online at any one time, making sure you are promoting content well is essential to helping it reach a larger audience.

Imagine if Ryan, a pet toy store owner, just spent a lot of time and effort creating an entertaining content piece about how to teach old dogs new tricks.

After all that work, he wants to make sure it will be seen by as much of his target audience as possible - which is where promotion can help.

For Ryan, the key to his content promotion strategy is understanding where his audience spends their time online. Is his audience on Pinterest? Instagram? Do his customers watch videos on YouTube or do they prefer to browse blogs? Understanding how his audience consumes content will help him get his strategy right.

Before you start creating a content promotion plan, it's important to consider the channels available. Identifying channels by Owned, Earned and Paid categories is a great place to start.

For Ryan, 'owned' refers to the marketing channels he manages, for example his website, blog, and social media profiles. Promoting content over owned channels is a great starting point because it's a typically flexible and low cost option.

Earned channels refers to anything that's picked up by a third party, such as another pet care blogger that shares Ryan's content. Earned channels can boost the reach of content and add credibility.

Finally, paid channels refers to promotion you pay for. This can allow you to target campaigns to a specific audience, based on your goals and budgets. Ryan could invest in advertising his blog post over social media, and reach more potential readers who regularly browse those channels.

Once you know which channels to promote your content through, it's time to create a content calendar. A content calendar is a detailed timeline that organises your content marketing activity. By clearly outlining what to publish and when, it can help make your content process consistent and efficient, as well as give everyone involved a clear action plan to follow.

Here are some tips to get you started on your own content calendar:

- ➢ make it achievable. Your content calendar should include realistic time frames - if it's not achievable, you'll fall behind schedule and your content won't reach its full potential
- ➢ highlight key dates. Things like public holidays or relevant events are great for releasing seasonal content

- consider multiple channels. Think about how a variety of marketing channels, such as a blog and social media, can work together to promote your content marketing campaigns
- remember the audience. Clearly define your audience at each stage of the calendar. If you segment your audience, specify which group you're targeting
- explore online tools. There's a variety of free and paid tools available to help you create a calendar, publish content to social media accounts, or collaborate on content with your team. These tools can save you time by automating some of the content creation and distribution process.

Now that we've covered how to promote your content online, think about which channels would work best for your business or brand, and consider how a content calendar can maximise the effectiveness of your content marketing campaign.

Check your knowledge 16.5

That's right, great work! Lydia needs to check all the channels that are available, and decide what content to create based on the needs of her audience. Once she has this information, she could consider building a content calendar to help her stay organised. Then, she can begin creating and publishing it, before promoting the content across online channels.

Question 1 of 1

Lydia is a business student working for a hotel's marketing department for the summer. She's responsible for creating and promoting content across the hotel's online channels. What should she do, and in which order?

1. Consider all the channels available
2. Decide what content to create, and when, based on the target audience
3. Create content
4. Publish content

5. Promote content

(answer: 1,2,3,4,5)

Activity 16.5

Next time you create a piece of content, try distributing the same piece via different channels.

For example, create a blog on your website and promote it via different social media platforms at different times of the day.

Record your findings to help inform your content marketing strategy moving forward.

Different audiences use different platforms, at different times of the day.

See what works for your audience.

Lesson 16.6
Measuring Your Success in Content Marketing

Key learning

Knowing how well your content performs once it's published online will help you understand your audience, as well as provide you with insights as to how to improve campaigns in the future. In this lesson, we'll explore:

- the tools available to help track the success of your published content
- key metrics used to measure the success of content marketing campaigns
- how to use data gathered to better meet goals in future campaigns

Knowledge:

While it may be tempting to focus on creating as much exciting content as possible, it's important to regularly sit down and review your goals. This ensures the time you are spending on your content is time well spent.

In this lesson we'll explore tools and software that can help measure the success of your content marketing, as well as identify key metrics to help you improve your campaigns.

Whether your target is to increase sales or spread the word about your business, if you don't monitor your progress against your goals, it will be hard to know if what you're doing works.

To start, identify your goals and objectives, and make sure they're measurable and trackable. For example, perhaps you wish to increase your YouTube channel subscribers by 200 people this quarter, or see a 10% increase in page views on your blog per month.

Once you identify your content goals, it will be easier to track what you set out to achieve.

Next, let's explore specific metrics that could help improve your content marketing. Consider where your visitors are located, their age and gender demographics, how long they spend on a specific webpage and what they search for when they land on your site.

Here's how this would look for an actual business. The Dog Diner produces premium dog food. To help achieve their goal of increasing product sales, they write fun, engaging blog posts and share them on social media.

Some of the metrics they could track are:

- the number of page views the blog receives
- the number of transactions made on the site
- the number of visitors that come to their website from social media channels.

Try comparing your metrics to previous results, such as last month's blog posts or the number of online transactions made during the last quarter. Tracking against past results will give you a clearer indication of whether new strategies are truly successful.

Now let's explore some of the online tools available to help measure the success of a content marketing strategy.

Many social media platforms provide detailed information about the people who follow or subscribe to business accounts. This includes gender, age, and location, as well as which posts receive the most engagement. Such data can give you an indication of which content is the most effective at meeting your goals, and which provides you with the best return on your investment.

Now that The Dog Diner has executed their content marketing campaign and have identified the important metrics to track, they need to understand how to use this information. Here's an example of how to draw insights from the metrics gathered:

The Dog Diner team has published two blog posts - one on dog food ingredients and the second on dog walking. Their Google Analytics account revealed that the first post had 200 views with users spending an average of 30 seconds on the page. In comparison, the dog walking post acquired 1000 views with users spending an average of 90 seconds on the page. From this data, The Dog Diner understands that blogs about dog walking are more popular with their audience and can focus on that topic when developing content in the future.

Analytics can also show them where their readers are coming from, such as from social media or a search engine, and how many of their readers made a purchase after reading a blog post. By looking at the data available, they could refine their content marketing strategy as they go, ensuring they meet the company goals and objectives.

Take some time now to think about the analytics tools at your disposal, and consider which metrics could help you measure the success of your content marketing campaign.

Check your knowledge 16.6

That's right, great job! Maria can use a lot of metrics to determine the success of her content marketing campaigns. In this instance though, her email subscriber list won't give her an indication on how well she is doing when it comes to increasing sales – but tracking clicks on the targeted CTA can.

Question 1 of 1

Maria has a pet shop in Bristol, and is writing fun blog posts about pets on her website, which are also being promoted on her social media accounts. Her goal is to try and increase product sales through content marketing efforts. Which metric is the most relevant in assessing which blog posts are contributing to increased product sales?

1. How long users spend on each blog post
2. Which websites are referring traffic to her blog
3. The number of new subscribers to her email marketing list
4. How many people click the "Buy Now" CTA at the end of each blog post

(answer: 4)

Activity 16.6

Open the analytics feature within one of your social media platforms.

Explore which posts were most successful by looking at metrics such as:

Views

Engagement (Likes or Comments)

Shares

Next, use this data to extract some top-level insights that will help improve the quality of what you are doing going forward.

Which posts performed the best this month?

Analyse these to work out why this might be the case.

Check your knowledge 16.A

Question 1 of 6

Which of the following is an accurate definition of what a content marketing campaign involves?

1. Creating and posting content ad-hoc when you have the time
2. The creation of time-sensitive content that can be published through various channels
3. Regularly emailing customers with news about a business's products or services
4. The creation and promotion of online materials with the goal of increasing interest in a product or service

Question 2 of 6

What does the following definition describe? 'The division of an audience into groups of who they are and what they like, with a goal of identifying a group most interested in your product/service.'

1. Marketing channels
2. Demographics
3. Audience segmentation
4. Group dynamics

Question 3 of 6

Fill in the blank: When describing the purpose of content, what is missing? 'To entertain, to inspire, to _____ and to convince'.

1. Humour
2. Please
3. Surprise
4. Educate

Question 4 of 6

Which of the following best describes why approaches to writing need to be adapted for online content?

1. Online readers have a reduced attention span, due to being flooded with information
2. Certain blogging platforms have a limit on the word count you can publish
3. Online readers only like to engage with long-form pieces of content
4. Online audiences are typically younger, so the language used needs to reflect this

Question 5 of 6

What are 'highlighting key dates' and 'considering multiple channels' best practices of?

1. Creating a content calendar
2. Designing illustrations to support content
3. Segmenting your audience
4. Identifying social media influencers

Question 6 of 6

Which of the following metrics could help you understand which blog post is resonating the most with your audience?

1. Session duration
2. Page views
3. Referral traffic
4. Unique page views

(answer : 4,3,4,1,1,1)

Module – 17: Connect Through Email

Email marketing is a great way to connect and stay in touch with your customers. From building a contact list to learning how to design emails that really stand out, this topic will teach you the basics of effective email marketing campaigns.

Lesson 17.1
Email Marketing Basics

Key learning

Sending newsletters and special offers to customers via email can play a key part in your overall marketing plan, building and strengthening relationships with your customers. In this video, we'll explore:

- developing a contact list
- targeting audiences based on interests
- building relationships with customers.

Knowledge:

Today, we're all bombarded with product choices. If you want to stay top-of-mind with your customers, try email marketing.

Email marketing is a great addition to your other digital marketing activities. Why? It builds customer loyalty and engagement without breaking the bank. And it works well on mobile.

In this video, we'll show you how to develop a contact list and how to speak to different audiences based on their interests. We'll also discuss how email marketing helps you build relationships with customers.

As with any type of marketing, your first step in email marketing should be to set goals.

Do you want to use email to showcase products and services, and bring more visitors to your website? Do you want to use email to drive business results, like distributing a coupon that brings in at least 10 sales?

No matter what your goals are, a good place to start is by building a list of people who've expressed an interest in your business.

So how do you find these people, and get their email addresses? Start by asking them.

Let's say you own a pet supply shop. When you chat with customers, offer to send discounts and special offers if they provide an email address. If you have a website, you can include a form and encourage visitors to subscribe online.

Keep in mind that people must give you permission to send commercial email, and many countries have laws that require consent.

Great. Now you've started building a list of people who want your emails.

Now let's think about the ways email marketing can help you achieve your business goals.

You don't want to overwhelm customers with too much content in one email, or too many emails in succession. Start with a friendly "hello" and introduction. Next, you might send information about your shop and the product lines you sell. At this point, you can ask them one or two questions to narrow down their interest a bit. (You don't want to send dog lovers cat food coupons).

Then, when you have information about your customers you can send specific offers, or content they might find interesting. For example, if you know that a group of these customers recently purchased dog food, you might showcase your most popular dog toys, collars and leads.

Be sure to include useful information and relevant offers, like tips for dog training, or a coupon for dog treats.

While you're educating your customers about your business, you can use marketing emails, to learn more about them as well.

Ask your subscribers if they are interested in receiving updates about other products or services. Then find out how they prefer to hear from you.

For example, do they want to receive emails weekly or monthly? Record what you learn in your email contact database for future email campaigns.

How about people who have been on your contact list for a long time? These loyal customers are really important to your business. And it's a good idea to build a positive, lasting relationship with them. So, how might you go about this?

Well, people appreciate when you anticipate their needs. Let's say certain customers have ordered a flea and tick treatment through your website in the past. Summer is approaching and along with hot weather comes tiny pests that can harm your furry friends.

So, you put together an email with tips for keeping your house, and pet, free of ticks and fleas. You might include an offer for 20% off a pre-season order of their preferred brand.

Or, from time to time, you might send your loyal cat owners a small gallery with some of the funniest cat videos on the Internet.

By making your content entertaining and useful, your subscribers will enjoy and appreciate your emails, and you'll likely remain their go-to choose when they're ready to buy.

Finally, you can use email to request feedback from your contacts about their shopping or customer-support experience, and then respond to them directly.

By knowing what went right, or what went wrong, you can offer solutions to their issues, or simply thank them for being a customer.

So that's it. Email marketing is a great way for you to develop relationships with both potential and existing customers.

As you identify your different audiences, you can customise communications, based on their particular interests. By offering useful and engaging content, you can build loyalty over time. A strong customer base will help your business grow.

If you want to learn more about email marketing we've got lots coming up. We'll discuss the different email marketing services and their specific features. We'll also show you how to write an email that will connect with your customers.

Check your knowledge 17.1

You can use email marketing to tell customers about products and promotions, and even to send out discount vouchers and special offers. If you know some of your customers' product preferences, you can send out emails with content tailored for them. Email marketing won't let customers contact each other over email, and they're often sent from a 'no reply' address, so customers wouldn't be able to reply to them with problems or queries. A dedicated customer service email address would be better for that.

Question 1 of 1

Steph runs an online pet supplies shop, and she has some ideas about how email marketing can help her business. Two of her ideas are correct and two are not. Can you weed out the wrong ones?

1. It's a good way of keeping customers informed about products
2. It helps customers talk to each other via email
3. It will let me send info about dog-related products to customers who have dogs
4. It lets customers email me if they have problems or questions

(answer: 2,4)

Activity 17.1

Consider the email newsletters to which you are subscribed.

Which ones do you read every time they arrive in your inbox?

Which ones do you delete, and why?

Are your favourite brands communicating with you according to your personal interests?

There are loads of email services available – just do a search to see some of your options.

The following list is a sample of available options, and does not imply any endorsement by Google.

Lesson 17.2
Your Email Marketing Options

Key learning

Many email marketing software systems will guide you through the entire process of setting up an effective email campaign. You can monitor how recipients interact with your emails in order to personalise the content. In this video, you'll learn about:

- common features of email marketing tools
- benefits of tracking email recipient behaviours
- personalising content according to customer information.

Knowledge:

So, once you're ready to start using an email marketing campaign, you'll need to know how to get started. An "email marketing service" can guide you through the process from start to finish.

We're going to discuss the typical features and benefits of email marketing services. We'll also talk about how these tools can give you insights into customer behaviour, so you can deliver more personalised content.

While there are many options to choose from, most email marketing tools share a few common features.

The first is a contact database that stores your customers' information. At minimum, the database needs to include an email address for each contact. Most software services allow you to include additional information, like name, mailing address, and other information.

Start building your email database by adding customer data you already have. Most services allow you to upload data from a spreadsheet, a handy feature if you have a lot of information to include.

Next, you want to give people the ability to subscribe (and unsubscribe) themselves. Most email services provide a online form that you can add to your website by copying and pasting a bit of code. Website visitors can then submit this form to sign up for your emails. This data is then automatically transferred to your contact database.

One thing to keep in mind: these forms are usually customisable, so you can ask for the specific customer information you want. But, your online sign up form should be short and easy to complete- you'll probably have more success growing a subscriber list if you don't require too much information. All you really need is their email address to get started!

If you do have information about customers, you can use it to sort them into lists. For example, let's say you own a pet supply shop. If you know that one set of customers own cats, you can group them in a Cat list and send them cat food offers. Customers who own dogs would be on the Dog list, and get different offers. The more information you have about your customers, the more relevant your emails can be.

Now you've got your database, let's think about the actual emails. Email templates allow you to create a design that matches your brand. You can reuse your template again and again, for similar email campaigns.

Keep in mind that many people read email on their mobiles, so be sure yours are mobile-friendly. Many email marketing tools allow you to preview your email on different devices before you send.

Another great feature to know about is the ability to schedule when your email goes out. You can send the email immediately, or choose a later day and time.

An email marketing tool can even be used to track what people do when they receive it.

You might find that most of your customers open their email first thing Monday mornings, or, during lunch on Friday. You can then use your email service to record those preferences and send future emails at more relevant times.

Email marketing services also track who clicks the links in your email. These links typically go to pages on your website. You can then track what those people do, once they're on your site. Like, whether they read an article, or make a purchase.

As you learn about your customers' behaviour, you can then deliver more personalised content.

Many email marketing services offer a personalisation feature that places relevant content into an email template, based on a person's interests. You can use this feature to send specific messages to different people within your database.

Remember those groups of cat owners and dog owners you set up? While most of your email will contain general information that all pet owners will appreciate, your email template can also include one or two fields for content that is specific for each pet-specific group.

By targeting each group with a personalised email, you increase the chances that they will not only read your email, but also click through to visit your website.

So, as you can see, email marketing tools make running a successful email program much easier.

Not only will they save you time, but you can track which recipients open, and take action on your messages. The more you know about your contacts, the more personalised content you can deliver.

Next, we'll explore how to craft a compelling email and how to best manage your campaign.

Check your knowledge 17.2

Email marketing services can automatically personalise emails by including the customer's name, but they're not smart enough to write the whole email for you – yet! Some email marketing services are free, but some do charge. Do some research and find out which works best for you.

Question 1 of 1

Steph is thinking about using an email marketing service to help her send out marketing emails for her pet supplies store. What benefits are there to using an email marketing service?

1. They make it easier for customers to sign up to receive marketing emails
2. They can help you create a customer database
3. They write marketing emails for you
4. They make it straightforward to send out personalised emails

(answer: 1,2,4)

Activity 17.2

Look up a few email marketing services and browse through their features.

Choose one and sign up for an account.

Often you can take advantage of a free trial for a limited time.

Use your free trial time to put together a test campaign to become familiar with how these services work.

There are loads of email services available – just do a search to see some of your options.

The following list is a sample of available options, and does not imply any endorsement by Google.

Lesson 17.3
Crafting Great Marketing Emails

Key learning

Your email marketing campaigns will change, but the goal remains the same. You want to craft attention-grabbing emails that encourage action. With a few tips, you can market your business like a pro. In this video, we'll explore how to:

- use subject lines to make a good first impression
- write concise content with strong calls to action
- include helpful links for customers.

Knowledge:

So you've signed up for an email marketing service, and you're ready to get started on your first campaign.

Let's now talk about grabbing your customers' attention with strong subject lines, keeping their attention with concise and relevant content, and offering links for more information.

Ok, let's say you own a pet supply shop. You've been collecting names, emails and 'pet types' of both prospective and loyal customers. And now, you're ready to launch your first email marketing campaign.

You want to send an email announcement aimed at dog and cat owners, telling them all about the latest and greatest all-natural pet foods you offer.

But in order to get customers to read your newsletter, you first have to get them to open the email.

It's all about making a good first impression here. Think about what customers see when they glance at their inbox. Will your email make them want to open it?

The two things they'll see, are your business name in the "From" field, and the subject line of your email.

Be sure to use a name and email address in your "From" field that clearly identifies your business. People are more likely to open an email, from someone they recognise and trust.

The subject line of your email can make or break your campaign. An effective subject line will compel people to open it. A poorly composed subject line might mean your email gets deleted or trapped in spam filters.

Keep your subject line short and simple-ideally under ten words. Try to capture the most valuable and relevant information contained in the email.

When possible, personalise or localise the subject line. For example: "Jane, is your pup the healthiest in London?"

It's best to avoid words like "free," "percent off," "reminder," and "specials," as well as pound (£) symbols and exclamation points. These are all known to trigger spam filters.

Now, you've captured your customers' attention, and they've opened your email. Congratulations! That's half the battle.

At this point, keep in mind how busy your customers are, and how many other emails they get every day. Even if you've crafted the most intriguing message possible, they'll likely just scan it. So keep your content concise, and get right to the point.

Your paragraphs should be short-maybe one to three sentences, and keep them focused on a single idea. You can always link to longer articles and additional information, on your website.

Make your writing as persuasive and engaging as possible. And use the right tone of voice for your audience. You want to have consistency across your brand, but email newsletters offer opportunities to be a bit more casual in tone.

Links in your email should include calls to action. Encourage recipients to click through, to offers on your website.

For example, a link could say something like "Click here to save 25 percent off your next order of all-natural cat chow". Or maybe "Click here for free shipping on orders over £50."

Use bold text and design, to highlight important offers and content.

There's one last thing you'll want to include. And that's some links at the bottom of the email that allow recipients to unsubscribe, change their email preferences, or update their contact information.

Providing an easy way for users to opt out of your newsletter, is not only good customer service, but it's also required by law in many countries.

So, remember: Take the time to craft a short, but strong subject line. Write concise content with a fun and engaging tone. And include helpful links that will improve your customer experience, and possibly lead to increased sales.

Each email marketing campaign will teach you more about what works, and what doesn't. Over time you can create better emails for your customers, which in turn can build your business.

Check your knowledge 17.3

The best option uses the customer's name and an engaging question or intriguing statement to get their attention. It's also short and snappy. The less effective options (answers 2 and 3) aren't very appealing. Using lots of pound symbols and exclamation marks can come across as unprofessional and salesy, and lots of email providers will automatically filter those emails straight into the spam folder.

Question 1 of 1

Steph is writing a marketing email to send out to customers who have bought puppy food and toys from her online shop. Which of the following options should she select to use in the subject line of the email?

Hi John, do you have a new puppy?

1. Save ££££son PUPPY FOOD!!!!
2. MEGASALE on food for PUPZ!

(answer: 1)

Activity 17.3

Sift through your own email inbox and look at the kinds of email newsletters you receive.

Which ones are you most likely to open, and why?

Practise writing short and compelling subject lines about your top-selling products using the guidelines mentioned in the video.

Lesson 17.4
Managing Successful Email Campaigns

Key learning

There's a lot to manage when running an email campaign – use these strategies to set yourself up for success. Here we'll explore how to:

- use A/B testing to improve engagement
- create relevant campaign landing pages
- measure the performance of your email campaigns.

Knowledge:

There's a lot to manage when running an email campaign. Today you'll learn strategies to set yourself up for success.

You can improve your campaigns, by testing your emails, creating relevant campaign landing pages, and measuring the success of all your hard work!

First, let's discuss how you can use something we call, A/B testing to get more people to open your emails, and click through to your website.

A/B testing is when you create two versions of an email to see which one performs better. You can use this technique to test different email approaches.

Let's say you are sending an email announcing a new product, but you're not sure what subject line to use. You can send half of your customers, Version A of the subject line, and the other half Version B.

Then, look at which email had a higher "open rate". That is the measure of how many people open your emails, compared to how many emails were delivered. Whichever version had a higher open rate, wins!

You can use A/B testing to test different subject lines, frequency, content and images. You could try sending emails on Tuesdays and Saturdays. Or, try sending emails weekly and monthly. See what your audience seems to prefer, and then adjust.

Keep in mind, that you don't want to overwhelm people by sending them too many emails. You should always provide the option for people to receive fewer emails, such as a monthly digest. That way they don't unsubscribe, simply because they want to hear from you less often.

Be sure to choose-or create- specific landing pages for your email campaigns. A landing page is the first page a person sees when they arrive at your website.

That way, when a person clicks a link within the email, they'll "land" on a relevant web page. You wouldn't want someone to click a link to learn about a specific product and end up the homepage, right?

Your email campaigns will be more successful if you send visitors directly to the page they want to see, so they can learn about the product, and maybe buy it!

Last, remember that people will read your emails, on mobiles, tablets, laptops, and desktops. That means your email landing pages need to work well, across all those devices.

Just like any type of online marketing, email marketing is easy to measure. Email services usually include analytics tools, so you can track and measure how well your campaigns are doing.

The reports can show you interesting data like "open rates," which can help you learn which subject lines are most compelling. You can see which content drives people to visit your site by looking at the "clickthrough rate," when people click a link within the email.

And finally, be sure to use web analytics to figure out what people are doing on your website, after they click on your emails.

As always, you should be looking for opportunities to improve the website experience for email visitors.

Let's review. You can regularly improve your email campaigns, by testing different versions, creating relevant landing pages and using analytics to see what's working best.

These tips will set you up for success and help you understand the value of your email marketing campaigns.

Check your knowledge 17.4

Analytics will give Steph the open rates (how many of her marketing emails are opened by customers) and clickthrough rates (how many customers have clicked links within her emails). Analytics can't tell Steph how frequently her emails were moved straight into the trash by a potential customer. Remember that as well as the analytics described above, Steph can use web analytics to find out more about how customers interact with her site. Check out the analytics topics on the Digital Garage to find out more.

Question 1 of 1

Steph is curious to learn how her customers react to email marketing campaigns. What kind of analytics data might she expect to get from her recent email marketing action?

1. Open rates
2. Clickthrough rates
3. Weekly sales
4. Trash rates

(answer: 1,2)

Activity 17.4

Write a sample marketing email.

Now come up with a few different subject lines that you could use A/B testing to choose between.

◆

Lesson 17.5
Measuring Success in Email Marketing

Key learning

Knowing whether your email campaigns are successful will help you take the right actions when it comes time to improving them. In this lesson, we'll explore:

- why email metrics are important in evaluating campaign success
- five useful metrics that can help you understand email performance
- how to draw insights from the email metrics gathered.

Knowledge:

When it comes to managing the success of your email campaigns, understanding your audience's behaviour is essential.

In this lesson we will explore the benefits associated with understanding email performance, as well as cover common metrics that can provide insights to help you optimise future campaigns.

First, let's look at why utilising email metrics can be a powerful addition to your marketing toolbox.

Let's say you own a pet supply shop and have gathered a strong email marketing list made up of interested customers. Using the analytics from your email platform, you can discover the number of people clicking from your email to your website, or how many complete any calls to action you've set, such as making an online purchase using a discount code.

This type of informed decision-making can lead to greater conversion rates, and help you refine any future campaigns for success.

So the benefits of reviewing email metrics are clear. But what story, or insights, can these individual metrics tell you? Let's take a look at five useful email marketing metrics:

An email campaign Open Rate is simply the ratio of people who've actively opened the email vs. the total number of people who received it. This is useful for understanding the effectiveness of your email subject line. For example, if a subject line of 'Things We Love About Our Pets' receives a higher open rate then an email titled 'Discounts and Offers on Pet Food', this tells you your audience favours emails that give them insight into life as a pet owner, rather than promotional content.

Once you know how many people opened the email, take a look at the Click Through Rate, or CTR. This offers a top level view of the success of the individual email campaign, and gives you the percentage of people that clicked on links to your website from every email that was opened.

The Click-to-Open Rate takes into account total number of clicks vs emails that were actually opened. This gives you a more realistic idea of audience engagement because if they opened your email and went on to click a link, you clearly did something right!

Another useful metric is Conversion Rate. Say you have a free pet grooming workshop coming up that you advertised in your email. The conversion rate would show how many people you sent the email to, compared to the number of people who actually ended up registering for the event.

Sometimes, when you send emails they 'bounce' back. The Bounce Rate is the percentage of emails that could not be delivered to subscribers and were sent back. There are two kinds of bounces to be aware of:

Soft Bounces: These are rejected due to a full inbox or size limit restriction on your audience's email server.

Hard Bounces: Your emails are blocked or the address you are using is incorrect. A breakdown of hard bounces per email campaign can show you which email addresses to remove, saving you time and effort for your next campaign.

Looking at the metrics and the story they tell will help you understand what's working and what isn't. The next step is to adjust any future campaigns accordingly, whether that be to refine the subject lines, review the type of content published, or clean up your subscribers list.

We've now covered some valuable email metrics that will help you uncover useful insights from your marketing campaigns. Take the time to review the metrics from the last email you sent - what story do these metrics tell you?

Check your knowledge 17.5

That's right, great work! The clickthrough rate looks at the number of times someone has clicked on a link and gone through to your website – it doesn't tell you the cause for a lower or higher rate.

Question 1 of 1

Amelia is a marketing assistant at a big clothing brand, and has just sent out her first email marketing campaign. She takes a look at the Click Through Rate, to understand how many people clicked on a link in the email in order to land on her website. What is the drawback of this metric?

1. The reason for the rate being higher or lower is not known
2. The less people that open the email, the lower the rate
3. It doesn't track the number of bounces

(answer : 1)

Activity 17.5

Develop three variations of an email campaign.

In each email, change up the subject line, the headline and the key images.

Measure which email performs better across all of the metrics we have covered in this lesson.

1. Pay attention to metrics like:

2. Open rate
3. Click Through rate
4. Bounce rate
5. What do these metrics tell you? What patterns start to appear?

Check your knowledge 17.A

Question 1 of 5

Which of the following will you need to start an email marketing programme?

1. A collection of email templates
2. A 'Contact Us' form
3. A way to collect people's email addresses
4. A set budget

Question 2 of 5

Which of the following is a common feature of email marketing platforms?

1. Personalised, custom templates
2. A free list of email addresses you can target
3. A feature allowing users to unsubscribe from your emails
4. Automation of your search ad campaigns

Question 3 of 5

Which of these is a good practice to keep in mind when sending emails to your contacts?

1. Run an A/B test on your subject line to determine which one works best
2. Send the same generic and simple message to your entire contact database

3. Include enough content in the email so there is no need for them to click away to read further elsewhere

4. Only include a call to action on the landing page you're linking to in the email

Question 4 of 5

If the open rate of your emails seems low, which of the following could help you fix that?

1. Redesign your website
2. Change the colour of the buttons inside your email
3. Send your emails to more contacts
4. Adjust the subject line of your email

Question 5 of 5

Which of the following statements is true when it comes to running email campaigns for a business?

1. There's no need to use sponsored ads within your email marketing
2. There's no need for analytics when it comes to email marketing
3. You need to include personal contact details
4. You can use any imagery, despite copyright

(answer: 3,3,1,4,1)

Module – 18: Advertise on Other Websites

By incorporating a mix of both display and search engine advertising, you'll be able to maximise your online visibility. Learn about the benefits of display and search ads, how they differ and how to find and target the right audience, so that you have the skills to correctly structure your ad campaigns.

Lesson 18.1
What Is Display Advertising?

Key learning

Display advertising allows businesses to reach specific groups of people on specific websites with their messages. In this lesson, we'll look at:

- what display advertising is
- how it works
- the goals it can help you reach.

Knowledge:

We're going to talk now about display advertising.

You know those adverts you see all over the Internet? Some are banners, while others are text-based or use videos. This is called "display advertising" and we're going to explore what it is, how it works, and how it can help you attract more customers.

Think of display advertising as the digital version of a billboard, print ad or TV ad you see offline. Businesses pay whoever owns the ad "space" hoping to get their ads seen by the right kinds of people. And then turn those people into customers.

In the online world of display advertising, ad space isn't on billboards or TV channels but on the websites we visit.

Display advertising gives businesses the chance to pay for their ads to appear when the right kind of person is on the right kind of page.

There are lots of ways to do this. You can make deals directly with the owners of a website, or you can use networks that match businesses with lots of different websites that have ad space to sell.

You can decide to show your ads on specific web pages, or to specific groups of people-or even both.

Let's imagine you're passionate about films, so you've created a podcast where you do film reviews. Now, you want to market it. Think about the people who might be interested in a film review podcast, and what else they might be looking at online... like cinema websites, official movie sites or film forums. The pages where your customers are is also where you should be.

Of course your customers won't always be looking at websites about film. With display advertising, you can still get your ads in front of them when they're browsing other things. So you can target people with specific interests - like film - while they are checking the weather, reading the news, visiting blogs, and browsing around all the other kinds of websites they might want to visit - even if those websites have nothing to do with film.

So display advertising offers businesses the ability to reach relevant audiences all across the Internet. That's actually quite amazing. And it's one reason why display advertising is a great way to build awareness of you and your business. For example, if you've just created your film review podcast, you'll need to make people aware that your new product exists. With display adverts, you can get noticed by just the people you want to reach.

But display advertising isn't only about getting your name out there. Display is also a great way to drive traffic to your website, build engagement with your visitors, and win new customers. How? Well, you might choose to show adverts to people who have visited your website, but haven't yet subscribed to your podcast. So, as they browse the news, check the weather or watch videos, your display advertising can remind them to subscribe with a special incentive or promotion customised for them.

This is called retargeting, and we'll cover this in more detail later.

Let's recap a bit, shall we? We know now that display advertising lets you be right where your customers are, and supports many different marketing goals. Next, we'll explore how display differs from search advertising, and how the different elements of a display campaign work. Then, we'll move on to talk about ways to find your ideal audience using different targeting options. Finally, we'll learn a bit about how to use retargeting to reach people after they've already interacted with you.

So I hope you're ready - it's time to explore the exciting world of display advertising.

Check your knowledge 18.1

A film production agency might be able to help with the creation of the ads if they specialise in digital formats, but they are likely to be costly and won't sell ad space themselves. Colin also shouldn't look for an online ad space in offline business directories. A forum for movie fans is a good idea – there are probably many people there that could be interested in visiting Colin's blog. Alternatively, if he doesn't know where he wants to post yet, he could contact a network that matches businesses with ad spaces.

Question 1 of 1

Colin has been running a film review website for his podcasts for the past two years. He'd like to start advertising his site to increase the number of subscribers. To do that he wants to contact some media owners. Who do you think Colin should contact?

1. A forum for movie fans
2. Film production agency
3. An offline business directory
4. A network that matches businesses with ad space to sell

(answer: 1,4)

Activity 18.1

Go to a few of your favourite websites and look at the different ads that are being displayed to you.

Can you think of why those advertisers might be targeting either you or the page you're on?

Lesson 18.2
Search Advertising vs Display Advertising

Key learning

Search engine marketing and display advertising can both help you find customers and grow your business, but they work differently. Here, we'll compare the two, explaining:

- how they both work
- where the different ads appear
- what those advertisements look like.

Knowledge:

Ready to delve into the two most popular ways to advertise online?

These are Search Engine Marketing and Display Advertising, and while both can really help your business, they're also pretty different. Let's look at how both kinds of ads work, where they show up, and what they look like so you can know how to best use them.

Ok. Imagine you've just seen the latest James Bond film and are feeling inspired to listen to some film critique. You open up a search engine and type in "film review podcasts."

What does this say about you? Well, we can see that you know what you want, and that you are actively looking for it.

With search engine marketing, advertisers use this insight to reach potential customers as they are actively looking for something.

So people tell search engines what they want online. And advertisers bid for their ads to show up in response to the words and phrases people search for.

For example, a person who is actively using a search engine to find podcasts about film reviews is almost definitely a potential customer - and this is the perfect time to tell them about your podcast.

Display advertising works differently. The person it targets isn't necessarily searching for business like yours, or showing interest in the products or services you offer.

The offline world equivalent might be billboards or magazine adverts. Perhaps people didn't actively seek out your product or service. But, you can choose where your billboards are located or the right publications to place your adverts in, which can help you get in front of the right kinds people who might have an interest in your business.

In the online world of display advertising, that means finding websites where your potential customers are likely to be spending time, or targeting people who have showed specific interests through the sites they visit or other online behaviours.

In our podcast example, your ideal customer is probably reading blogs about films or looking up local cinema listings. So those could be the places to show them your "billboard" online.

Here's another difference between search and display: where the ads show up.

Let's say someone searches for film review podcast, and your ad appears-but they don't click it. Maybe they clicked on one of the other results instead.

With search engine marketing, your ad can only show up when people are searching. So when they've left the search engine and are browsing around the web, you can't reach them with search engine marketing.

But with display advertising, your ads can show up on any website that's offering advertising space, and it means that you can tap into millions of additional websites beyond search engines.

There's one last difference between search and display: the ads themselves. The ads on search engines are usually just made up of text. There's typically some kind of a headline, some descriptive text, a link you can click, and maybe a few other things, like an address or phone number, depending on what options the search engine offers.

Display advertising, on the other hand, gives advertisers a lot more creative options: different sizes and formats, images, video, and more. This means there are lots more opportunities to get a potential customer's attention.

So now you can see how search and display advertising differ, but hopefully you're also getting a sense of how these can work together. Grabbing someone's attention with a dazzling display ad is a great way to get on their radar. Later on, when they're looking to act or make a purchase, they're likely to head to a search engine. If your ads then appear on their search, they might recognise you and go for the click!

To sum up, search and display advertising can both attract new customers, just in different ways.

Knowing how they work, where ads can be shown, and what ad formats are available can help you get the right message in front of the right people no matter where they are online.

Check your knowledge 18.2

Colin's search ad would only show up when people are searching for keywords on a search engine. This is known as search engine marketing (SEM). Search ads are text based so they're an ideal way to put content in front of people who already have an interest in a specific subject. In this case, film fans. Once a person moves away from a search engine, search ads can no longer target them. This is where display ads come in. These can appear on any website where paid advertising space is available. As display ads can contain graphics, audio and even video, they can be a lot more engaging. If Colin puts a display ad on a cinema listings page, he can draw in cinema-goers who may not otherwise search for his website.

Question 1 of 1

To maximise the hits on his website, Colin wants to target two different audiences using both display ads and search advertising. His two target audiences include cinema-goers and home movie watchers. Which type of approach would work for each audience?

1. Home movie watchers – Create a search ad with keywords based on Colin's film reviews
2. Cinema-goers – Place a display ad on a cinema listings site

(answer : 1,2)

Activity 18.2

Think about how you might be able to use display advertising in your marketing strategy.

Write down the audiences you'd like to advertise to, noting the attributes they share and the websites you may be able to find them on.

What messages would you like to give them early in the consumer journey?

How can you tie those messages in with search campaigns?

Lesson 18.3
The Ins and Outs of Display Advertising

Key learning

Ready to create a display advertising campaign? First you've got to understand how to use all the different components of display, including:

- how to find and target the right audience
- how to create different kinds of adverts
- how to organise your display campaigns.

Knowledge:

It's time to cover the different components that make display advertising work, including how you'll find and target the right audience, how you'll build your adverts, and how you'll organise your campaigns.

First, you're probably going to be using a display advertising network - that is, a system that lets you advertise on many different websites - to help you build and run your display campaigns, and almost all of them will allow you to decide where your adverts will show up, and who will see them.

Like all digital advertising, display advertising platforms offer many targeting options. You can limit your ads to people who speak certain languages, or to certain days or times. You can even combine multiple things together. For example, you can target local people heading out on their morning commute by choosing to advertise to English speakers who are using smartphones within 20 miles of your shop in the morning. But there are many more - so let's take a look some targeting options that are unique to display adverts.

For example, you can really zero in on where you want to be advertising by defining specific websites, individual pages on those websites and even specific areas on those individual pages that you want your adverts to appear on.

These are known as a "placements." The idea here is that if you know the kinds of sites your target audience is likely to be visiting, you can get your ads in front of them by targeting the exact placements you want.

Or, you can aim for a broader audience. If we take our example of a film review podcast, you could decide to show your adverts on any website that fits into general, high-level topics like "cinema" or "art" instead of targeting specific websites.

You can even target specific groups of people, and even the things they do online, regardless of the sites they're browsing.

Depending upon what options your ad network offers, you might be able to target by gender or age group. Or by very specific locations, such as people who are located on a university campus. You can even target people who have demonstrated an interest in film based on the kinds of websites they have visited in the past.

Finding the right audience to target is essential, but your display campaign also needs actual adverts to show them. With display advertising, you have lots of options for what form they might take or how they can look.

There are banner adverts in all sorts of shapes and sizes, and video adverts that can use motion and sound to show what's going on behind-the-scenes of your podcast.

There's no reason why you can't use many different kinds of adverts. In fact, you'll be maximizing all the potential places where your adverts might appear. Just remember: you'll want to match the content with the audience you are targeting.

So now you're probably seeing how to accomplish your different advertising goals using many different combinations of audiences and adverts. And you're probably also realising just how important it is to keep things organised. That's why nearly all display advertising solutions allow you to keep things under control by creating and managing what are known as campaigns.

You could have one display campaign aimed at indie film fans, with adverts featuring your interviews with up-and-coming directors.

At the same time, another campaign could be dedicated to everyday moviegoers. These adverts might target cinema sites or film review sites. They could run on specific days of the week, like Fridays and Saturdays when people are going out to the movies. The message could be different as well, perhaps suggesting people come to decide which films to watch this weekend.

Display advertising can be used to target very specific audiences, and even multiple audiences at the same time, depending on the message you want to send. Thinking about who you want to reach and what you want to tell them will not only keep your campaigns organised, it will also help you figure out the message, the tone, and the style your display advertising should take.

Understanding how these things work together will help you match the right message with the right people-and you'll be well on your way.

Check your knowledge 18.3

The best sites to advertise on are the ones where the target audience is likely to be visiting. That way, Colin knows his ads will be seen by people who are likely to be interested in his site. Colin could also draw in more visitors by putting the ads in the cinema listings page on Fridays and Saturdays when a lot of people are going to the cinema. He could even alter the message according to the time and location. Technically, the more locations Colin can place his ad, the more people he can pull in. The news site or his friend's blog might still get him a few hits, but the less targeted audience means he won't get as many as he would from a more relevant site, like the filmography page.

Question 1 of 1

Colin's favourite director has launched a new film. Colin has written a review and wants to use it to bring in visitors with a digital campaign. Considering he has a limited budget, which of the website pages would not be ideal for his digital ads?

1. Filmography page of the director
2. His friend's culinary blog
3. Cinema listings
4. Local news website

(answer : 2,4)

Activity 18.3

Take a moment to write down a few possible display campaigns you might be able to run.

Note the kinds of adverts you might run, the messages you might want to get across and the target audience you want to see those adverts.

Check your knowledge 18.A

Question 1 of 4

If you own a film blog, which type of customer can you expect to reach with display advertising?

1. People who use ad-blockers and are interested in your subject
2. People who haven't read your blog before but are interested in your subject
3. Only people who have read your blog previously
4. Only people interested in films and movies

Question 2 of 4

Fill in the blank: The ads on search engines are usually made up of _____.

1. Audio
2. Video
3. Text
4. Images

Question 3 of 4

When using search engine marketing, where can your ads appear?

1. Only on search engines
2. Only on websites
3. On search engines and websites
4. On websites and social media

Question 4 of 4

When setting up display advertising campaigns, who can you target?

1. People with specific names
2. People who speak different languages
3. People who already own specific products
4. People with a specific address

(answer: 2,3,1,2)

Module – 19: Deep Dive into Display Advertising

To make display ads succeed, it is important to first understand how advertising networks connect businesses who want to advertise, with websites with ad space to sell. You can then harness the power of retargeting solutions to stay top of mind and really move potential customers through the sales funnel.

Lesson 19.1
Making Display Ads Meet Your Goals

Key learning

From the start, you should design your display advertising campaigns to help you achieve your goals. Here we'll go over some of the many things display advertising can do for you, including:

- making a great first impression
- moving customers through the sales funnel
- turning interested people into paying customers.

Knowledge:

If display advertising sounds like something that might be interesting to you, before you start, it's important to understand what display does well and decide what your goals are. This can not only help you set the right expectations, it can also help you focus and get the biggest benefit for your business.

So, what are you hoping to do with display advertising?

Get your name out to people who might not know about you? Tell existing customers something new about your business? Bring customers back again and again? You can use display advertising to do all these things, but it helps to decide what makes sense for you and then build your display advertising campaigns around those goals.

If you have lots of goals, a single ad or a single campaign can't do it all. But don't worry. If you clearly lay out what you want to achieve up front, you can then build out different adverts targeting different people for all the right reasons.

A simple way to break down what you want to achieve with display advertising is to think about the different steps of the customer journey as a funnel. The widest part at the top is awareness.

Let's go back to our film podcast example. Before you can turn people into subscribers, they need to know you're there. Display advertising can help you here, giving you a way to reach a broad target audience.

So if building awareness of your business is a goal, you'll want to target a broad audience and use adverts that make a great first impression.

This is a good time to think about what might catch someone's attention - remember, they're not actively searching for you when your adverts show up.

Is your film podcast the most popular one online? Do you feature exclusive interviews with the best directors? These could be great attention-getters. You can even consider giving film fans a taste of your brilliant content in a rich media video advert.

See how setting your goals can help guide you as you build out your display advertising campaigns?

OK, let's keep going. The next stage in the funnel is all about shaping people's opinions of you, and making sure that they remember you in the future when they want what you're selling.

So, if this is one of your goals, you can create new display advertising campaigns that use messaging to reinforce your competitive advantages and really highlight the benefits of whatever product or service you offer.

At this point, you might narrow down your audience a bit more to include people who have been to your site before, or maybe people who are really interested in the products and services you offer.

Next on the sales "funnel", is to focus on people who are already considering the solution you're offering. Here, you might really refine your message, zeroing in on what exactly makes your product or service so great.

So, for your film podcast, you could talk about how many subscribers you have, or use testimonials from happy customers. Remember, you won't be targeting everyone with this message...these adverts will be limited to people who you know have been looking into you.

The last step in the sales funnel is the purchase. If your ultimate goal is to get people to become paying customers, you need to focus on conversion. For example, you can use adverts with special offers or incentives targeted at people who you know have shown interest in your podcast, but who haven't become subscribers.

Retargeting is especially useful at this point in the funnel. Remember, you want to target people that you know have been researching you online, and get them to consider you and eventually convert. Well, retargeting is a way to accomplish that. It lets you show adverts to people after they visit your website, or do specific things that indicate their interest.

Say someone visited your podcast's website after spotting an ad, looked at some pages, and even made it all the way to the subscription page - but they didn't quite make the final leap.

With retargeting campaigns, you can define these "near misses" as your target audience.

Then, you can show this very specific audience adverts to help entice them back to your site. This time, they might visit your site and finish that subscription form. Just like that, you've got yourself a new customer!

Defining exactly what you want to get out of your display advertising will help you create campaigns that are focused on your different business goals. So whether you want more people to know about your business or you'd like to turn more visitors into paying customers, display advertising can help.

Check your knowledge 19.1

The text-based advert is quite basic, but could contain subscription information about the film podcasts. The second video ad might appeal to film fans, but the video itself is too big and takes up the whole of the ad space. The third, illustrated advert is more general. Through engaging graphics it could show Colin's wide range of podcasts and even some of the benefits for subscribers. The advert could also include a testimonial to support the benefits.

Question 1 of 1

Colin distributes a popular movie review podcast called 'Film Talk' from his website.

He wants to use display advertising to attract new visitors to his site.

Take a look at the three adverts. Pick the one you think will draw the most visitors.

1. Text-based ad
2. Video ad
3. Image and text ad

(answer: 3)

Activity 19.1

Take a moment to write down some of your business goals at each stage of the sales funnel.

How could you support those business goals with display advertising campaigns that convey those messages to the right audiences at the right stages?

Lesson 19.2

Understanding Ad Networks

Key learning

Advertising networks connect large groups of websites offering advertising space with people who want to advertise on them. This video examines:

- how websites and businesses work together
- common things advertising networks do.

Knowledge:

Well, you've seen all those display ads all over the Internet, and by now, you've hopefully got a pretty good understanding of how they work. Now, you might want to start thinking about where you want your ads to appear. But how do you find websites with advertising space to sell? And how do you connect with them? Well, that's where display advertising networks come in.

Display advertising networks are like a middleman, connecting businesses who want to advertise, with websites with ad space to sell. Now, let's find out how they can help your business find, and advertise on, the right websites for you.

Let's go back to our film review podcast. Say you found a specific website you wanted to advertise your podcast on. Well, you have a few options here. First, you could contact the site directly to work out the details, and that's certainly something that happens. But with all the websites out there that offer advertising opportunities, you can imagine this can get pretty time consuming. This is where display advertising networks come in. They handle both the buying and the selling of display ads, linking businesses to websites that want to sell advertising space.

Another way to think of it is as a marketplace that brings businesses and websites together, helping manage the transactions. There are quite a few of these networks out there, like Google Display Network or Yahoo, and they all offer different features, but there's a few things most all of them have in common.

First and foremost, they all offer businesses looking to advertise ad space on websites.

Websites that offer these ad spaces can become a part of these networks, and they can do things like set minimum prices for how much money they expect for showing ads.

Your business can then bid for the spots you want throughout all the websites in that network, deciding how much you're willing to pay. Buyers and sellers are connected every single time pages are loaded, and the ads that win the right to fill the ad spot are shown.

Of course, each network has its own rules, its own features and its own processes and bidding systems, but the key is that they all match buyers and sellers to fill available ad spots.

Networks can also help you target specific audiences through two main routes: the topics of the web pages where the ads appear, and general information about the people viewing the content. While the exact criteria you can use to find your audience, or the way you actually go about running your campaign, could vary from network to network, targeting is essential to get your ads in front of the right people.

Another thing networks do is handle the money involved. Buying and selling ads happens every second of every day, and the networks collect money from businesses and pay the websites that show the ads.

Finally, and perhaps most importantly, advertising networks collect and share data with businesses.

They can tell you how many times your ads are shown, how many times they're clicked on, how much they cost you, where they've been showing up, and how all of this varies between the websites and audiences you're targeting. Many networks even let you add tracking to your web pages so you can see if your ads are resulting in conversions on your website.

If you want to use display advertising to promote your business across the web, advertising networks are a great place to start. They'll bring you together with the websites that want to sell you ad space. They'll let you decide where your ads will be seen, and who will see them. They'll manage the money for everyone involved. They'll even provide you the data you need to know just how well your campaign is getting on.

Check your knowledge 19.2

Ad networks such as Google Display Network or Yahoo are a great, cost-effective way for Colin to get the attention of individual websites. Ad networks find ad spaces on websites, and sort out payment so he won't have to. Colin can also tweet the link to his video, and post it on his Facebook profile. However, this approach can be time-consuming and he can't be sure his video is appearing on the most relevant sites. It's probably better for him to use a dedicated service, and spend his time growing his business.

Question 1 of 1

Colin has created his first video ad, and identified quite a few film-related websites where he'd like to display it. What one solution will allow Colin to easily place his ad on as many relevant websites as possible?

1. Tweet the video link to his friends
2. Email website owners to ask if they will feature his video
3. Use an ad network such as Google Display Network
4. Share the video on his Facebook page

(answer: 3)

Activity 19.2

Go to your favourite search engine and do a search for "display ad network".

Take a look through the results and get familiar with some of the various ad networks and what they have to offer.

Lesson 19.3
How Retargeting Works

Key learning

Retargeting allows you to advertise to groups of visitors to your website based on the things they did when they visited. Here we'll cover the basics:

- tracking what people do on your site
- using that information to identify people you want to target
- creating ads specifically for those people.

Knowledge:

One really powerful type of display advertising is called retargeting, and lets you use what people do on your website in order to target them with a specific advertising message, even after they've left. In this video we'll show you how it works, and help you decide if retargeting is right for your digital strategy.

Let's use our example of a film review podcast once more. A potential customer comes across your website searching for something new to listen to on their morning commute. They are interested and start to subscribe, but halfway through filling out the subscription form are suddenly distracted by phone call. So they leave your site before hitting "Subscribe".

While you're probably glad they visited your website, you'd be happier if they had finished subscribing. They might forget about your podcast. Or find something else to subscribe to instead.

Here's where retargeting comes in.

Your first step in re-targeting is to define your target audience.

There are lots of retargeting solutions out there to choose from, and many display networks offer this feature as well. But no matter which you use, you'll first need to define who will be in your audience.

So, you could define your target audience as people who started to fill out a subscription form, but didn't complete it.

Your retargeting service might need you to add a little code to your web pages, or integrate it in your web analytics tool, so it can start collecting a list of people from your website who match this criteria.

Again, this won't be a list of individual people with any personal information, such as names or email addresses. Instead, it's an anonymous list (often called a retargeting list) of users that match your criteria who can be retargeted with ads.

So, now that you've defined an audience, any visitor who started to subscribe but didn't finish will be added to the list. Now it's time to create ads specifically for them.

These ads can be pretty focused, because you know everyone seeing them has already started to subscribe on your website. So you might include things like special offers for extra content, a free gift for signing up, or some other incentive that's aimed at getting them to come back and finish subscribing.

With a campaign set up to show ads to people on the retargeting list, you can now reach potential customers even after they've left your site.

So later on they might see one of your ads, click on it, and finish signing up.

Once they've subscribed, there's no need to show them ads with subscription incentives anymore. So you might want to create a new retargeting list for current subscribers. Then, you can target them with a different ad campaign, perhaps convincing them to come back and explore all the other podcasts on offer!

So that's how retargeting works. It tracks what people do on your website and then creates an audience based on their actions, letting advertisers design specific ads for people who have - or haven't - done specific things.

Hopefully this sparks some ideas of how you might be able to use retargeting for your own business to re-engage visitors, turn them into customers, and bring them back again and again!

Check your knowledge 19.3

Retargeting ads are a way of bringing potential customers back to a site. A tailored ad that asks someone to return wouldn't be relevant for people who are searching with the keywords 'TV podcasts' because they've not actually visited his website yet. This is the same for film forum users from other sites. These two audiences would need to be targeted using a different advert. However, website homepage visitors, 'almost' subscribers and those who download the e-catalogue are all aware of the website and can be retargeted to draw them back.

Question 1 of 1

Colin is getting a lot of traffic to his podcast website, but not many subscribers. He has budget to design three display ads to encourage people back to his website to subscribe. Colin came up with a list of target groups that he'd like reach with his ads. Help him to cross off the two least useful target groups from his list.

1. People who visit his site
2. People who search for TV-related podcasts
3. People who have started (but not finished) the subscription process
4. People who download his e-catalogue
5. Commentators on film forums

(answer: 2,5)

Activity 19.3

Go to your favourite search engine and do some searches for commercial retargeting options.

Browse around each of the solution providers' websites to get a feel for what they offer and what might be right for you and your business.

Check your knowledge 19.A

Question 1 of 5

In what way can display advertising be effective?

1. It guarantees more visitors to your site
2. It guarantees increased sales
3. It drives traffic to your website
4. It improves your ranking in search engines

Question 2 of 5

Which of the following is an example of the type of data that advertising networks automatically collect and share with businesses?

1. The number of sales you make from the ad
2. The cost of each ad you publish
3. The cost of creating the ad
4. A prediction of sales you can make from your ad

Question 3 of 5

Which of the following is true when purchasing ad placements on an advertising network?

1. You always need to contact the owner of the website to buy ads on their page
2. The network provides data on the click-through-rate
3. The network provides names of the people who click your ad
4. The network will continue to show your ad for 7 days once your budget has expired

Question 4 of 5

If a person adds a product to a shopping basket but then leaves the website, which of the following tactics is most likely to encourage that person to return and purchase the product?

1. Retargeting with a display ad encouraging newsletter sign-up
2. Redesigning your website
3. Creating a Facebook page for your business
4. Retargeting with a display ad that has a discount coupon

Question 5 of 5

What is the first step of display retargeting?

1. Sourcing keywords
2. Defining your audience
3. Writing content
4. Setting a call to action

Module – 20: Make the Most of Video

Today, video is a vibrant and popular part of the online experience. Connecting with customers through this versatile medium can open up valuable advertising and content marketing opportunities. Learn how to integrate video into your online strategy, plan and produce videos on a budget, and promote them so that they're seen by the right people.

Lesson 20.1
The Rise of Online Video

Key learning

As technology has improved, the popularity of online video has skyrocketed. Now, it's a powerful tool in marketing. In this lesson you'll learn:

- how technology has improved online video
- why online video is here to stay
- ways to promote your business with video.

Knowledge:

As technology continues to improve, more and more people are watching videos online. The popularity of online video-and the increasing quality-means huge opportunities for your business.

In this lesson, we'll discuss how technology has boosted online video consumption, why online video is quickly becoming a go-to marketing tool, and ways you can take advantage of these trends in your marketing efforts.

Remember the old days, when you connected to the Internet with a dialup modem? If a friend emailed you a funny cat video, you would probably have time to go make a sandwich before the video would load.

Then, while enjoying your sandwich and the cat's piano solo, the video would sputter... then start...then stop as it continued to load.

Back then, the issue with online video was that it required a lot of juice-that is, a fast Internet connection-to work properly. Sending a video, even a low quality one, put a huge strain on the typical Internet connection.

So, it's not hard to see why advertising with online video wasn't popular at the time.

Fast forward to today. Video technology has progressed significantly. The cost of Internet connection is much lower and the speed is much faster. New software delivers higher quality videos that use your Internet connection efficiently.

These days you can watch video on your computer, tablet, or mobile-at home, at the gym, or on a plane. You can even use the Internet to watch online videos on televisions, thanks to gaming consoles and other devices.

Thanks to such easy access, video can now be used for entertainment, education, information and advertising. You can even use video to learn about how to use video, as you're doing right now!

Now that video is a mainstay for the web, it's a valuable tool for the online marketer. So how can you make the most of it?

There are several ways to reach customers through online video. You can create a video and share it on websites like YouTube or Vimeo. Or you can embed your video directly on your own website.

Another option is to buy ad space in other people's videos. You could display a text ad at the bottom of the video, or run a short commercial at the start.

Advances in Internet technology have made online video marketing a viable option for loads of businesses, large and small. And experts only expect its influence in marketing to grow.

As access to fast Internet connections continues to spread, the popularity of online video will only keep growing-which makes video marketing an ideal way to showcase your business.

If you stick with us, we'll help you create a plan for marketing with online video. We'll show you how to create and share your videos, and how to advertise on video sharing sites.

We'll also discuss ways that you can measure how well your videos are performing.

Check your knowledge 20.1

YouTube, social media sharing, online ads and video website content are all great ways for Justin to reach his target audience through online video. Online video is an ideal option to reach your target audience. People all over the world like the movement, energy and messages that can be contained so concisely in videos. According to analysts, one minute of video is worth 1.8 million words! They are a great way to communicate with the world. Videos can go viral and be targeted at the same time to reach a broad audience. As access to fast internet connections continues to spread, the popularity of online video will only keep growing – which makes video marketing an ideal way to showcase your business.

Question 1 of 1

Justin is a passionate cook. He runs a vegetarian cooking website where he shares recipes and sells speciality ingredients. How could Justin reach his customers through online video?

1. Upload cooking videos to YouTube
2. Advertise on other videos to promote his recipes
3. Add video to his own website
4. Advertise on online games
5. Buy a TV commercial slot
6. Share video on his social media pages

(answer: 1,2,3,6)

Activity 20.1

Do a search on YouTube for videos that are relevant to your business.

Note the types of text ads and video ads that are presented.

Make a list of ways your business could take advantage of these opportunities.

Lesson 20.2
How Video Fits into Your Online Strategy

Key learning

Businesses of every size can use videos to promote their products and services. In this lesson, you'll learn about:

- how video can further your business goals
- expanding your online presence with video
- ways to advertise using video.

Knowledge:

Let's take a moment to think about all the videos your potential customers are watching. Worldwide, people watch more than 300 million hours of video on YouTube per day!

And it's not all funny cat videos-in fact, online video has become an important way for businesses to show off their products and services, and reach new customers.

In this lesson, you'll learn how video can help you expand your online presence. We'll also take a look at some of the ways you can advertise with video and achieve your business goals.

As you incorporate video into your online marketing plan, consider how it will support your business. Nailing down your goals will help you decide the most effective way to use online video.

While it's important to create goals that align with your mission, keep in mind what your customers may be looking for as well. Get those two together and you are well on your way to success.

Here's an example. Say you're a passionate cook, and you have a website where you share vegetarian recipes and sell specialty ingredients related to them.

Through your experiences cooking and baking, you've developed a recipe for the perfect vegetarian lasagna. You want to help others make the dish-and video can be a big part of that.

What if you made a video showing how to make the lasagna, step-by-step? And what if that video went viral, with people spreading the word that this lasagna is even better than the meat version?

Using video is a great way to get people excited about what you have to share, and gain exposure to new fans or customers.

But what if some components of your food blog don't lend themselves to being featured in videos? Or what if you don't want to get involved in producing videos just yet? You can still take advantage of this opportunity by advertising your blog on other people's videos.

Think back to your goals. You're trying to get the word out about your cookie recipe (and perhaps sell some of the specialty ingredients, like the vegan chocolate you recommend).

Even if you don't make your own video, your audience is still likely to watch someone else's cooking and baking videos. Since your audience enjoys cooking, why not advertise on other cooking videos?

With video advertising, you can select certain types of videos, or even specific videos, where you'd like to advertise. You could pick someone else's channel on cooking, or a specific video about vegetarian cooking and advertise there.

Your ad could direct viewers to your website, or tell them about your products.

To sum up: Video marketing offers several ways to reach lots of customers, and you don't even have to make an actual video. With all the possibilities that video represents, make sure you always focus on your business goals to help guide your online video strategy.

Check your knowledge 20.2

Emails, YouTube channels and ads on other cooking websites are great ways to get people excited about what you have to share, and gain exposure to new fans or customers. Email is also one of the fastest and most direct ways of communicating new products and services, and by embedding video in the email Justin can increase the content's engagement rate. Posting videos to relevant YouTube channels is a great way to share content as this audience is already looking for cookery related videos. If Justin isn't ready to upload his own videos just yet, he could always advertise on other people's channels and sites.

Question 1 of 1

Justin's created the perfect vegetarian lasagne, and he wants to share his recipe with the world. Can you help him plan where to put a promo video so it will most effectively reach his target audience?

1. In an email to his customers
2. Cookery section of YouTube
3. Websites selling speciality vegetarian ingredients
4. Local directory listings

(answer: 1,2,3)

Activity 20.2

Write out your online marketing goals.

How can you make use of videos to achieve those goals?

Do you need to produce video content, or could you simply advertise on other relevant videos?

Take some time to write your next steps into using video.

Lesson 20.3
Creating Video Content Within Your Budget

Key learning

Having an online video presence for your brand is more important than ever. Find out how you can cash in on this medium without a Hollywood budget. In this lesson you'll learn:

- how to be creative with your resources
- simple planning tips for videos on a budget
- video editing resources for beginners.

Knowledge:

Videos are all over the Internet. Need to change the oil in your car? There's a how-to video for that. Need an afternoon pick-me-up? There's a funny cat video that will do the trick.

The average viewer watches more than 20 hours of online video a month. As the popularity of online video grows, more and more businesses use it as well.

In this lesson, you'll learn the keys to creating video without breaking the bank with careful planning, creative resourcing, and smart video editing.

The first step to creating video on a budget is to plan your content.

Remember-videos can be entertaining, educational, informative and everything in between, as long as they reflect what your company stands for and further your business objectives.

Let's say you are a food blogger and you want to add video to your site. You'd like to use it to showcase your culinary tastes and talents and increase your subscriber base.

You might decide to do a cooking demonstration in one video. In another you'll tour the kitchen of a popular local chef. In a third, you'll stage a recipe contest.

By planning ahead, you can shoot several videos at a time-with less effort and fewer resources.

To outline the content for each video, use storyboards.

Storyboards are visual plans of your story-showing what will happen scene-by-scene, including action and dialogue.

Once you've got the content of your video planned out, it's time to think about production. Producing video on a budget means being creative with your resources.

Not too long ago, you would have had to hire a crew, rent a studio, and pay a small fortune for equipment before you even began shooting the video.

Now, all you need to produce a video is your mobile or laptop's built-in webcam-or a high-def video camera if you or a friend of yours have one-and basic video editing software (some computer operating systems include that for free).

There are other factors to consider. You can save time and money on finding props, actors, and locations by asking yourself a few questions:

Can you find props at home, among friends, or in thrift stores?

Do you or someone else you know secretly long to be in front of a camera?

Can you use your home, office, or recreational areas as a video location?

Once you've planned your videos, arranged your sets, and booked your crew, now it's time to film.

A steady camera, plus good lighting and sound can make all the difference.

Here are some key points:

Any high-def camera will do-whether on your mobile or an inexpensive digital camera-as long as you keep it steady with a tripod or other stabilizer.

Consider using an external microphone for high-quality audio.

Make sure the room is well lit.

When it comes time to edit your footage, you can find online tutorials to guide you.

A variety of video editing tools-such as iMovie, Windows Movie Maker, or YouTube Video Editor-can help you edit and combine videos, build smooth transitions, and even add music. Little tweaks in the editing process will give your videos a more professional feel.

Making videos is not only a great marketing tool for your business, it's also fun to do! Embrace the chance to tap into your creative side and show the world what your business is all about.

Remember that a tight budget doesn't have to limit your video content.

With advance planning, a little practice, and some creative resourcing, you can make a scene without breaking the bank.

Check your knowledge 20.3

The correct order is: 1. Plan the video release schedule 2. Storyboard the video content 3. Decide on a location and source props 4. Find a video crew and film the videos 5. Edit then upload the videos By planning ahead, you can shoot several videos at a time – with less effort, fewer resources and a smaller budget. Using mobile phones to film your videos and editing with the software that comes with your computer operating system can help keep costs down. Remember, storyboarding your video content is an essential step to make sure you get the audio script, graphics, movement and angles right before you start.

Question 1 of 1

Justin wants to do some video interviews with other local chefs. He wants to add the videos to his blog. Can you help him order his to-do list?

1. Plan the video release schedule
2. Storyboard the video content
3. Decide on a location and source props
4. Find a video crew and film the videos
5. Edit then upload the videos

(answer: 1,2,3,4,5)

Activity 20.3

Brainstorm three video ideas you could film using the same location and actors, say a series of video how-tos.

Remember – you don't have to produce a major motion picture!

The most popular videos are relatively brief.

Lesson 20.4
Sharing and Promoting Your Videos

Key learning

Whether you upload videos to your website, video sharing sites or social media, there are many ways to share and promote your video content online. In this lesson you'll learn how to:

- organise videos on your website
- share videos via social media and email marketing.

Knowledge:

Once you've put a lot of hard work into creating great videos, you'll want loads of people to watch them.

In this lesson, you'll learn how to post and organise videos on your website and video sharing sites like YouTube. We'll also discuss how to grow your audience using social media and email marketing.

Let's say you are a food blogger, and you've filmed a suite of cooking demos. A first step would be to upload your videos to popular video sharing sites, like YouTube or Vimeo.

Be sure to use accurate titles, relevant keywords, and detailed descriptions of each video's content. Not only will this help viewers know what to expect, but it can help your videos appear in search results.

Include calls to action to encourage your audience to take the next step. For example, ask viewers to share the video, visit your website, subscribe to your email newsletter or write a comment.

The next place to post videos is your own website. You could place your videos on pages that correspond to a certain type of cuisine or cooking technique.

Keep your content fresh by uploading new videos frequently. Archive or remove outdated videos-such as a promotion for a local food festival that has already taken place.

After people watch your videos, encourage them to spend more time on your site by showing previews to other videos, and making it easy to find them.

Group videos based on their purpose, such as cooking tips or recipes for brunch.

Sharing video through email marketing and social media is another effective way to engage and grow your audience.

Keep in mind that some popular email programs don't support video playback, so you may direct people to your site rather than embed video directly into an email. You can insert a still shot of your video that links to a page on your site page where the video can be viewed.

On social media sites like Facebook or Twitter, post videos that people might want to share with friends, family and followers, such as interesting cooking tips or interviews with celebrity chefs.

Another way to share videos? Use hashtags.

Adding hashtags to your posts can improve your visibility on certain social sites. For a food blog, you might use hashtags like #cooking, #cookingtips, and #foodies.

To sum up: Uploading videos to your website and popular video sharing sites is the first step to distributing and promoting your video content.

Once there, spread the word by sharing links through email and social media.

Check your knowledge 20.4

Posting on a number of sites and encouraging sharing is a very effective way of making videos more popular. When uploading your video use a suitable title, set of search terms and description. These will make sure people find your video. And when posting on social media, always use a relevant hashtag. And finally, you should encourage people to do something when they've watched your video – for example, ask them to share your video or visit your website.

Question 1 of 1

Justin is uploading some new videos. What can he do to increase the chance of them being promoted and shared?

1. Post it on his website as well as other sites
2. Use a title and keywords that the target audience will use to search
3. Have a call to action such as a 'share' option
4. Add hashtags to your videos for social networking sites

(answer: 1,2,3,4)

Activity 20.4

Consider your current website pages and social media profiles.

Create a list of pages and topics where adding videos might be useful and engaging for your target audience.

If you have any video content already created, practise uploading to YouTube or another video sharing site and practise using the features, such as adding titles, tags, keywords and descriptions.

Lesson 20.5
Advertising On Video Sharing Sites

Key learning

Advertising on video sharing sites is one of the many effective ways to grow your online audience. In this lesson you'll learn:

- top video sharing sites
- ways to advertise on video sharing sites.

Knowledge:

As you probably know by now, people are spending loads of time watching videos online. That means they're spending time more time than ever on popular video-sharing websites, like YouTube, Vimeo, Daily Motion, and many others. With large audiences engaging with content, they care about, video sites can be a great place to advertise your business. And you don't even need your own videos to do it.

Today you'll learn about the various ways you can take advantage of the boom in video sharing to advertise your business.

The first step is to define your target audience and identify the types of content they will be most likely to view. Let's assume that you've got a cooking blog, and your readers like websites about cooking at home, TV shows featuring famous chefs and cooking demo videos.

Start by looking for video channels featuring content that matches the interests of your readers - YouTube can be a great place to start. These channels have the audience you want to reach, and advertisements on these videos can introduce new people to your food blog.

Think about some ways you can pique the interest of cooking video enthusiasts. Do you have similar types of recipes and tips? Do you have your own interviews with celebrity chefs?

Once you have some ideas of your audience's interests, you can use the Google Ads program to advertise on YouTube. Other video sites often allow advertising as well. You don't need videos of your own to advertise on these sites - you can use images and text instead. There are even free tools, like Google's Ad Gallery, that will help you create professional-looking banners, for example.

Be sure your ad gives viewers a reason to visit your website and that they find something compelling when they visit. You already know that this audience likes visual content, so guide them to pages with stunning photos or your own videos, if you have them. Remember, you want them to keep coming back for more.

Let's say you've decided to advertise on YouTube. Once you have your ad ready to go, use an Google Ads account to run your campaign. Within Google Ads, choose the category of people you want to reach on YouTube, such as cooking enthusiasts.

When your target audience is watching videos on YouTube, your ad will then appear next to the video, or even within the video itself, depending on the type of ad you choose.

As with any online advertising, you'll have to define a budget for your YouTube campaign. Monitor your campaign and optimize based on what you learn.

Let's review.

There are loads of ways you can promote your business on video sharing sites. You don't have to create your own video content to advertise in places that show mostly video. It's more about reaching an audience who will find your business relevant and engaging.

Find out which videos and websites your target audience is interested in and place relevant advertisements on those sites.

Check your knowledge 20.5

The correct answers are: - Home cooking - TV chefs - Cooking videos When you create your keywords, you need to think like your customer. What will they be searching for? Being specific is often better as it means your content will be more relevant to the search and increase the likelihood of someone visiting your site. Be sure your ad gives viewers a reason to visit your website and remember, you want them to keep coming back for more.

Question 1 of 1

Justin wants to do more video advertising. He knows his blog audience likes cooking at home, TV shows featuring famous chefs and cooking demo videos. Which keywords should he choose for the Google Ads programme?

1. Home cooking
2. TV chefs
3. Instructional videos
4. Cooking videos
5. Chefs
6. TV shows

(answer: 1,2,4)

Activity 20.5

Visit some of your favourite channels on YouTube.

What types of advertising do you see?

Which types best grab your attention?

Lesson 20.6
Measuring Video Performance

Key learning

Analytics can give you insights into the people who watch your videos and how they engage with your content. With this information at hand, you can improve your videos and grow your audience. In this lesson you'll learn:

- how to determine who watches your videos
- ways to find out what they like and don't like
- opportunities to improve and engage new audiences.

Knowledge:

One of the great features about marketing with online video is that you can measure your results. Whether you're creating videos for your own website, sharing them on social media, or advertising on popular video sites, you can measure the results of your efforts.

In this lesson, we'll discuss how to use analytics to learn who your viewers are and how they interact with your videos. We'll also look at opportunities to improve your video performance and engage new audiences.

Video analytics reveal a lot about the people who watch your videos, like their age, gender and location. When you know your audience, you can create video content they're interested in watching.

Say you are a food blogger who creates videos about your culinary experiences in foreign locales. Your analytics reveal that most of your viewers live in London, and your most popular videos feature French cuisine.

If you want to increase traffic to your blog, you might create more videos and content for these viewers-perhaps a cooking demo with a famous French chef?

If you have videos in different places-such as your website, Facebook page, and YouTube channel-analytics on each site will show you where people are watching your videos the most.

Knowing where people watch your videos is key to promoting your content. If most of your audience watches your videos on YouTube, focus on uploading more fresh content to that site.

You can also see what day and time people are most likely to watch your videos. If most people watch on weekends, then consider uploading fresh content on Friday nights.

When measuring the performance of your videos, you can find out if people watch your videos start to finish. The length of your video may depend on the content.

In most cases, short videos work best. You can increase the likelihood that people will play your videos and watch them to the end by keeping them brief.

If people only watch the first few seconds of a video, it might not be meeting their expectations. Consider updating your preview images, video titles or descriptions so that people have a better idea of what they're about to watch.

Also look at the average length of video viewed. If most people spend only a minute watching your demos, try creating videos that are 60 seconds or less.

Other common indicators of your videos' performance are: likes, dislikes, comments and shares. This information from viewers provides insightful feedback. Another tip: keep an eye on the reactions your videos receive through comments and social media.

If people share your video, it's a strong measure of engagement. After all, they liked it enough to pass it along to someone else.

To recap: You can use analytics to learn who is watching your videos, identify what they like and don't like, and find opportunities to engage new audiences. What you learn can help you when creating your next video.

Check your knowledge 20.6

In most cases, short videos work best. You can increase the likelihood that people will play your videos and watch them to the end by keeping them brief. Statistics show that after one minute, 45% of viewers will stop watching. Also, checking comments can be a useful way to find out why people aren't watching the video through to the end.

Question 1 of 1

Justin is studying his food blog's analytics. He notices that most people give up on his videos after 60 seconds. He's brainstormed a list of fixes. Cross out the ones that you think are wrong.

1. Change his preview image and video title
2. Update the video description
3. Keep new videos under 60 seconds
4. Review the comments to see what viewers have said

Activity 20.6

If you have a video channel on YouTube, Vimeo or another video sharing site, review the site's analytics tools.

1. How are your videos performing?
2. Which of your videos are most popular?
3. What's the average length of time people watch your videos?

Check your knowledge 20.A

Question 1 of 6

When incorporating videos into a digital strategy, which of the following tactics provides value to customers?

1. Setting up live streams of the business's physical shop on their website
2. Publishing a how-to video on their website
3. Producing sale campaign videos
4. Sharing personal vlogs

Question 2 of 6

What can using video as part of your online presence help you create?

1. Content that will go viral
2. A channel to engage with customers
3. A variety of different brand perceptions
4. An online following and fanbase

Question 3 of 6

Fill in the blank: As a small business, creating videos to showcase your business or product requires only _____.

1. An agency, professional crew and equipment
2. Creativity, lots of experience and a large budget
3. Creativity, planning and any budget
4. Creativity, planning and high-quality equipment

Question 4 of 6

Using videos in email marketing and social media is an effective way to do what?

1. Increase word of mouth referrals
2. Engage and grow your audience
3. Guarantee sales of your product or service
4. Lower the cost of developing content

Question 5 of 6

How can you take advantage of video for your product/services without actually making a video?

1. This isn't possible
2. Advertise on other people's videos
3. Use images with a call to action instead
4. Share other people's videos

Question 6 of 6

When looking at your video analytics, you discover people are only watching the first few seconds of your video. What should you do?

1. Consider removing the video from the platform
2. Consider re-shooting your video based on comments
3. Consider updating your preview images, video titles or descriptions
4. Consider asking people to watch the whole video in the description

(answer : 2, 2, 3, 2, 2, 3)

Module – 21: Get Started with Analytics

Web analytics can provide a world of information when it comes to understanding your web users. By clearly outlining your business goals, you can then utilise analytics data to help you refine and improve your website and meet your objectives.

Lesson 21.1

What Is Web Analytics?

Key learning

Web analytics can answer questions about what people are doing – and not doing – on your website. In this video, you'll learn about:

- the kind of data web analytics can provide
- how to understand that data
- how simple it is to get started.

Knowledge:

Welcome to our introduction to web analytics. In this video we'll be going over what web analytics is, a quick overview of the kinds of insights it can give you, and a taste for how to get started with analytics yourself.

Okay, let's get started.

So, what is web analytics, exactly? Well, it's all about using the data you can collect from your website to give you insights about your business.

There are lots of web analytics tools out there, and they can do a variety of things. Since we're just getting started, we'll focus on the basics, and talk about the ways analytics can help you, no matter which specific tool you use.

Web analytics helps you by providing data. First, let's look at the different types.

A "metric" is basically anything you can count. "Unique Visitors" is a good example. "Time Spent On Site" is another. If you sell things on your website, you can track how much money you're making or how many of a certain product you're selling. If your goal is to get people to read your website, you can track the number of times someone looked at a blog post or the amount of time they spent on it. All of these things are "metrics."

Next, you'll generally analyze your metrics by using what are called "dimensions." But let's come back to that in just a minute.

When you're first starting out with analytics, you might feel like you're swimming in an ocean of metrics, but you'll quickly get used to having all this data.

So, what do you do with it?

Well, you can use web analytics tools to learn more about your website visitors.

Let's say someone places an order, downloads driving directions to your shop, fills out a contact form, or does something else that you want them to do when they're visiting your site. This is known as a "conversion."

Web analytics tools can tell you if the "conversion rate", or the amount of people that visit and then convert on one of your goals, changes based on where they came from, whether they'd been there before, or even the type of device they're using.

So let's look at that last one. If you know which devices your site is working best and worst on, you can identify specific areas of strength to build on and areas you'll need to improve.

You'll notice in that example that we were comparing "metrics" of conversions or conversion rates, but we were breaking it down by the device they used. The "device" data we're collecting is called a "dimension," and as promised, it's time to talk about those next.

Generally, a dimension is any kind of data you can use to describe something you're tracking with words.

Dimensions include things like the device type, what browsers visitors use, their geographic locations, and much, much more.

By taking your metrics and "slicing" them with dimensions, you can find answers to very specific, detailed business questions, like "which devices are people finding it easiest to convert on the goals of my website?"

And that's just one of many questions you can answer with web analytics.

Want to know what time of day most people are visiting your website? Take your "Visitors" metric and break that down by an "Hour of Day" dimension.

How about finding out which marketing campaigns are making the most sales? Take your "Conversions" metric, and break it down by a "Campaign" dimension.

As you dive into your own web analytics reports, you'll be able to see all the metrics and dimensions being tracked, and you can combine them and slice and dice them to answer the questions you care most about.

If you haven't started with an analytics tool yet, you'll want to select and install one. Most have a pretty similar set up.

First, you'll need to copy and paste some special code onto your web pages. Next, while these tools will track a lot of things on their own, you might want to configure them to track the specific things that are unique to your business and your goals.

We hope you're getting excited about all the amazing insights you can get from web analytics tools. It's another important tool in your online arsenal, but if this seems like a lot to take in, don't worry.

If you stick with us, we're going to cover all the terminology and the basics of how you can use web analytics to measure how you're doing with digital. We'll cover how to see whether visitors convert on your goals, and how to find out which kinds of visitors perform better than others. On top of that, we'll even go into using analytics to measure and improve your paid and organic search engine campaigns.

Check your knowledge 21.1

Metrics are measurable, numerical data like time spent on site or pages viewed. Conversions are data on how many users have completed a desired action on your site, for example buying a product or signing up for a newsletter. Dimensions are groups of user data that can be used to generate a report, such as their device type or location. Imagine Linda had 1,000 visitors to her website last week – 1,000 is a metric. 500 of those visitors are from France, 300 from Italy and 200 from Germany. Those countries are dimensions - they organise visitors into groups sharing common characteristics, such as their country of origin. Finally, let's say 300 of last week's visitors signed up for Linda's newsletter. Those 300 signups are conversions - visitors who did something on Linda's website that is important for her business.

Question 1 of 1

Linda runs a guesthouse with a website where people can book their rooms online. She's been using web analytics to monitor how customers interact with her website. Linda uses the information to improve the site and the visitor's experience. Take a look at the following terms – do you know what they mean in the web analytics world?

Time spent on site

Metric / Dimension / Conversion

Visitor's device type

Metric / Dimension / Conversion

Visitor's location

Metric / Dimension / Conversion

Signing up to the newsletter

Metric / Dimension / Conversion

(answer: Metric, Dimension, Dimension, Conversion)

Activity 21.1

Do a search for "web analytics tools" and open an account with one of the tools that you like.

Google Analytics could be a great place for you to start.

Lesson 21.2
Making Web Analytics Work for You

Key learning

One of the biggest benefits of going online is that digital marketing is extremely measurable. Throughout the entire customer journey, web analytics provides insight on where your website visitors are coming from, what they're doing and how you can get more of them to "convert" on your site. In this video, we'll cover:

- why web analytics underpins everything you do in digital
- the kinds of insights you can gain using analytics
- how to use data to support your business goals.

Knowledge:

In this lesson, we'll be going over how you can make web analytics work for you-no matter what kind of business you own.

You'll learn about how analytics helps you track and measure what visitors do on your website, and use that information to help you achieve your business goals.

Let's get started.

Used properly, web analytics can become the foundation of the online portion of your business. That's because analytics can measure the performance of just about any kind of online marketing you decide to do. From search to display advertising, social to email, and everything in between.

At the same time, analytics measures your website visitors across the entire digital customer journey - from the first time a person visits your website, to the time they become a valuable repeat customer.

To see how this all comes to life, let's look at an example, say, a guesthouse or "bed and breakfast."

One goal for for a bed and breakfast is to have website visitors make a reservation online - after all, that's how they make money.

Analytics can help measure how many reservations are being made, but it will also capture important insights about the things that lead up to and follow that reservation. All throughout the entire customer journey.

So what exactly does that mean? Let's play out an example of the journey a customer goes through before they make a reservation. If you were looking for a guest house in, say Cologne, Germany for a trip you'll be making three months from now, the first thing you might do is go online and search for a term like "guesthouses in Cologne."

After you search, you end up on a search results page. And from there, you might spend some time clicking around on some guest house websites that interest you. You're in research mode.

Once you're on a website, you might do any number of things. Like check out the daily rate. See what kinds of rooms are available. Browse some reviews or testimonials to get a better idea of what the guesthouse is really like. You might even look at some pictures to get a sense of the place. At this point, you're probably not ready to actually book a reservation - you're still looking around. But you might decide that this one is on your short-list, and you might even sign up to receive email updates from the guesthouse to make sure you don't miss out on any promotions.

Now, two weeks later, what do you know? An email shows up in your inbox offering 10% off the normal rate, for the same dates you were planning to travel!

At this point, you've done quite a bit of research, but you haven't booked yet, and that email was just what you needed to make your decision. So, you click on the email, go back to the website, and make a reservation.

The power of analytics is that it can help a business measure what's going on at every stage of that customer journey. Want to know how people are initially becoming aware of your business? It can tell you which search engines people are finding you on and which kinds of pages they're being sent to.

It can then tell you if people are actually engaging with your business when they get to your website. For example, do they browse around and sign up for your email updates? Or do they just click the back button in their browser and move on to the next option?

Analytics can also measure whether people are converting on the goals you want to track - in our example, there were actually two: First, that email newsletter signup, and second, the reservation itself.

Analytics can tell us whether people are coming back and becoming repeat customers. And when properly set up, analytics can even tell us if those loyal customers are becoming our advocates - for example, are they sharing our content with others on social networks?

A great way to turn analytics into a powerful tool that helps you understand how people use your website and improve accordingly, is to set clear, specific, quantifiable goals at every stage of the customer journey.

Then, use analytics to measure your progress toward those goals, and identify bottlenecks that are getting in the way of achieving them. For example, the guesthouse may have a goal of getting at least 50 reservations per month. Using analytics, they might find out that people are getting confused by their booking system, which is causing interested potential customers to abandon the website... and probably book somewhere else.

This isn't good news, of course, but it's great information. It identifies what needs to be fixed, and hopefully, drives a decision to spend some time and resources making the booking process quicker and easier. And that's the key - data without action isn't going to help anyone.

We've covered a lot of ground here, so let's recap. Analytics can become the foundation that measures and supports all of your digital efforts.

It can help you measure what's happening and understand the different stages of the online customer journey, highlighting things you're doing well and showing you where you need to improve. So set your goals, measure your progress, and then use your data to take your business to the next level.

Check your knowledge 21.2

Before making big changes like sending more newsletters or stopping them altogether, Linda should review the newsletters to find out why people are unsubscribing. How many is she sending a week? Is she sending too many? Is the content of the newsletters the best it can be? Linda should focus on improving the quality of the newsletters and monitor whether the numbers of people unsubscribing drops.

Question 1 of 1

Linda's analytics data shows people unsubscribing from her newsletter after two weeks. These people also aren't booking rooms at her guesthouse. Linda gets some advice from her friends. Whose advice should she take?

1. "Stop sending newsletters as people aren't reading them"
2. "Review the content of the newsletters to check they're suitable"
3. "Check you're not sending too many newsletters"
4. "Send more newsletters reminding customers to book a room"

(answer: 2,3)

Activity 21.2

Think about the big-picture goals for your business.

Are you trying to maximise revenue?

To improve margins?

To cut costs?

How do your website and your online marketing campaigns help you achieve those goals?

Write down your thoughts – this will help focus your efforts with analytics.

Lesson 21.3
Tracking Specific Goals With Web Analytics

Key learning

Used properly, web analytics tools can give you valuable information to help you meet your objectives. You can do this by setting up your web analytics tool to track the specific goals that you care about. Here we'll explore:

- examples of goals and conversions
- why it's important to create and configure goals
- how to determine what your own goals and conversions should be.

Knowledge:

Web analytics tools can give you a mountain of data, straight out of the box - and that's a great opportunity for businesses. But in order to really make use of all that data, it's important to make sure you're measuring progress toward your own particular goals. That means you'll want to customise your analytics a bit, to make sure you're tracking things that really matter to you.

Seeing some examples of goals and conversions, and looking at why it's important to create them, will help you figure out what yours should be.

So, you've taken your business online for a reason, right? Well, just about anything you hoped to achieve with your website can be tracked and measured with web analytics as a goal you hope to achieve.

"Conversion" is the word commonly used to describe what happens when a website visitor completes a goal. And by now, you know that web analytics tools have the ability to break down loads of data about your visitors and what's happening on your site to give you information that can help you get more of those conversions.

Let's use the example of a guest house to see just how important goals and tracking conversions can be.

Say you sign in to your web analytics tool and start looking at numbers.

First, you notice that the guest house website had 10,000 visitors last month. You compare that number to the past, and see that your visitor count is up from 5,000 during the same month last year.

Great, right?

Well, not necessarily. Visits alone don't help your business move forward, and without understanding the value of those visits, it's really hard to figure out what to do with this information.

So let's try to figure out a little more about the value of those visits. Maybe you look at some reports and notice that the average visitor spends two minutes on your website, about the same as last year.

We're starting to learn a little more, but we're still not really getting to the business value of those visits. Is two minutes enough time to make a valuable visit? Is it too little? The truth is that we don't know.

Just looking at stats like these really limits our ability to make any decisions.

What we need is data that can very clearly show the value of these visits to the business. With that data you can start to really use your web analytics tool to show you things you can do to constantly improve.

And that brings us back to the very basics of what it is we want to achieve online.

One reason you'd create a website for a guest house is so that people could reserve a room online. So a completed reservation is definitely a goal that you'll want your analytics tool to be tracking. That's one down!

But what other goals might your guest house have? What else can people do that is valuable to your business? Well, maybe you want people to know where to find you.

How would you set up an analytics tool to measure that? Well, maybe visiting the page on your site with a map and directions would be something you could consider a goal and configure that as a conversion.

Or maybe you want people to sign up for your email newsletter so that you can send them special offers and keep them up-to-date with improvements you're making. If they sign up, they're signaling that they're interested in your guest house and giving you an opportunity to reach them, so that's really valuable!

And that means completing the signup form could be another goal that you track.

There are all kinds of goals you can find that can be tracked as conversions inside web analytics and show you the real value of what's happening on your website.

Once you've figured out your goals, you'll need to configure them in your web analytics tool. While the processes for doing that can vary, it's usually pretty painless.

Once it's done, looking at the reports in your web analytics tool becomes much more productive.

Instead of simply looking at how many visitors you've gotten or how long they spend on your site, you can start seeing reports showing the things you actually care about. Like maybe only 2% of your visitors coming from social media sites are signing up for your email newsletter.

So what can you do? How about putting out some social media posts offering a 10% off coupon when people sign up for the email newsletter?

Or maybe you find out that your reservation rate jumps from 3% up to 6% on weekends. Your next step? You adjust your advertising campaigns to advertise more heavily over the weekend, when people are more likely to take action.

If you're thinking this is all starting to come together, then you're getting the hang of what web analytics tools can do for you.

Just remember: you'll get the most out of these tools when you use them to measure your specific goals.

Now go forth and analyze!

Check your knowledge 21.3

When it comes to analytics, it's important to focus on the information that has the most impact on her business. In this case, Linda should focus less on the number of visits to the site or the amount of time people spend on it. It's also not hugely important how many pages people look at on average. Instead, she should be monitoring specific goals like the percentage of orders that comes from customers on their smartphones, or the number of people who click on the content in her newsletters. This information is much more valuable as it gives feedback on the new elements she's recently introduced to her business.

Question 1 of 1

Linda runs a guesthouse and has been using analytics to gather information about how people interact with her website.

She's recently revamped her newsletter, and has made the site responsive to appeal to users on mobile devices.

Which elements of the analytics should Linda focus on to measure the effectiveness of her changes?

Number of visits to the site per month

Number of site pages users explore on average

Amount of time visitors spend on the site

Number of people clicking on the links in her newsletters

Percentage of orders made on smartphones and tablets

Activity 21.3

Take a look at your website.

Why do you have a website?

Write down every answer you can think of, because that's a goal you can track with analytics.

Check your knowledge 21.A

Question 1 of 3

Fill in the blank: Website analytics can tell you _____.

1. What time of day your website gets the most traffic
2. How many mentions or likes you get on social media
3. How well your competitor's ad campaigns are doing
4. The email addresses of visitors to your landing pages

Question 1 of 3

Analytics can give you immediate valuable information about which type of customers?

1. Previous and current customers
2. Current and future customers
3. Previous and future customers
4. Offline and online customers

Question 1 of 3

If your key business goal is to get people to book rooms at your guesthouse, what data are you most likely to be interested in?

1. How long people spend on your 'How To Find Us' page
2. Which day of the week is most popular for bookings
3. Whether your funny Tweet goes viral
4. How many people visiting your site book a room with you

(answer: 1,1,4)

Module – 22: Find Success with Analytics

Analytics tools provide loads of data, but they don't always give easy answers. Dive a little deeper into web analytics, and you'll soon be able to measure organic search analytics, understand SEM data and master segmentation techniques.

Lesson 22.1
Web Analytics and Organic Search

Key learning

Web analytics is great for measuring all kinds of traffic to your site, including traffic from organic search results. But you can do much more than just count up your website visitors. In this video, you'll learn:

- what kinds of data web analytics can give you about search traffic
- how to evaluate trends in your search traffic
- how to discover opportunities to make your website more relevant to searchers.

Knowledge:

Are you curious about how you can use web analytics tools to see how you're performing in organic search results? In this video, we'll touch on monitoring organic search traffic, using data to gain valuable insights about how your site is evaluated by search engines, and how you can troubleshoot SEO issues uncovered by analytics.

OK, let's jump in.

Search engines are an important source of traffic for most websites. In fact, they're very often the single biggest source of traffic to a business's website. But are you getting more or less of that traffic from search engines over time? What do all of those searchers actually do after they get to your website? And most importantly, how can you improve your website to make sure the search engines are sending you people who are interested in your products and services?

If you're thinking that web analytics has the answers to these questions, you're spot on.

No matter which web analytics tool you're using, you'll be able to monitor how many visitors are coming to your website from organic search results from the different search engines. If you're paying an agency or consultant to maintain your website for you, you should ask them for access to your website's analytics data.

Once you've got access to that data, one of the first things you'll want to check out is how your traffic from search engines is trending over time. If you're getting more visitors from search engines, that's great. But, if your traffic is trailing off, you've probably got some work to do. Either way - before you can make any decisions, you'll need to know the "why", and that means we need to dig deeper.

If you're using Google Analytics as your web analytics tool, you can dig deeper by learning which keywords people are typing into Google before they reached your website. That data doesn't necessarily come from the analytics tool itself, but because Google Analytics can integrate data from Google Search Console, you get to see that kind of information.

Remember our example of the guesthouse? You might see that people are searching for things you wouldn't have expected, like "luxury guest houses in Glasgow" or "cheap Glasgow bed and breakfast" to find your website. This can help you get a sense of what your visitors are really looking for, and you can respond to that by building the right content and pages to fit their needs.

You'd also be able to see whether you're getting more or fewer visitors from any given keyword theme, as well as whether or not visits to those pages end up with actual bookings.

Let's say you're noticing that you used to be getting more traffic for a certain search term, but that traffic has been gradually declining. What can you do to turn things around? Well, you might start by taking a look at some of the content on your site. How can you ensure that your content is as relevant as possible to users who are looking for that luxury guest house? Could you rewrite some of your text to focus on the fact that you've got a high-end guest house? Remember, you're not re-working your content to suit a search engine. You're working on it to make it match your existing business better. And to make it as relevant and useful as possible to people who are searching for luxury guest houses. If you want to know even more about optimizing your pages, check out some of the other videos on SEO.

Now, what about the opposite scenario? Maybe you've found that you're getting more traffic from people searching for keywords around that luxury guest house theme. That's great - but how can you build on that? Again, you want to focus on what's relevant to the people who are searching. What are some of the exclusive, high-end features of your guest house? Have you included content on your website that talks about your gourmet breakfast? The fancy cocktails you're offering on Saturday afternoon?

Adding more useful content about the luxury aspects of the guest house could help search engines point more relevant users to your website.

If you've invested some time in improving your content, you'll want to know what the impact is, and web analytics can show you this. If you're expecting your content to be more relevant to people searching for luxury guest houses, Google Analytics can show you whether that effort is translating into more visitors reaching your website. Pretty smart, huh?

So far, we've been focusing on analyzing the amount of traffic, or visitors, that are reaching your website after searching. That's really important. But keep in mind that even more important than the amount of traffic you're getting is the quality of the traffic that you're getting.

After all, what's the use of attracting loads of people to your website if nobody's going to book a stay at your guest house? Remember, analytics doesn't just tell you where people are coming from, it also tracks what they do on the website.

So take a look at the themes that are driving conversions on your goals, as well as visits. If all this work on luxury themes has got you more traffic, but people aren't engaging with your content, they're not signing up for your email newsletter, and they're not reserving their rooms, you may want to investigate why, or even consider shifting your focus somewhere else.

Web analytics can be a great tool for your SEO efforts, helping you measure how much traffic you're getting from search engines, where you might be able to make improvements, and the impact of changes you're making to your website.

So if you're focused on SEO, put on that analysis hat and start digging into your data!

Check your knowledge 22.1

Analytics can tell Linda a lot of interesting information about her organic search performance. However, it won't tell her explicitly whether her site's content is relevant to her keywords. To understand that, she can look at information such as how long visitors spend on her site, or the bounce rate, to see whether her site is giving her customers the information they are looking for.

Question 1 of 1

Linda runs a guesthouse. She wants to use analytics to measure traffic coming to her website from organic search results. What can she learn from analytics reports?

1. Which search engines visitors use
2. How traffic is trending over time
3. How relevant the content is for keywords
4. How many visitors are using mobile devices

(answer: 1,2,4)

Activity 22.1

Looking at your web analytics tool, note the top pages on your site that are getting organic traffic from a search engine.

See if you can find any pages that get surprisingly little traffic – perhaps those are your opportunities for improvement.

Lesson 22.2
Tools To Measure SEM

Key learning

When it comes to SEM, you're paying real money for every click that brings visitors to your website. Here's how you can use web analytics to make sure you're getting the most out of your investment. We'll look at:

- which keywords are paying for themselves
- how to understand which ads are working
- how to use analytics to help you bid smarter.

Knowledge:

It's time to talk about using analytics to get the most out of your Search Engine Marketing, or SEM, campaigns.

We're going to look at how you can use analytics to figure out which keywords are the best ones for you to bid on, how to tailor your ads to make them more effective, and how to decide how much to bid for the spots that are the most cost-effective for you.

Let's get started. With search engine marketing, you're spending money. The good news is, with analytics you can track what you spent where, and understand where it was spent most effectively.

Remember that guesthouse we've been talking about? Well, let's take this a bit further and pretend that it offers three themed rooms: King Arthur, Modern Romance and Football Fanatic. To promote each of these, let's say you decide to run separate search campaigns with the goal of getting people to visit your website and take a video tour of one of these rooms.

Business is pretty good, but you'd like to take it to the next level.

With an analytics tool, you can check the keywords you're using for each of your campaigns, and immediately see which are the most effective.

Let's say you're looking at your "Modern Romance" campaign. You notice that when your keywords, 'romantic guesthouse' and 'guesthouse for a romantic weekend' were used, the visitor took a video tour of that room about 5% of the time. This is known as a 5% "conversion rate" for the goal of taking the video tour.

But when people search for keywords like 'luxury romantic guest house' or 'luxurious romantic guest house' the conversion rate drops to only 1%.

You've just found something you can improve, and there are lots of ways you might choose to do it.

First, you might look at the relevant pages on your website and see if there are changes you could make.

Take a look at all your luxury adverts and test some different messages that might really highlight either the video tour itself, or the luxury aspects of the guest house.

Whatever you decide to do, the key is that you'll still be tracking what happens after you make your changes, and that means you'll be able to see if your fixes raise that conversion rate from 1% to something better!

That covers a few different ways you can measure the keywords you're bidding on, but that's just one part of it. Analytics can also help you understand the impact of the actual ads you're running.

You know that you want to write ads that are clear and compelling to the user, but ultimately, those users will decide what clear and compelling means to them. And that's where analytics can help.

Sticking with this Modern Romance campaign, let's say you have two different ads with two different headlines. One reads "Lockhart House" and the other reads "Romantic Weekend Accommodation".

Analytics tools can show you how these compare, side by side. You can see which one is more likely to get a click and send someone to your site, and which one is more likely to get the visitor to take that video tour.

This will tell you which one you should be using. And you can even use the insights you learn here across other campaigns and other areas of your website!

Last, analytics tools can help you understand just how much you should be bidding for ads, to make sure you're getting a good return on your SEM investments.

By using Google Analytics, which integrates deeply with Google Ads, you can see the keywords and ads driving people to your website and what they do when they get there, but you can also see quite a bit more. For example, how much you had to pay for each of those clicks, and how high up on the results page your bids put your ads. This gives you a lot of clarity into both what you're getting for your investment as well as if it makes sense for you to bid higher or lower, to reach different positions that work for your business.

Let's say you're not the only guesthouse in town, and you've got some competition from "Stuart's Guest House". You might see that when you bid enough to out-do Stuart and your ad is in the top spot, it results in a conversion rate of 2%.

But, if you keep digging, your analytics tool might also tell you that when you bid lower and end up underneath Stuart, you get a little less traffic, but your conversion rate jumps up to 4%!

Of course, the ideal position and bid for you will depend on lots of things, and you might find that it's better to be higher or better to be lower, but the key is that by using analytics, you'll know exactly where you perform the best, and that means you'll be getting more out of your investment than your competition.

Whether you're analyzing your keywords, your ads, or how you're bidding in your campaigns, analytics tools are essential to get the most out of your SEM investments. So, before you make another update to your campaigns, make sure you drive those decisions with data!

Check your knowledge 22.2

Linda can use analytics data to see which of her SEM investments are working and which aren't. The key is not just to track the number of clicks on an ad, but more importantly the conversion rate. So whilst the 'Family friendly guesthouse' campaign gets the most clicks, it needs work, because it has the lowest conversion rate of the three ads. That means people are clicking on the ad, but not booking a room as often as people who click on the other ads.

Question 1 of 1

Linda owns a guesthouse and has a website where customers can book and pay for rooms in advance. Linda uses SEM to create targeted ads for her rooms. She's now looking at the analytics data for the different ad campaigns she runs. Take a look at the analytics data for the three campaigns. Which one campaign is performing least well?

Cosy guesthouse in Guildford town centre Get away from it all in a relaxed setting Book a room today! 478 clicks 6% conversion rate

Family friendly guesthouse Lots to do nearby Come and see what we have to offer! 830 clicks 2% conversion rate

Romantic guesthouse getaway in Guildford Plan a special trip with your loved one Book online now 630 clicks 4% conversion rate

(answer: 2)

Activity 22.2

Take a look at your analytics reports.

Find two keywords that are performing well.

Why do you think they are doing well?

Then, find two keywords that aren't performing as well.

What do you think you can do to improve their performance?

Lesson 22.3
Breaking Down Your Data for Insights

Key learning

Analytics tools provide loads of data, but they don't always give easy answers. To understand why things are happening differently for different groups, you can use a simple technique called segmentation. Here you'll learn:

- what segmentation is
- why it's valuable
- how to do it.

Knowledge:

In this lesson we're going to take a look at a web analytics technique called "segmentation."

Segmentation helps you break down and understand the data you get from web analytics in smaller chunks to help you get more insights and improve your website's performance.

Let's go back to the guesthouse example, where one of your goals is to get people to book a room at the guesthouse.

If you use your web analytics tool and look at your high level data, you might learn that only 3% of all your website visitors are indeed signing up.

To understand this a little better, you can use segmentation to break down all those visitors by different groupings.

First, let's break it down by geographic segments, starting with country. As it turns out, when we look at our visitors by where they live, there are some big differences in whether or not they book a room, and that makes sense.

People in the UK, for example, represent a big percentage of our visitors, and they're converting at 6%, which is twice the average rate! When we look at visitors from the US, though, we see a fair bit of traffic, but a really low conversion rate of 1%. Immediately, you've got a good idea: adding a bit of content tailored to American visitors could help you get more bookings. For example, adding some information about the best ways to get to the guesthouse after landing at Heathrow would help.

Let's dive deeper. We'll break down the UK segment even further into specific cities.

Here, we can see that London and Leeds stand out as more likely to make a reservation. Perhaps running some local advertising campaigns in those cities could help you get more bookings.

So, what's the big deal with segmentation? Well, as you're starting to see, segmentation gives you some insights you can action.

Fun, right? Let's back up and segment by something different. How about the ways people are getting to our website.

This can help us answer questions like: "Are people who come from social media more likely to book a room?"

When you break down your visitors by where they came from, you can see the differences between your organic search traffic, paid search traffic, social media traffic, and more.

And this can help you decide where you want to invest your time and resources as you build up your digital marketing campaigns across lots of different channels.

Let's do one more. This time, we'll chop up our visitors by the kind of device they're using, and we'll be able to see any differences between things like desktop computers, tablets, and smartphones.

Here we get more valuable information. People on computers and tablets are booking to the tune of 4%. But people on smartphones almost never make a reservation.

To improve things, you could work on making your website more mobile-friendly or see if there are issues with how your online booking process is working on smartphones that you can fix.

And that might help increase the number of bookings that you're getting- another impactful insight!

So that's segmentation. Of course, you can slice and dice by just about anything that piques your curiosity, but the general idea is this: break things down into smaller groups and find insights that can help you figure out how to improve.

So dive in, start segmenting, and see what kinds of answers you can find!

Check your knowledge 22.3

Linda can get lots of data through segmentation, such as the devices her visitors use to access her website, and what country and city they're accessing from. The number of clicks on a page is broad information that can still be segmented. Linda can use segmented information to find out where people are visiting her guesthouse from, and how many conversions she gets. She can also find out if many people book using their mobiles, or if they prefer booking on their computers. With this information Linda can make improvements to her website and keep monitoring results.

Question 1 of 1

Linda runs a successful guesthouse in the centre of Guildford. She promotes the guesthouse online and has a website where customers can book and pay for rooms in advance. Linda wants to use segmentation to break down her analytics data. What information about the visitors can she gather by using this?

1. Devices used
2. The visitor's city
3. The visitor's country
4. The number of clicks on a page

(answer: 1,2,3)

Activity 22.3

Consider your online goals.

How would you segment your data to find out how to achieve more success?

By geography, mobile device or something else?

Write down your ideas.

Check your knowledge 22.A

Question 1 of 3

Most web analytics tools can tell you what information about the user?

1. Their contact details, their behaviour and their operating system
2. Their location, type of device they're using and pages visited
3. Their location, type of device they're using and contact details
4. Their interests, when they delete their browser cookies and their location

Question 2 of 3

Fill in the blank: If an ad is not performing well, one effective tactic is to _____.

1. Try a different search engine
2. Tweak the ad's copy and analyse the results
3. Hire a professional ad agency
4. Delete the ad and try again

Question 3 of 3

Which section of Google Analytics can tell you whether visitors have found your website via social media?

1. Site search

2. Acquisition
3. Behaviour
4. Search Console

(answer: 2,2,2)

Module – 23: Turn Data into Insights

Knowing how to turn digital data into actionable insights can improve your online campaign results and help you meet your goals. In this topic, you'll learn about the data cycle, how to draw actionable insights from raw data, and which tools can help you manage digital data efficiently. We'll also cover how to present information in a way that will make the most impact with a target audience.

Lesson 23.1
Using Data to Understand Audiences

Key learning

Collecting and analysing data can offer many benefits to online businesses. To take advantage of these benefits, it's important to first understand the types of data available to you as well as the best way to gather it. In this lesson, we'll explore:

- the differences between quantitative and qualitative data
- how online data can be used to complement your offline business approach
- common ways to collect data.

Knowledge:

Years ago, the only way to get to know your customers was to ask them questions face to face. Today, the internet provides a wealth of information right at your fingertips.

In this lesson we'll explore how online data can be utilised to develop your business as well as how to combine online and offline data to maximise results.

Collecting and analysing data should be a key part of your business strategy, and should regularly factor into your overall approach. The better you understand your customers and business, the more targeted and efficient your marketing efforts can be.

Because we are surrounded by so much information, it's important to have a targeted strategy to get the answers you're looking for. A good way to do this is to break down your digital data into the two groups: quantitative and qualitative.

Quantitative data is anything that can be numerically measured, like the number of people visiting a website or the amount of sales a site makes in a month.

Qualitative data is essentially any descriptive information that you can't put a number to. This could be people's opinions about a new product, or the sentiment and language people use on social media when talking about a brand.

The right approach will vary depending on what information is most relevant to your business scenario. If you want to know how people feel about your products or service, take a qualitative approach and ask them directly. If you want to know something quantitative, such as the amount of time someone spends on one of your blog posts, use an analytics tool to review that specific metric. Often, combining quantitative and qualitative data will provide you with a richer overall picture.

So where can you find all this data? Quantitative data can often be pulled from tools such as Google Analytics or from the analytics features offered by most social media platforms. This can be great for finding out information about demographics, search habits, and the journey a customer has taken across your digital assets.

Alternatively, qualitative data is often gathered through connecting directly with people, such as having a review section on your website or asking customers to fill out an online survey.

Combining different forms of data is a great way to identify what is working and what isn't, and can give you valuable insights about who interacts with your business.

Online data can also be used to complement your offline business approach. For example, offline data like in-store customer surveys, can be combined with social media poll results to give you a more detailed picture of customer needs and opinions. This allows you to make informed business decisions - from deciding the time of day to post on social media, to understanding how to improve products or services.

In your own business scenario, try using a mix of quantitative and qualitative approaches to help build a clear summary of your activity. Have a think about the benefits of digital data and make sure you are collecting the relevant data you need to help inform those big decisions.

Check your knowledge 23.1

That's right, great work! Analytics tools allow you to collect and review data in real time, enabling you to gain valuable insights by analysing this information. Data in itself doesn't reach more customers, but understanding it could help you create a plan, or revise an approach, resulting in you reaching more customers.

Question 1 of 1

Charles is thinking about taking his business online. He has many questions, but first he wants to understand what benefits data can have in online marketing. He needs some advice. What are the benefits of data in online marketing?

1. Data can be accessed and analysed in real time
2. Data helps you make informed decisions
3. Data allows you to regard every customer as a number, removing the need for personalisation
4. Digital data reaches more customers

(answer: 1,2)

Activity 23.1

If you haven't already done so, setting up analytics on your website is one of the best ways to start collecting data.

This will give you some good baseline information to take forward, allowing you to make adjustments and improvements to your strategy.

If you already have analytics installed, start recording some of your monthly figures in a table to monitor progress.

What changes do you see?

Lesson 23.2
Understanding the Data Cycle

Key learning

One of the benefits of working in the digital world is the amount of data and information available. This data can help you continuously improve what you do, allowing you to meet your goals. In this lesson, we'll explore:

- how the data cycle can help improve your efforts online
- which tools can be used to capture your data
- best practices to help you get the best results from the data collected.

Knowledge:

When it comes to evaluating what's working in your online strategy, knowing what to measure and how to interpret your marketing data is a useful skill have.

In this lesson we'll explain what the data cycle is, its benefits, and how you can use it in day to day activities to help achieve your goals.

The data cycle is a popular way to help you make the most of the information collected from various online marketing activities. Use it to help you prepare, action, and inform your business decisions online. The four main stages of a data cycle are: Plan, Do, Check and Act.

Let's explore the data cycle in action. Imagine a marketing team working at the local town hall want to organise a digital advertising campaign to encourage people to cycle to work.

In the "Plan" stage, the team would identify their goal for this campaign and outline how they plan to promote it. They decide their goal is to see a

25% reduction in commuter traffic over the next three months using search advertising and social media marketing.

Next up is the "Do" stage of the cycle. This is when the team designs the ads and launches the campaign.

A few weeks after the campaign has ended, the team measures how many people clicked on the ads and assess whether the campaign had an impact on the number of people cycling to work. They notice that while the search ads drove a substantial amount of new traffic to the website, very few people saw or engaged with the social media campaign. This insight highlights that the town hall's social media campaign should be reassessed and optimised for improvements. This is the "Check" stage of the data cycle.

Finally, the "Act" stage reveals where a business can use their findings to improve future campaigns. In this case, the marketing team could decide to vary the social platforms used, review the content they're publishing, or post at different times of the day and see if these changes help improve engagement.

Now that we've discussed the data cycle, let's look at some tips to help you get the best results from the data you collect.

Don't get overwhelmed trying to collect as much data as possible. Focus your efforts on the data sets that are most relevant to your goals and work to capture the right information at the right time.

Review the information you gather at periodic intervals. This will help you stay aware of any data anomalies that may appear during the year, such as spikes or drops in sales due to seasonal dates like national holidays.

Utilise online tools to help you gather the data you need and draw out the relevant insights. Tools such as Google Analytics, Adobe Analytics and Webtrends can provide data on website visits, including pages visited, time spent on site, and whether users have completed a target action, like completing a contact form.

Finally, if you have access to historical data or data of past trends, use it and learn from past experiences.

When it comes to your business scenario, think about how you can apply data to inform your decisions. How could the data cycle support you in optimising future marketing campaigns?

Check your knowledge 23.2

The data cycle is an effective process to help Jo make the most of data when running her campaign. The four main stages of a data cycle are as follows: - Plan - Start by identifying the goals of the campaign - Do - Then, begin collecting the relevant data - Check - Once you have that, review your data - Act - Lastly, take action to test the hypothesis.

Question 1 of 1

Jo is about to launch a new online campaign, and wants to know how data can be used to make the campaign as effective as possible. Rearrange the steps below in the correct order to help Jo understand what should happen first.

Identify the goals of the campaign and plan the next actions to take

Collect the relevant data

Check and investigate the findings

Take action to test the hypothesis

Activity 23.2

Create a post for one of your social media platforms, then use the analytics tools built into the platform to see who is looking at your posts and when.

Compare this information to the data on other posts you've published previously.

Using the Plan, Do, Check and Act cycle we discussed in the lesson, build and improve upon your social post, using data to inform your next steps.

What would you do differently?

Lesson 23.3
Creating Actionable Insights from Your Data

Key learning

Actionable insights give you tangible actions to take away, and can be used to improve your website or online campaigns. In this lesson, we'll explore:

- what an actionable insight is, and how it differs from a regular insight
- how to take action based on the data you've analysed.

Knowledge:

Website analytics can offer a wealth of information about who is visiting your website and where they came from. But while collecting data is important, knowing what to do with this information is what can truly add value to a business.

In this lesson we will explain what actionable insights are, how to identify them, and how you can use metrics to turn your data into a story that can help improve your business.

So, how do we define an insight? To put it simply, it's analysing 'why' something has happened. Insights are critical to determine actions and help you focus on what is important to your business goals. An actionable insight takes this analysis one step further and determines what to do next, so that you can successfully improve and refine what you're doing.

To uncover your own actionable insights, try following these six steps:

- Define your goal: Clearly outline what your campaign aims to achieve

- Collect the data. Gather and organise any statistics or information relevant to your goal

- Interpret the data: Analyse trends and any deviations from those trends to see how this has affected meeting your goals

- Develop recommendations: Provide justified suggestions on how to improve business practices based on what you have learned from your data analysis

- Take action: Put your recommendations into practice and create an action plan to test your assumptions, and finally

- Review your outcomes: Evaluate whether your actions have had the desired impact and make note of how you can further optimise to improve results.

Let's look at an online example that explores how data can lead to actionable insights.

Susie is part of a team responsible for planning a charity fun run, and this year her goal is to get 250 people to register. As her goal is to increase attendance, the data she collects from her analytics software could include how many people completed the sign-up form, which online channel they used to register, and how many people shared posts on social media.

Analytics reveal that social media channels are the main source of sign ups, so next Susie wants to determine which social media posts were most effective at driving registrations.

When interpreting the data, the trend emerges that registered runners who shares the charity's social media posts on their personal accounts generated the highest number of new registrations.

By looking at these insights, Susie can conclude that registered runners become powerful ambassadors and are able to spread the word of the race quickly and efficiently, encouraging more sign-ups.

So, to turn this into an actionable insight, Susie now needs to combine the data gathered with an action that can put her research to good use. For example, she could design a series of social media posts that provide easy instructions on how registered runners can promote the Fun Run across their own social network.

Let's look at a case study from a real business that used actionable insights to help them reach their goals.

Now that we've explored how to draw actionable insights from data, think about how you can use your online data to help make a decision you're currently facing. What would you like to learn from the information you have available and how can an actionable insight help bring you closer to your goals?

Check your knowledge 23.3

That's right, great work! Lee is having much more success on social media than he is via his emails. Focusing his attention on the platforms that are working for him will help increase his success. In addition, his audience are online between the hours of 5.00 p.m. and 7.00 p.m., which could be because they are commuters, or professionals who have finished work for the day. Optimising when he publishes his posts will also result in being able to reach more of his audience at the optimal/peak time.

Question 1 of 1

Lee is currently trying to promote a free eBook download on his website. He has spent time creating compelling emails and posting updates on his social media accounts. He decides to use data to work out if actionable insights can improve the success of his non-paid promotional efforts. Here are the highlights of the data that was gathered:

1. Develop additional email marketing content, ensuring emails are delivered during the off-peak eBook download time.

2. Post content across all social media channels during off peak eBook download time, and send email marketing content during peak eBook download time.

3. Reduce his efforts on the email marketing campaign and expand on social media promotion, specifically on Facebook and LinkedIn.

4. Schedule engaging Facebook posts to be published between 5.00 p.m. and 7.00 p.m.

(answer: 3,4)

Activity 23.3

Using social media metrics, create insights based on the data at your disposal.

Use this information to improve future posts:

What works for your audience, and what doesn't?

Does posting at a particular time of day likely to make it more successful?

Are posts with images more engaging?

If you tag another person or business in the post, do you see more success?

This information should form part of your strategy going forward, and help you to improve future campaigns.

Lesson 23.4
Managing Numbers Using Spreadsheets

Key learning

Sometimes having so much data at your disposal can seem a little overwhelming. Using spreadsheets gives you a way to manage this information and make the most of the data provided. In this lesson, we'll explore:

- what a spreadsheet is, and how you can use it to collate and analyse data
- basic spreadsheet formulas that can help make life easier.

Knowledge:

Dealing with data related to your business can feel a little overwhelming when there's so much of it. Spreadsheets allows you to break this data down into useful information, and can save you a lot of time in the process.

During this lesson we will cover the benefits of using spreadsheets, introduce basic functions, and explain and these functions can be used to help you manage specific data.

So, let's start with the basics: What is a spreadsheet?

A spreadsheet is defined as an interactive software application designed to help organise, analyse and store data. Put simply, spreadsheets create a grid of data, using a principle of rows and columns. Once numbers are added into the spreadsheet, you can use automated tools and functions to analyse the information and find the answers you are looking for.

Spreadsheet software like Microsoft Excel, Google Sheets and Apple Numbers are incredibly useful when dealing with large amounts of data, such as financial budgets, project plans and databases.

For example, if you were in charge of collating census information for a town, you could use a spreadsheet to keep track of addresses, names, dates of birth, and how long residents have lived in the town. You could then apply a filter to work out how many people are under the age of four; which would be valuable information to consider when planning school capacity.

Here are some key features that make spreadsheets beneficial:

Information can be presented in different ways. For example, you could produce a graph highlighting the population of the town based on gender or a table showing the different age groups that attend local sporting clubs.

Filter tools allow you to quickly organise your data into a specific order, whether that be alphabetically or by date.

Not everything in a spreadsheet is just a plain number. Percentages, currency, dates and duration are just some of the common formats you can use depending on your data.

Functions can be used to instantly recalculate values based on a change. Applied to the census example, you could create a formula that would automatically work out the average age of the town at any point in time.

There are many functions and formulas built into spreadsheets - with many of the basic ones available in all popular spreadsheet software. Let's take a look at some functions that could help you to organise and make sense of the census data.

The function SUM() allows you to calculate the total of two or more spreadsheet cells. This is handy if you wanted to know the total number of people in the town.

Average, or "AVG()" returns the average of the numbers selected. It could be used to work out the average age of the town's population.

The COUNT () function counts how many times a certain value occurs. For example, the number of people who have lived in the town for three years or less. This might give you a good indication of the amount of people moving to the town.

Now that we've explored how spreadsheets can help you manage and analyse your data, spend some time considering how you could utilise them in your business scenario. Explore which functions can save you time, and which spreadsheet features can put your data and insights to good use.

Check your knowledge 23.4

Question 1 of 1

Cassie has been using spreadsheets to keep track of how her email campaigns have been performing. She has created three different graphs using all of the data at her disposal. Which graph best shows that the open rate of her emails has decreased over time?

1. Pie
2. Bar
3. Line

(answer 2)

Activity 23.4

Spreadsheets are a great place to store and manage your digital marketing data.

Think of your social media data and try creating a spreadsheet that can be used to track all of your social media metrics on a daily basis.

1. Create a row for each social media channel
2. In the columns, input the following in the first row: number of followers, total number of 'likes' (or other social media metrics from each platform), engagement (for example, for Twitter this would be retweets/replies, for Facebook this would be shares/comments), and

any other metric useful to your specific goals (such as hashtag use or conversion rates).

3. Use formulas to calculate the totals and averages.
4. Be sure to update the table regularly with the latest data so that you can review how each social media channel performs over time.

Lesson 23.5
Presenting Data Effectively

Key learning

Once you've gathered and analysed your data, the next step is knowing how to present it in a way that will resonate with your audience. In this lesson, we'll explore:

- how to present your data in a clear and understandable way
- popular visual formats to use when presenting data
- how to match your data to the right format, based on your audience's needs.

Knowledge:

With so much data and information at our disposal, presenting it in a way people understand is essential to getting your message across successfully.

In this lesson, we'll explore how to present information based on the specific needs of your audience, and introduce you to popular presentation formats. You'll also learn how to select the right visual format based on the type of data collected.

We all interpret things in different ways. Some people like colourful image-based visuals, likes graphs and infographics, whilst others absorb numbers and text more easily in tables or lists. Because of this, it is important to base the presentation of your information on the needs of your audience.

Ask yourself the following questions to help you identify your target audience:

➢ what roles or positions do people in my audience hold?

- what level of knowledge does my audience have? and,
- which industry does my audience work in?

For example, let's consider a town's census data. If you were presenting this data to the Mayor, the key stats could relate to the number of residents eligible to vote in the next election year. This means you would focus on presenting this in a way that the Mayor could easily and quickly understand - perhaps in a bar chart, representing how many people from different age groups are registered to vote. For a meeting with the transport director, you would probably want to highlight different areas of the census data. Their focus would be the transport methods people use to get to work - which could be presented in a pie chart, showcasing the number of people who walk, or take a train, bus, car or bicycle to commute to work.

Regardless of whether the data is being presented in a meeting or published in a report, overwhelming your audience is the fastest way to lose their attention - so avoid packing in too much information and aim present it in an easy-to-digest way.

So, now that you know why it's important to understand your audience, how do you decide which format to display your data in? When it comes to presentation, aways choose a visual format that best displays the story you are trying to tell. For example, if you wanted to present a trend over a period of time, consider a line graph, which makes it clear to an audience how things have progressed or changed over a given period. Here are some other visual formats to try out, and the data that works best with them:

Tables can be used to display smaller data sets, allowing for comparisons to be made quickly.

Pie charts are useful to display percentages or proportional information in an easy-to-digest way.

Bar charts, are great for comparing related items in a group, where the length of each bar is proportionate to the value it represents.

Line graphs are useful for understanding how data changes over time, for example, whether your website traffic has increased over the past month.

Heat maps are often used to represent performance by area, such as which parts of your website people are clicking on most.

We have now covered why understanding your audience is such a big part of presenting data, and how once you know the needs of your audience, you can then shape the visuals to tell your particular story. Go online and explore the different ways information can be displayed, and see which formats would work best for you.

Check your knowledge 23.5

That's right, great work. The bar graph is the correct choice in this scenario. It clearly shows each year's data, and the growth experienced year to year. Pie charts are better for illustrating percentages, rather than growth or trends. The heat map can show location data, as well as increased demand for parking. However, the location data might not be useful to the investors, and it is harder to clearly see the year on year increase in this format. The table may have too much data to be clear and concise.

Question 1 of 1

Anya is working on a presentation for potential investors. They would like to see how the demand for public parking has grown in the past three years. Anya has created the following four graphics to illustrate the growth demand. Which graphic would be the clearest and make the most impact on the investors?

1. Image of a table of figures
2. Image of bar graph
3. Image of pie chart
4. Image of a heat map

(answer: 2)

Activity 23.5

Extract certain data metrics, such as number of visitors to your website, from your online analytics tools.

Present this information in a few different formats.

Try sending the different options to colleagues or friends, and see which visual display they prefer.

Check your knowledge 23.A

Question 1 of 5

Which type of data relates to a metric that can be represented with a number?

1. Quantitative
2. Qualitative
3. Holistic
4. Customer

Question 2 of 5

What makes the data cycle useful?

1. It helps you make the most of the data collected from marketing activities
2. It helps you evaluate your competition
3. It provides information about what users like about your website
4. It presents collected data in a visually appealing way

Question 3 of 5

Fill in the blank: Actionable insights can be described as explaining the _____ of an online marketing campaign.

'Why'

1. 'How'
2. 'When'
3. 'Who'

Question 4 of 5

Which of the following is a benefit of using spreadsheets?

1. Vast quantities of data can be stored, sorted and analysed quickly
2. Data can only be accessed when all users are online
3. Valuable customer and market insights can be delivered quickly
4. Spreadsheets are the only way to collect data and extrapolate results

Question 5 of 5

If you needed to showcase which parts of a website are being clicked on the most, which presentation type should you consider?

1. Bar chart
2. Pie chart
3. Table
4. Heat map

(answer: 1, 1, 1, 1, 4)

Module – 24: Build Your Online Shop

Tap into the world of e-commerce and learn how to effectively sell your products online. From the tools you'll need to build your online shop from scratch, to payment methods and managing orders, this introductory topic will get you on your way.

Lesson 24.1
Using E-Commerce to Sell

Key learning

Whether you're a traditional retailer, a service business, a wholesaler or even an Internet start-up, there are many ways you can use e-commerce to reach more customers and increase sales. In this video, we'll cover:

- what e-commerce is
- varying levels of e-commerce used in business
- how to match your needs to the options available.

Knowledge:

Let's talk about e-commerce. We'll help you learn what it is, discuss the different ways it's used for business, and help you choose the best e-commerce option to match your needs.

Sound good? Let's get started.

So first, what is e-commerce? Well, it's really just a fancy name for selling things online.

People have been making online purchases on websites and mobile applications for a while now. And all kinds of businesses are finding ways to make use of e-commerce to achieve their sales goals online.

These goals vary, depending on the business. You might start with a simple goal, like "I want to offer customers the ability to send payments through the web." Or, maybe you want a lot more-a website that allows people to view and search your inventory, create customer accounts, and set up recurring orders.

The sky's the limit.

So how do you get started with e-commerce for your business?

Your first step might be to simply offer a way for customers to transfer money to your business through the web. You can easily add payment services like PayPal to your website that make online payment easy. In many cases, your customer doesn't even need to setup a PayPal account and can pay through credit card or direct debit.

If you're starting to sell online from scratch, you might try an "off-the-shelf" service that includes e-commerce, like Squarespace or Wordpress. These services not only accept payments, but they usually offer templates so you can easily add product pages to your website.

If you're going for the gold, you might decide on a customised e-commerce service like Magento or Shopify. There are many options available, with feature like product search, inventory management, checkout, customer accounts, order management and more.

E-commerce often brings to mind a sort of retail or shop-like experience. Any business that sells products in a physical shop can also sell their products on a virtual shop online.

Offline customers can walk through the door of your furniture shop and browse the couches, bookcases and beds on display. While online, customers should be able to see those same products by clicking around the pages of your online shop.

Even though customers won't be able to sit on that couch for sale or feel the fabric, your online shop can bring your products to life. You should include lots of photos, detailed descriptions, customer reviews, and even videos of the products.

This high-quality imagery and well-written content is like your online "product display". Done well, it can help narrow the gap between a customer's retail and online shopping experience.

After you've sorted out how to sell products on your own website, you want to sell more products, in more places. So, your next step might be to look into other online marketplaces.

For example, you might also sell your furniture through sites like Amazon and eBay. If this is one of your goals, and you haven't yet selected an e-commerce provider, make sure that they support your multi-channel selling.

To sum up, whether you plan to offer a full-blown virtual version of your physical shop, or you're just looking to accept payments online, e-commerce can be a really powerful tool for your business.

Next we'll be helping you take those first steps into e-commerce. We'll be examining your different options in more detail so you can know which one works best for your business. We'll also be showing you how to re-engage with customers after their initial connection with you.

So stick with us.

Check your knowledge 24.1

Question 1 of 1

Jo owns a furniture shop, and she's just started using the internet to boost sales. She has some ideas on what to do to sell products on her website. Help Jo decide on one idea and cross off the rest.

1. Publish her inventory on a third party site
2. A forum to get feedback on her services
3. Use a money transfer provider to take customer payments online

(answer: 1,2)

Activity 24.1

Think about how your business will use e-commerce, and write down a list of features and requirements you'll need to achieve your business objectives.

Lesson 24.2
Taking Payments and Manage Orders

Key learning

If you decide to sell products and services online, many tools and solutions are available to help. This video will walk you through:

- handling online payments
- managing orders.

We're now going to talk about how you can accept payments and manage orders as part of your e-commerce activities. And we'll show you how this can help your business.

One of the primary features of your e-commerce shop is being able to accept payments online. There are many options that can do this for you, and they range from relatively simple to fairly complex.

Let's say you're a furniture craftsman who offers limited edition artisan pieces, such as bookcases, tables and chairs. You have a website that showcases a gallery of bespoke furniture. But as it stands, customers have to ring, or visit your shop, to make an actual purchase.

Of course, you want to make things easier for your customers, by accepting payments online. You can do this using any number of online payment solutions, or what's known as third-party payment processing, with services such as PayPal and Nochex.

These types of payment solutions let you add a button to your website, which customers can click to make a payment. This takes them to a separate payment website, which takes care of the transaction for you. Then after the order is complete, the customer is sent back to your site.

As transactions occur, you will receive all the information you need to fulfill the actual customer orders. So this approach means you can just focus on your business, while someone else takes care of the complex electronic transactions.

At some point, you might want to integrate the transaction experience into your website, such as offering online payments and a shopping cart that lets customers buy multiple items in one session.

Despite the additional costs, this integrated process provides very real benefits. One way to start is to use an "off-the-shelf" service, like Squarespace. These services give you more control over the shopping and checkout process and let you make changes and improvements.

For example, you might want to customise the thank-you page with specific offers. Or promote other furniture designs relevant to what the customer has already purchased.

Another benefit? You can track the entire customer experience, including the digital marketing campaign that brought visitors to your site. You can get more information about these people and see what website content they interacted with. And, you can learn what the most likely prospects tend to do on your site.

Now, let's say your furniture design business has grown. And now you want to expand and offer furniture sets for every room, in every possible wood finish, to customers throughout the UK.

When you have loads of products to sell online to a broad audience, it's probably time to consider a full e-commerce solution. There are many on the market- such as Shopify, Volusion or Magento.

Some are free, others you'll need to pay for. And they all offer a wide range of features. But one common thing many of them offer is the ability to create and manage a fully functional online store.

A fully functional online store has a big benefit: a backend system with order management.

Let's take a closer look at how a backend system can help you.

Well, first, your customers can create accounts and manage their personal information, billing preferences, and shipping addresses. You can offer them coupon codes, integrate multiple payment options, and even customise the checkout process.

And rather than program all of this yourself, you can use these e-commerce services to upload and manage product and inventory details, create and organise category, subcategory and product pages, and offer advanced product search.

Many solutions manage orders, track shipping and fulfillment details, and integrate with your financial and accounting systems.

Let's sum up.

As an merchant growing your business online, you'll need the right tools to accept payments and manage orders. Depending on your needs, a variety of options are available: from simple, third-party payment processing services to a fully developed e-commerce platforms.

Whatever option you choose, selling online is a great way to grow your business.

Check your knowledge 24.2

A fully functional online store doesn't push customers towards over-the-phone payments, but it does make it easy to buy through the site itself. It gives you a backend system that allows you to easily manage orders and track shipping. You'll then have control over the features of your online store, which will allow you to design it so that it feels more like a real shop for customers.

Question 1 of 1

Jo wants to create a fully functional online store. Can you check which of the following features are available in most fully functional online stores?

- Order management via a backend system – Yes / No
- Customer reviews pane – Yes / No

- Products browser – Yes / No
- Over-the-phone payments via a web-based calling system – Yes / No

(answer: Y, Y, Y, N)

Activity 24.2

Think about your current website and your own business needs.

Are you ready for a full e-commerce platform?

or

Would it be easier to start out with a third-party payment processing solution?

Check your knowledge 24.A

Question 1 of 4

What would be beneficial to include on a product description page?

1. Previous versions of the product
2. Links to other suppliers
3. Reviews of the product
4. Price comparisons

Question 2 of 4

Which of the following is an advantage of e-commerce?

1. More relaxed checkout procedure
2. Low operational costs
3. Minimal interaction required with the customer
4. Segmentation of audiences

Question 3 of 4

To an owner or administrator, what is a functional benefit of having an online store?

1. It collects the addresses of your online store visitors
2. It provides a backend system with order management
3. It provides a quicker checkout process than a physical store
4. It allows you to feature more sales and discounts than a physical store

Question 4 of 4

What is the name of the process that describes what happens when a customer is taken to a separate site to complete a transaction before being sent back to the original site again?

1. Second-party payment processing
2. Third-party payment processing
3. External payment processing
4. Internal payment processing

(answer: 3,2,2,2)

Module – 25: Sell More Online

Once your online shop is set up, it's time to ensure everything is optimised correctly so that customers have the smoothest user experience possible. Each touchpoint is an important communication opportunity between you and your customers: from signing in and browsing to checking out and receiving promotions about sales.

Lesson 25.1
Creating A Smooth E-Commerce Experience

Key learning

Once you've taken your first steps into e-commerce, your next job is to improve the shopping experience. From getting more people to use your online shopping basket to streamlining the checkout process, there are lots of ways to improve your site for shoppers. In this video, you'll learn how to use analytics to optimise:

- for different devices
- navigation and search
- product pages
- checkout by using customer accounts.

Knowledge:

So, you've started selling online and customers are buying right from your website. Great. But are your customers as happy as they could be? Is the shopping experience and checkout process as smooth as possible?

We're going to look at how you can use analytics to continually improve your customers' e-commerce experience. We'll cover optimising for different devices, improving navigation and search, optimising your product pages, and finally, using customer accounts to enhance the checkout process.

The first step to optimising the e-commerce experience is ensuring that the purchasing process works smoothly on all the different devices your customers might use. These days, that means more than just laptops and desktop computers.

Say you look at your analytics data and learn that plenty of people visit your site from their mobiles, but they rarely make a purchase. That's a clue that shoppers on mobiles or tablets may not be able to properly see your product pages, or move smoothly through the payment process. You've got some work to do.

One great option is to implement a "responsive design" into your website. This type of design can adapt to different screen sizes. Or, if you want to guarantee a more consistent shopping experience on smartphones, you could even create a dedicated mobile website.

OK, that's got you covered for all types of devices. Here's another opportunity for improving the shopping experience. Say your analytics show that lots of people visit your home page, but they aren't taking the next step and actually looking at your products.

You'll want to make it easy for your visitors to browse and find what they're looking for. This starts with navigation that your customers can easily understand and use. Typically, you'll use categories and subcategories to organise your inventory in any number of ways.

Let's use the example of a furniture maker. You could start out with broad categories of, say, different rooms in a home. Then, you could add subcategories of furniture pieces in each, like "bed frames" or "desks" or "dining room tables."

So what's the best way to go about this? Well, the answer is the one that your customers like best. You can conduct formal testing to see how your visitors react to different arrangements, or you could simply survey your friends, family and some trusted clients to see what they prefer.

No matter how you arrange your site navigation, there will always be people who prefer to search for something specific rather than browse through various categories and subcategories. That's why it's best to cover both options and include a search function on your website.

Your product pages are another great way to optimise the shopping experience. What if you're seeing that lots of people visit your product pages, but they don't add any products to the shopping basket?

You might add video of a craftsman in action, or a gallery of photos from various angles to help customers get a closer look at a particular piece of furniture. Make sure those photos are professional quality, and load quickly.

You can also write up great descriptions and provide all kinds of details and measurements-whatever helps customers feel confident that they're ready to buy.

The last thing we're going to look at is how you can optimise the e-commerce experience by using customer accounts.

You might notice in your analytics data that customers shop on your site, and put products in the cart, but then leave before completing their purchase. Encouraging customers to create an account can streamline the process so this happens less frequently in the future.

As a customer completes an online purchase, you can allow them to store their shipping and billing information and payment preferences in an account on your site. This will also make future purchases that much easier.

If you're ready to get super advanced, you can also use a customer's past purchases, recent searches, or recently viewed products to recommend specific items that might interest them. If they just purchased a dining room table, for example, you might recommend the best sets of chairs to go with that design and wood finish.

And of course, you can always reward your loyal customers with offers and discounts tailored especially for them-lots of shopping cart solutions offer these features by default.

To sum up: Optimising e-commerce is an ongoing process that requires a consistent experience across devices, smart site organisation, and smooth checkout using customer accounts.

Taking this approach will help you on your quest to provide current, and future, customers the very best service possible.

Check your knowledge 25.1

If she sees people access her shop a lot from their mobiles, Jo can introduce responsive design to improve her customers' browsing experience. Adding a search feature will help people search for and quickly locate specific products. Improving product pages could be the answer if lots of people visit but don't buy from her shop. Finally, customer accounts can simplify the check-out process, helping people complete their purchases more easily.

Question 1 of 1

Jo wants to use analytics data and visitor surveys to make some improvements to her e-commerce website, but she only has limited time and budget. What actions could Jo take for each of these findings? (Choose the right one)

- Customers access the shop a lot on mobile

    Introduce responsive design

    Add a search feature

    Add customer reviews

    Create registration for customer accounts

- Customers want to find a specific product

    Introduce responsive design

    Add a search feature

    Add customer reviews

    Create registration for customer accounts

> There are lots of website visits but no one is buying the products

Introduce responsive design

Add a search feature

Add customer reviews

Create registration for customer accounts

> Repeat customers add products to their cart but are not checking out

Introduce responsive design

Add a search feature

Add customer reviews

Create registration for customer accounts

(Answer: Introduce responsive design, add a search feature, add customer reviews, Create registration for customer accounts)

Activity 25.1

Write down some ideas of ways you can optimise your e-commerce site, and prioritise what you'll tackle first.

Lesson 25.2
Product Promotion and Merchandising

Key learning

If you have an e-commerce store, you probably offer a number of different products. Sometimes it can be difficult for customers to find the best match for their needs. Product promotion and merchandising can help. In this video, we'll look at:

- promoting products and specials
- predicting products your customers might like
- showcasing products visitors might not normally see.

As you build out your online shop, promoting your full inventory of products can be challenging. Here, we'll examine the best ways to promote products and special offers. We'll show you how to predict which products your customers might like. And help you showcase products your visitors might not normally see.

The first step is to set up your online shop. That way it's easy for your visitors to browse all of your products. You'll want to create the right hierarchy of categories and subcategories, which will help a customer navigate your site and the products for sale.

Promoting products in an online shop isn't too different from a high street shop. Think about the last time you visited a furniture shop. You probably didn't just walk in and see a map of the shop's aisles pointing to where the products could be found. More likely, you walked in to see a really comfy sofa near the door that you could sink right into.

Like a brick-and-mortar shop, online shops also display very specific, featured products. If it's the end of summer and kids are going off to university, the furniture shop might have desks or bookcases on display and on sale. This is an example of product merchandising.

You can do the same thing online, starting by promoting certain products right on your homepage. Your promotion might be to help shift old inventory, or feature a best-selling item you want more customers to see.

Using part of your homepage to showcase products, or even running online advertising campaigns with dedicated landing pages, can be a great way to merchandise online.

And that's just the beginning. Imagine if you walked into an offline furniture store and the front door display magically transformed based on your interests. And as you browsed, all the promotions you encountered were customised to what you had previously looked at.

That's exactly what online shops can do! As visitors browse the pages of your site, you're collecting data about what interests them. Now, you can use this data to predict what they are likely to be interested in next.

Think of the last time you were shopping online. You might have been shown "recommended products" after viewing certain items, or putting them in your cart. For instance, if you were on a custom furniture website, and you were looking at kitchen tables, you might have seen a promotion for chairs, or window shutters to match the room.

Many shopping cart providers, such as Magento, Volusion, Prestashop and Shopify, offer these product recommendation engines.

Next up in product promotion and merchandising is finding ways to showcase products that your visitors may not have otherwise been looking for. This can be a really effective way to cross-sell.

How does this work? Well let's imagine an office manager is looking for a new executive desk for the big boss. Something grand and ornate. But he might not have been thinking about matching bookcases, or custom doors. Now is the perfect time to remind him. Promoting related products can help increase sales.

The world of e-commerce offers you plenty of great ways to make sure your customers see and interact with relevant products on your site. You can create a virtual display as they enter your site. Or use data to suggest what they might buy next. So get out there and start selling!

Check your knowledge 25.2

Jo can use product recommendation engines to show related products and introduce customers to new products they might not have considered before. Adding a video tour or evaluating who is visiting the site won't help increase people's awareness of different products.

Question 1 of 1

Office sets are steady sellers for Jo. How can she suggest office furniture items to customers who might not have considered them yet?

1. Create a 'Suggested products' banner
2. Use analytics to understand who is visiting the site
3. Add a video tour of the shop

(answer: 1)

Activity 25.2

Write down a few items you'd like to promote to shoppers as they land on your website.

Now, write down some recommendations you might want to make to customers based on what products they've shown an interest in.

Lesson 25.3
Retargeting For E-Commerce

Key learning

After shoppers have interacted with your website, product retargeting campaigns can help you get them back by showing them related ads across the web. In this video, we'll look at:

- what product retargeting is
- how product retargeting works
- tips for successful retargeting campaigns.

Knowledge:

Did you know your e-commerce website can track shopper behaviour, and respond with dynamic advertising? And that this can be used to bring visitors back to your shop, even after they've left to visit other sites?

This is called product retargeting. Now, let's explore what it is, how it works, and tips for running your own successful retargeting campaigns.

We've all browsed an online shop, put a product in our shopping cart and then, for whatever reason, decided not to buy it. Think of the last time you did this. Did you then suddenly start seeing ads for that product you didn't buy on other sites around the web? Yeah, well that's what we call retargeting.

The way a shopper behaves on an e-commerce site can tell that shop owner a lot about which products they're interested in, and even what they were on the verge of buying.

This is very useful information for your business. Because it allows you to create very specific advertisements aimed at people who have showed interest in certain products. That's what product retargeting, or remarketing, is all about.

Let's say someone is shopping online for bespoke furniture. They visit your e-commerce site and fall in love a beautiful kitchen table you're offering. But halfway through the checkout process, they decide to hold off and see if another shop had any specials first.

Luckily while they were browsing your online furniture store, you were using a product retargeting solution. This is a small bit of code placed on the pages of your website. This code tracks which products on that page a shopper is interested in.

Of course, this tracking code uses anonymous methods. No personal information is exchanged. But what has happened is that your website tracked a behaviour. It now knows that the shopper wanted that kitchen table AND that they didn't actually buy it.

That online shopping behaviour is great information for you as an advertiser. Now, you can use this information to take ACTION. This is where product retargeting solutions come into play.

There are a number of product retargeting options out there. All of them will allow you to collect information, and then target audiences with customised ads based on that information.

So let's say the shopper leaves your furniture shop and clicks over to a news website. They're reading an article and off to the right of the page what do they see? Yup, your digital ad with an image of the kitchen table they were just looking at! You may even include a 20 percent discount here too. That incentive just might be enough to persuade them to make the purchase after all.

That's basically product retargeting. There are many services available, like Google Ads and Criteo. The services share some basic functions, so let's talk a bit more about that.

It starts with that bit of code we mentioned that tracks shoppers' interactions. This information is then sent to your product retargeting service.

As an advertiser, you can go to your product retargeting service and set up rules and parameters.

So when a person browsing your site meets those parameters, the service will then start targeting them with advertisements over one or more of the Internet advertising networks.

Since the service knows exactly which products your shopper was interested in, those advertisements can be very specific and dynamic.

Now let's look at a few guidelines for running these kinds of campaigns.

First, you don't always have to offer a discount right away. While in the earlier example we considered price as a reason the shopper didn't buy, in reality there are loads of reasons people leave websites without making a purchase. And if you always offer a discount, you could be selling yourself short.

Next, it's good to know when to STOP showing these ads. It's certainly possible that the visitor found the same product somewhere else and bought it, or simply changed their mind and isn't going to buy it at any price. Most retargeting solutions allow you to set limits and experiment with just how many times you'll show the same ad to the same person, and for how long.

As with any advertising campaign, it's important to measure and optimise the performance of your product retargeting campaigns over time. This means tracking conversion rates, testing new types of ads, tweaking your parameters, and using analytics to manage these campaigns.

Product retargeting can be a great way to re-engage visitors that might have otherwise not returned. Knowing how it works, how to do it and how to optimise over time can make these campaigns a great addition to your digital marketing plan.

Check your knowledge 25.3

Jo can measure how customers interact with each ad type. She can also check her campaign's conversion rates to see how customers respond. Checking comments on her social media profile is unlikely to be as effective as the other options as it won't show in detail how customers interact with the retargeting campaign. Finally, looking at how many pages visitors check before they leave the site won't tell her whether those users are potential customers.

Question 1 of 1

Jo has noticed that some of her customers leave her site without making a purchase. She's set up some product retargeting ads, and wants to measure the performance of her campaign. What parameters should she look at to see if she's attracting potential customers?

1. Conversion rates
2. Number of people clicking on each ad type
3. Comments on her social media profile
4. How many pages visitors check before they leave the site

(answer: 1,2)

Activity 25.3

Go to your favourite search engine and search for product retargeting services.

Browse around and see what features and offerings are available to see what service might be right for you.

Check your knowledge 25.A

Question 1 of 3

Which of the following is a sign that customers are having trouble using a particular device to make purchases?

1. Analytics shows you have a lot of mobile visitors, but very few purchases through mobile
2. A specific product is not selling much compared to your other products
3. You get a lot of questions about your return policy
4. People are having trouble using a promo code for a current sale

Question 2 of 3

What is an example of product merchandising?

1. Running an ad for your products
2. Adding a way for customers to filter your products
3. Displaying very specific, featured products on your home page
4. Cross-selling products in the checkout process

Question 3 of 3

Which of the following statements is true when describing how retargeting ads work?

1. Retargeting ads are visible to people who haven't been on your website yet
2. Once a user visits your site, the code drops an anonymous browser cookie
3. Once your customer purchases, you can not turn off the retargeting ad
4. Retargeting will always drive customers to your site

(answer: 1,3,2)

Module – 26: Expand Internationally

Ready to dive into the global market? Before launching products or services to an international audience, it's important to validate your new markets, know the difference between translation and localisation and ensure you have the technical infrastructure to manage it all. Once you have a solid set-up, consider advertising across borders so that your marketing messages are seen by the right people, wherever they are.

Lesson 26.1

Introduction To International Marketing and Export

Key learning

Digital marketing gives you easy and instant access to a global marketplace – and this makes expanding your business to other countries an attractive possibility. Before you dive in, you'll want to evaluate your business's readiness. In this video we'll explore:

- how to evaluate international markets for your product
- practical and cultural issues of expanding internationally.

Knowledge:

You've heard people talk about the global marketplace, and today digital advertising makes it easy for almost any business to think beyond borders when seeking new customers.

We're going to look at the opportunities and realities of international marketing, focusing on how to evaluate international markets for your product and which practical and cultural issues you need to be ready for.

Let's say you have a vintage record shop with a stellar reputation. Your high-end equipment and expertise have helped you stand out and attract an elite customer base. Business is good, but you want to reach more of those customers. You've eyed some of the markets abroad and reckon it'd be a good move to sell your products in Europe-and beyond.

So where do you start?

First, you need to learn about the target market in each area you're considering, and find out how best to reach them.

For instance, with digital advertising, look at search traffic, competition and pricing. This will give you a clear view of your potential markets, so you can decide where your products will be well-received.

You can use search trend reports, geographic data in your web analytics, and marketing insight tools to help determine which markets would be the best place to start expanding your business.

Once you know where you want to go, you may need to overcome language barriers. How do you communicate and market to customers and prospects without losing anything in translation?

You might need to translate and localise your website's content. Automated translation services are rarely 100% accurate, so it's probably a good idea to have a native speaker who can help you confirm the content has the right tone.

Your new customers and prospects from different cultures and languages will need to communicate with you, too. Be ready from the start with a plan to support those customer service needs.

Next, think about your infrastructure and the systems you'll need to properly support your expansion into international markets.

Don't forget about packaging considerations for fragile components, VAT, and any legal or regulatory issues.

Once that's resolved, it's time to review your e-commerce and payment solutions.

Although many e-commerce systems are able to set up multinational transactions, you'll have to customise payment options and other settings. We'll discuss this further in a later video.

Even with great cross-border e-commerce systems, you'll still want to think ahead to the next step-getting your products to your new international customers.

What's required to ship and deliver your orders? What about refunds? Customer service and support?

Marketing to new customers in international markets is an exciting prospect and one that could expand your business tremendously. Mapping out your plan in advance sets the stage for success.

Are you ready to fully explore international expansion?

In the next videos, we'll explain how to research and validate the market for your product in new countries. Then we'll help you handle translation and localisation, and discuss the infrastructure and support you'll need.

Finally, we'll go over adapting your e-commerce and delivery processes for an international market.

Stay tuned, and your business will be positioned for success in these exciting new markets!

Check your knowledge 26.1

Matt can identify the best markets for his business by using helpful business tools like web analytics, trend reports and geographic data. This can help him narrow down which markets have most demand for vintage vinyl. After Matt has chosen his new market, he can then use translation services to adapt his website for foreign customers.

Question 1 of 1

Matt runs an online vintage record store in the UK. He wants to expand into new markets, but doesn't know where to begin.

1. What tools can help him choose his new market?
2. Market insight tools
3. Search trends by location
4. Translation services

(answer: 1,2)

Activity 26.1

Write down the countries you are interested in marketing your products and services to.

Next, log in to your web analytics tool and review your geographic reports for the last six months.

What are the top regions or countries?

Are engagement or conversion metrics showing interest?

This exercise can help determine if your business already has a certain level of interest from other countries, and can be one way to help prioritise the market you target first.

Lesson 26.2
Validating Your New Market

Key learning

Bringing your business to new markets in other countries has never been easier, thanks to the simplicity and availability of global advertising. Understanding which markets have the best potential will be the key to success. In this lesson we'll explore:

- how to identify potential markets using analytics
- researching search terms for international customers
- advertising on social networks.

Knowledge:

You've come to the right place to start the process of expanding your business into new countries.

Before you start selling your products or services abroad, it's really important to decide which countries make sense for you. Which markets have the most demand for what your businesses offer? Do some pose legal or logistical challenges that you need to be aware of?

We'll walk you through how analytics and tools can help you decide which markets offer the biggest opportunity for you.

Let's say you've got a online shop selling hard-to-find vintage records. Business has been going really well at home in the UK, so you're starting to wonder if expanding into new markets could be your next big step forward.

The question is: where? From Portugal to Finland, and Ireland to France, there are some markets where your products could be a hit - and others where you'd be less likely to find success.

Fortunately, there are lots of tools you can use to gauge the situation in advance.

You could start by looking at Google's Market Finder. This free tool allows you to quickly analyze search traffic on keywords that are important to your business. For example, where do people do a lot of searches for vintage records?

Countries that show a lot of search traffic for terms like these could be markets with lots of demand for your products.

On the other hand, countries that don't tend to generate a lot of searches for these terms probably aren't your best bet.

By using the Google Market Finder, you can make more informed decisions about where to invest in expanding your business.

Once you've found some countries that do a lot of searching for your products, use tools like Google's Keyword Planner or Bing's Keyword Research Tool to find out how much competition there is for search ads.

This will help you know whether you're entering a market with few competitors, or whether you'll be entering an already crowded space.

Another handy tool is your web analytics.

Whether you're using Google Analytics or any of the other common analytics tools, you can check whether people in other markets are already showing interest in your business.

For example, imagine you've only shipped your products within the UK so far. You might notice that you're getting a lot of website visitors from France.

They're browsing your website and learning all about you, only to realize that they can't buy your products ... yet. This could give you the insight that you might have a customer base waiting for you in France.

So far we've looked at tools to help you understand market demand and competition. Of course, there are some other considerations you should take into account when deciding which markets to focus on.

For example, some countries may pose more legal, regulatory, or tax issues than others. You'll want to get an idea of this before you start investing in a project to expand your business. Some markets may seem appealing you to "on paper," but doing some research into these kinds of issues will help you avoid any nasty surprises. Fortunately, many governments have websites where you can find resources to help you answer these questions.

So let's recap.

Expanding your business into a new market could be a great way to grow.

Before you jump straight in, use online tools to help you understand where there's strong demand for your products.

Then, make sure you're not wandering into any legal or regulatory issues by doing some background research first. Once you've done that, you're well on your way to growing your business in a new market.

Check your knowledge 26.2

Google Market Finder can show Matt that there is high search traffic on vintage record terms from Portugal. To Matt this may imply that a lot of people are looking for records out there. Low competition on search ads in Portugal would mean Matt wouldn't be up against lots of other vintage record sellers. Google Keyword Planner is a useful tool for looking at the volume of search ads. If people in Portugal are looking at his website already, then Matt can be fairly sure that there would be potential buyers. Google Analytics can help Matt keep track of things like who's looking at his website and what pages they look at most and adapt his strategy as needed.

Question 1 of 1

Matt has found out there's a growing market for vintage records in Portugal. He now needs to identify insights on his new audience using a variety of tools.

Can you help him match the correct tool with its corresponding insight?

High search traffic on vintage record terms from Portugal – (Google Keyword Planner, Google Analytics, Google Market Finder)

Low competition on search ads in Portugal – (Google Keyword Planner, Google Analytics, Google Market Finder)

People in Portugal are looking at his website – (Google Keyword Planner, Google Analytics, Google Market Finder)

(answer: Google Market Finder, Google Keyword Planner, Google Analytics)

Activity 26.2

Visit a tool such as the Google Global Market Finder (http://translate.google.com/globalmarketfinder/g/index.html).

Enter a keyword you are interested in researching.

Select your location and language, then filter by your target market.

Do you see any countries that might be worth researching in more detail?

Lesson 26.3
Being Understood Abroad

Key learning

To expand globally, you need to communicate in other languages and provide support to customers wherever they are. In this video we'll explore:

- the difference between translation and localisation
- how to do it right.

Knowledge:

Have you been thinking about marketing your products or services to potential customers who live in other regions and speak other languages?

If you have, you've probably wondered how to take the first step. This is where translated and localised content comes in. In this video, we'll explain the difference between translation and localisation-and how to do it right.

Imagine you own a vintage record shop that specialises in rock 'n' roll vinyl and you're ready to sell your products to customers in other markets. You've done your homework, and you think Italy and France would be great places to sell your products.

Start by thinking about the countries you want to market to.

How will French and Italian customers discover your products? Through advertising? Search engines? Social networks? Chances are, it'll be a combination.

To help your website appeal to customers in different countries, you need to think about two things: translation and localisation.

Translation is the process of changing your content from one language to another. After all, when potential customers in new markets find your website, you want them to be able to understand what it says.

But simply translating content might not be enough. Words and phrases that work in an Italian market may not resonate with a French audience.

Localisation is the process that makes locals feel like you "speak their language".

For example, you might want to make sure your translated website reflects that region's units of measure, currency, and addresses. You might want to change the website navigation. You might even change specific cultural references to feel local to the customers you're marketing to.

It seems like a fair bit to think about...but there are many companies and freelancers out there who specialise in exactly this type of work. Once your site is translated and localised, it's worth the effort to have a native speaker review the work.

To sum up: branching out of your home market is an important step for growing your business.

Translating and localising your website can help potential customers find you, and understand what you have to offer.

Check your knowledge 26.3

Localisation is where you adapt content to suit the culture. For example, removing or rewriting colloquialisms, idioms or humourous content, and generally making the site feel as if it's tailored to the needs of the new market. Localisation might also include changing things like currency, addresses and cultural references to bring the content in line with the local market.

Question 1 of 1

Matt needs to make sure his website is suitable for his Portuguese customers. He's made a list of translation and localisation tasks.

Which items on his list relate to localisation?

1. Adjusting colloqualisms so they make sense in Portuguese
2. Adding his UK office's address to the main site
3. Calculating prices of the products in local currency.
4. Adjusting humourous product descriptions so they make sense in Portuguese

(answer: 1,3,4)

Activity 26.3

Make a list of the countries you want to target and note the languages spoken in each.

Can you support the languages with your current or future translation plans?

Before getting started, be sure you're able to properly support customers in other countries.

Lesson 26.4
Advertise Across Borders

Key learning

When you're expanding into a new market, you should definitely have a solid marketing plan in place. Fortunately, there are loads of online advertising options that can help spread the news about your business. In this video, we'll look at:

- search advertising
- display advertising
- advertising on social networks.

Knowledge:

If you're planning to expand your business into a new market, you'll need a plan to help you advertise effectively in a new country.

It's possible that customers in a new market will find you through organic search results, or through word-of-mouth. But investing in advertising can help get your name out there much faster. Let's take a look at search advertising, display advertising, and advertising on social media, and how they can work together.

Let's go back to our vintage record store example. If you're planning to expand your business from the UK to Germany, you'll probably want to get your website translated and localised into German. That way when people search for terms like 'vintage records' in German, they might come across your website and become your new customers.

But if you want to get your business in front of lots more potential customers, it's a good idea to advertise.

Advertising on search results is a great way to get in front of people who are already looking for products like yours. If you're already doing this in your home country, great! Just translate and adapt your keywords and ads. Then, make sure that your ads point people to a landing page that's written in the local language.

If you're wondering which keywords are commonly searched in your new market, try using a tool like Google's Keyword Planner or Bing's Keyword Research Tool. These tools can tell you which keywords are popular, as well as other useful information. Like how much they might cost, and how many competitors you're likely to face.

But what about people who aren't already searching for your products? Remember, when you expand into a new market, people are unlikely to be familiar with your business already.

Display advertising and social media are two great ways to raise awareness.

You could start by advertising on the websites your audience is visiting online. So, if there's a popular site where German audiophiles go to discuss their favourite records, this could be the perfect place to show your ads. If you need a little help, check out tools like the Google Display Planner. They can provide detailed info about where your audience is spending time online.

What about Germans on social media? Well, it's a good idea to research which social media sites they're using. Is it Facebook and Twitter? Or are there other popular networks? Maybe even one unique to Germany? Once you have this information, you'll be able to use social networks to advertise to Germans who are really interested in vintage records.

By using a combination of advertising options, you'll set yourself up to win customers in your new market.

Ok so let's say you've started to get some traction with customers in your new market. You could now gear your advertising to continue engaging with them, and build loyalty. Email marketing is a great way to keep in touch with interested customers over the long term. You can send updates when you have new records in stock, or special promotions. Just keep in mind that each market may have different email marketing laws.

You could also try retargeting. This lets you advertise to people who have visited your website, based on the things they did there. So, you can show ads to people who are interested in your business, and encourage them to come back to your site. If someone reads your blog twice a month, they're obviously interested in vintage records. So, try using retargeting ads to convince them to buy.

We've covered a lot. So let's recap quickly. When you expand into a new market, customers probably don't know about your business yet. So, you'll want to do some advertising. You can use lots of different forms of advertising, all working together. Search ads are great for growing your business in a new market. While display ads, social media ads, email, and retargeting can also play a really valuable role.

Check your knowledge 26.4

Matt can run ads when people search for keywords or phrases (such as 'vintage records') in Portuguese. It's a good idea to get a native speaker to check his text when translating keywords. Sending English emails out might raise awareness locally, but isn't a great way to attract potential Portuguese customers. Facebook would be a good place to advertise. However, Matt would need to engage a native speaker to manage the page, so he can have meaningful conversations with Portuguese fans.

Question 1 of 1

Matt's chosen his market, now it's time to find new customers.

He has a few ideas, but not all of them will reach his Portuguese audience.

Can you help him choose his best advertising ideas?

1. Advertise on Portuguese music websites
2. Send English emails to current UK customers
3. Use search ads driven by translated search terms
4. Set up a Portuguese fanpage for his store

(answer: 1,3,4)

Activity 26.4

Do some research into social media sites in the countries you're considering targeting.

Do they have social networks unique to their region?

Are Facebook and Twitter just as popular there?

Lesson 26.5
The Support Systems You Will Need

Key learning

Expanding into new markets is exciting – but it isn't just about marketing. You need the right technical infrastructure, a strong supply chain and compliance with laws and regulations. In this video we'll cover:

- making your business accessible to new customers
- managing the supply chain
- possible legal and regulatory implications.

No matter where your company is physically located, you can expand into other regions or countries with the click of a button.

Now that marketing tools have made international advertising campaigns so much easier, it's tempting to dive right in. But before you do, stop and think about how you can best serve your new customers.

In this video, we'll look at technical capabilities, managing your supply chain, and what local rules or regulations you may need to follow.

Addressing these details will help reduce risks and identify potential issues before you're too far down the line.

First, you might want to check how your website performs in the countries where you want to sell products. Some regions may have slower Internet connection speeds-make sure your web pages can load and your site works well in places where you want to sell.

Next, look at your supply chain and make sure you're able to deliver your products to all the far corners where you want to sell them.

Don't forget to review all taxes and laws affecting businesses in these markets. Local government agencies can sometimes provide this information and may offer consulting services to help you figure out what you need to know about the market you plan to export to.

Remember, you want all your customers to be able to reach you, no matter where they are. An easy way to start is to provide customer support via email and contact forms on your website.

At some point you should probably establish a way to communicate beyond just your website, like through a telephone line. If you use a toll-free number or freephone number, make sure it's properly formatted so that customers in other countries can easily call you.

Now, think about how a customer would interact with your business, starting from discovering your products and services all the way to placing an order. Do you need to make any adjustments to your processes to keep things running smoothly?

Reviewing your business processes-especially supply chain management-will play an important part in your success.

Say you own a vintage record shop in the UK. You heard that the vintage vinyl scene in Lisbon is booming. So you want to start selling your records in Portugal to get in on the trend. Managing your supply chain might include sourcing local suppliers, factoring in shipping supplies, and determining the most efficient way of getting the product to the customer in Lisbon.

Let's imagine you've just received an order for 2,000 vinyl records that have to be delivered in two weeks, but you don't have the full quantity in your local inventory.

Given the rapid turnaround time, receiving the remainder of the order, repackaging the products, and shipping to the customer in less than two weeks sounds like a risky proposition, so in this case, you might decide you need to source from a local supplier.

As you look to expand your business into global markets, you'll also need to explore local laws and regulations for doing business in each target area. Beyond any cultural barriers, these legal hurdles can pose challenges to expanding into a certain region or country.

Look at the tax requirements and import or export restrictions for your products and services. Some countries have agreements that may impact tax collection, and additional customs or tariffs could affect your bottom line.

The way your business is incorporated may also make a difference in your ability to operate across borders. Some countries may require that you register with proper authorities in order to sell there.

To recap:

Make your business is accessible to new customers.

Examine your supply chain processes and how they'll work across borders.

Research legal and governmental regulations that affect doing business.

Expanding your markets into new regions and countries may seem like a lot of work, but taking these steps will ensure you're properly set up for success.

Check your knowledge 26.5

Before Matt can work out whether or not expanding into Portugal would achieve the growth he wants, there are a number of things he should check, including: - Customs duties or tariffs - Portuguese taxes - Exchange rates - Product safety requirements - Whether he needs insurance cover The Portuguese government website would be a good starting point for finding these things out.

Question 1 of 1

Portugal seems like a good market for Matt to move into. He's looked into the legal requirements of trading records in Portugal and is pleased to find there aren't any. But what other financial or regulatory requirements should he check?

1. Custom duties and tariffs
2. Portuguese taxes
3. Exchange rates

4. National holidays
5. Product safety requirements
6. Insurance cover

(answer: 1,2,3,5,6)

Activity 26.5

Go online and research business agencies and customs laws for your target markets.

Call or visit your government taxation and business office to gain an understanding of your own country's export rules.

Put together a list of your discoveries and then consult with a legal or governmental expert.

Lesson 26.6
Helping Customers Abroad Buy Your Products

Key learning

When it comes to expanding your business globally, don't assume that your website processes are 'one size fits all'. In this video, we'll look at what you need to check off your list to make sure that the following things are international-friendly:

- your site itself
- the e-commerce system
- the payment process.

Knowledge:

This Lesson is about the technical side of expanding your online business into other countries.

We'll show you how to think beyond your home turf and give you a checklist to help make sure your website, e-commerce system and payment process are friendly to international visitors.

Imagine you own a vintage record shop in Brighton. Your reputation has spread, and you're starting to get some inquiries from international collectors. There's never been a better time to take your online sales global! Let's look what you need to do to succeed.

Step One: Language and Localisation.

We have an entire lesson on this with more details, but here's the basics: If you're growing into an area that primarily speaks another language you'll need to translate your site. And it's probably best to have it done by a native speaker - rather than an automated translation service.

Along the same lines is localization. Essentially, this refers to making sure things like your forms where customers submit information or inquiries is compatible with, let's say, the ways other countries write addresses or phone numbers.

OK, on to Step Two: Payments.

Different countries have different preferred payment methods, so you'll need to investigate each to include them in your target markets. Online payment services like Paypal and Worldpay may be an easy solution, since they work worldwide. Remember that some customers may not have access to credit cards so will prefer to use those services, or even their debit cards.

Also, look into using an e-commerce system that adapts for different currencies and taxes, helping your customer pay without having to think about exchange rates or additional tax. When a customer doesn't have to make these calculations themselves, he's much more likely to buy.

Finally, Step Three: Review.

Take some time to go over your entire site from the point of view of an international visitor. Look at the site objectively and run through the process a visitor from your target market would take to make a purchase or engage with you.

Is it a clear path? Are there familiar terms and formats? Currencies? Payment methods?

If everything's ready, congratulations! But make sure you come back on a regular basis to check everything's working as it should.

Being able to advertise to customers from international markets is a potentially lucrative opportunity. Making your website friendly to visitors, wherever they're from, will help remove any barriers to sales.

Check your knowledge 26.6

Matt needs to make sure that: - His payment system can be used in Portugal, and accounts for different currencies and taxes. Paypal and Worldpay are two systems that have an international focus. - He knows enough about Portuguese culture and the music scene to tailor his products to his customers. - His site works from an international point of view. Matt needs to run through the process a visitor would have when they access his site. Automated translation services can give people an idea of meaning but won't translate the content as well as a native speaker would. Matt doesn't need to visit Portugal – that's the benefit of online shopping. However, the occassional trip to the country, and learning the language, could help him better understand his customers' culture.

Question 1 of 1

Matt's found out that Portugal has fast internet speeds, which is great for accessing his website. What things will Matt definitely need to do now he has customers in a new market?

1. Use an international payment system
2. Research the Portuguese music scene
3. Visit Portugal frequently
4. Use an automated translation service
5. Learn to speak Portuguese
6. Check his site from an international point of view

(answer: 1,2,6)

Activity 26.6

Using a search engine, research the top payment methods in your target markets.

If you're not currently set up to accept this payment type, investigate adding it to your payment options.

Lesson 26.7
Delivering To Customers Across the Globe

Key learning

You might have all your systems in place to accept international orders. But can you deliver your products accurately and on time? What about customer service and support? Are you prepared to handle refunds and exchanges across borders? In this video, we'll explore:

- processes involved in deliveries
- choosing reliable shipping partners and services
- post-sales customer service and support.

Knowledge:

In this lesson, we'll explain the process of international product deliveries, how to choose shipping partners, and the importance of post-sales customer service and support.

If you've ever made an online purchase, you've experienced product delivery-or order fulfilment-in action. From the customer perspective, you simply visit a website, select a product, give the merchant your payment and shipping information. Then wait for your order to arrive. Afterwards, if you have any issues, you contact the business for assistance.

As a business, you'll follow a similar process as you expand into international markets-but now you've got borders to deal with, currencies to exchange, possible returns to handle, and more customers to support.

Imagine ordering a product from a business in another country, but you receive the wrong item. What happens if you're unable to communicate with the business, or you're unable to return it back across borders?

You'd be quite an unhappy customer.

As a business owner, you can avoid this scenario with the proper preparation. Let's look at some things to consider for international deliveries.

Let's say you own a vintage record shop. The new reissue of The Beatles' Revolver on vinyl has become so popular there's a run on orders.

Let's have a look at your inventory and supply chain process. You'll want to monitor demand and ensure your products are adequately stocked so you can fulfill orders as they come in.

And as your orders are received, they'll need to be shipped in a timely manner according to the promised delivery dates.

Have you thought about your ability to ship, and the time and costs involved? Shipping across borders may involve extra costs that you'll need to factor into your pricing model.

Now let's think about shipping partners. Not all shipping companies have access to all markets, so you'll want to partner with a reliable cross-border shipping company or agency.

Some cross-border shipping partners may have better access to certain markets, as well as the ability to collect and pay import or customs taxes on your behalf.

Your shipping company-or companies, if needed-can also advise you on packaging and labelling for shipping across borders.

Be sure to explore all your options. Reliable shipping partners can truly drive your success when orders are shipped accurately and received in a timely manner.

Even when a customer has successfully received his order, your job isn't finished. This post-sales period can be a crucial time for your business as you try to cultivate this one-time customer into a loyal, repeat buyer.

What happens if your customers in other markets need to return or exchange their purchase? How will your business handle exchanges? How will you process refunds? It's really important to provide clear, up front instructions to your customers about the policies and processes involved in refunds or exchanges.

No matter where they're located, customers expect prompt and friendly service. You can provide support online or via the telephone, but either way, you want your customers to be able to contact you directly.

As you put these processes in place, be mindful not only of language differences, but possible cultural differences as well, so that you provide the best possible customer service, during and after a sale.

To sum up:

Before offering product delivery to international customers, think about your inventory and supply chain, cross-border shipping, and customer support-no matter what their location.

When you take the time to properly adapt your process, you'll be setting up your business for international success.

Check your knowledge 26.7

Matt needs to check the shipping process and the time and costs involved before he starts selling records to his Portuguese customers. Shipping across borders can be complicated and more costly. Not all shipping companies support international shipping, and many require specific labels to ship, so Matt will need to do his research. Matt will also want to make sure customers have a way to contact him from abroad in case of any issues.

Question 1 of 1

Matt's getting ready to sell his vintage records to Portuguese customers online. But there's one unhelpful task on his to-do list.

1. Can you cross it out for him?
2. Research label requirments for international shipping
3. Set up a few Portuguese social media accounts
4. Choose an international shipping partner
5. Set up customer service for international orders

(answer: 2)

Activity 26.7

Explore the websites of the top shipping companies that serve your target markets and compare prices and cross-border services.

Be sure to take into account your packaging sizes and any extra packaging requirements that may impact costs.

Are there any savings when you compare companies?

Does the company website note any additional services for shipping to your target country?

Following your research, factor these estimates into your expansion costs.

Check your knowledge 26.A

Question 1 of 7

What is the best way to translate the content on your website for a new market?

1. Google translates
2. Native speakers
3. Translation software
4. Language guide

Question 2 of 7

Before starting to promote products to other countries online, what could you use to gauge demand for your product in that specific market?

1. Translation software
2. Keyword planning tools
3. Interviews with people from that country
4. A range of search ads in different countries

Question 3 of 7

When adapting your website for customers who speak a different language, what should you do?

1. Have a 'translate' button that pulls a translation from an external provider
2. Translate your content with consideration to particular words and phrases
3. Translate your content directly, word for word
4. Localise the name of the business owners

Question 4 of 7

Which of the following is primarily meant to target new customers online?

1. Email marketing
2. Print advertising
3. Retargeting advertising
4. Search advertising

Question 5 of 7

What should a business do first, when considering going into a new market?

1. Hire an agency to translate its website into the local language
2. Open a new office in the capital city
3. Determine its ability to deliver products and review all tax and legal information
4. Invest in major ad campaigns to raise brand awareness

Question 6 of 7

When selling to people in different countries, what payment form should you consider using if you aren't already?

1. Debit cards
2. Credit cards
3. Paypal or Worldpay
4. Bank transfers

Question 7 of 7

Which of the following options is important to research when planning to expand delivery of products and services to customers across the globe?

1. What times of the day international shoppers are online
2. The legal and tax considerations in that market
3. Which social channels are popular in that market
4. Which couriers offer the cheapest services for global shipping

(Answer: 2,2,2,4,3,3,2)

www.ingramcontent.com/pod-product-compliance
Lightning Source LLC
LaVergne TN
LVHW061538070526
838199LV00077B/6823